D1760389

SOVIET EDUCATION UNDER PERESTROIKA

Soviet education, like other areas of Soviet society, has been undergoing rapid changes since 1987–8, but at the same time restructuring has been inhibited by economic constraints and by unreformed attitudes and behaviour. The situation has been further complicated by increasing decentralization of authority. This is the first book to provide a description and analysis of these complex developments across the educational spectrum. A historical survey, written partly with the non-specialist in mind, makes particular reference to the influence of the 'new' (progressive) education on state schools, and the story of educational policy and innovation in this sector is continued to the start of the 1990s. Curriculum case-studies deal with computing; music, art and literature as aesthetic education; and stances for living (the incipient transition from atheistic to religious education). Provision for disadvantaged children features in contributions on the impact of perestroika on earlier innovations to help slow learners, and on a charitable initiative, the Lenin Children's Fund. Changing demands on and policies for vocational education are scrutinized. Two complementary studies of higher education consider policy development and implementation in this sector and analyse newly released statistical materials. A study of nationality education and culture focuses on the Soviet Koreans, and the book concludes with a discussion of challenges facing comparative research. The book will be essential reading for academics and students concerned with comparative education and with Soviet society and politics in the Gorbachev era.

John Dunstan is Senior Lecturer in Soviet Education at the Centre for Russian and East European Studies, University of Birmingham, UK. He was formerly the Centre's Deputy Director. His publications include *Paths to Excellence and the Soviet School* (1978), the edited volume *Soviet Education under Scrutiny* (1987), and many contributions to other books and journals.

SOVIET EDUCATION UNDER PERESTROIKA

Edited by
John Dunstan

Papers from the IV World Congress
for Soviet and East European Studies
Harrogate, UK, 1990

London and New York

First published in 1992
by Routledge
11 New Fetter Lane, London EC4P 4EE

Simultaneously published in the USA and Canada
by Routledge
a division of Routledge, Chapman and Hall Inc.
29 West 35th Street, New York, NY 10001

© 1992 John Dunstan

Typeset by LaserScript, Mitcham, Surrey
Printed and bound in Great Britain by
Hartnolls, Bodmin, Cornwall

British Library Cataloguing in Publication Data
A catalogue record for this book is available from the British Library.
ISBN 0–415–06947–5

Library of Congress Cataloging in Publication Data
Soviet education under perestroika : papers from the IV World Congress for Soviet
and East European Studies, Harrogate, UK, 1990 / edited by John Dunstan.
p.   cm.
Selected papers from the congress.
Includes index.
ISBN 0–415–06947–5
1 Education—Soviet Union—History—20th century—Congresses.
2 Perestroika—Congresses. 3. Educational change—Soviet
Union—History—20th century—Congresses. I. Dunstan, John. II. World
Congress for Soviet and East European Studies (4th : 1990 : Harrogate, England)
LA831.82.S57 1990
370′.947–dc20   91–31163
CIP

CONTENTS

CONTENTS

TABLES

CONTRIBUTORS

Harley D. Balzer is Director of the Russian Area Studies Program at the Graduate School, Georgetown University, Washington, DC. In addition to higher education, he has researched and published on technology and society in the tsarist era and on Soviet science and technology policy.

Youn-Cha Shin Chey is Executive Director of the Korean Center, Inc, San Francisco, Ca, and President of the San Francisco Institute of Language and Technology. She is also Research Associate at the University of California at Berkeley. In the mid-1970s she established the Department of Russian at the Korean University in Seoul.

Detlef Glowka is Professor of Pedagogy and Comparative Education at the University of Münster, Germany. Areas of special interest to him are school reform in the Soviet Union and in Great Britain.

Stephen T. Kerr is Professor of Education and Associate Dean for Professional Programs in the College of Education at the University of Washington, Seattle, WA. His work on Soviet education focuses particularly on questions of reform and restructuring.

Friedrich Kuebart is a Research Fellow in the Comparative Education Research Unit at Bochum University, Germany. His academic work is mainly concerned with education in the Soviet Union and Eastern Europe.

Jane M. Lommel is Director of Educational Computing at the Indianapolis Public Schools and Adjunct Professor of Education at Butler University, Indianapolis, IN. She has published on computer literacy in the USSR.

James Muckle is a Senior Lecturer at Nottingham University, UK. His recent publications include *A Guide to the Soviet Curriculum* (1988) and, following a period as exchange teacher in Moscow and Leningrad, *Portrait of a Soviet School under Glasnost* (1990).

Landon Pearson is the author of *Children of Glasnost: Growing up Soviet* (1990). Formerly at the Canadian Embassy in Moscow, she is Chairperson of the Canadian Council on Children and Youth, and was an official delegate to the World Summit on Children in September 1990.

Avril Suddaby has a degree in Russian and has done research on various aspects of Soviet education, resulting in several publications. She has worked as a teacher in Eastern Europe and in the UK.

Jeanne Sutherland served for many years in the British Embassy, Moscow. She is a graduate of London University and the author of articles on perestroika in the Soviet general school.

INTRODUCTION

In the late 1980s and early 1990s, freer access to information and more open conditions of debate have shown the problems of the USSR's education system in ever higher relief, while increasing decentralization of authority has compounded their complexity. Our book bears witness to this. We have been faced with the gradual demise of 'Soviet education' as a fairly homogeneous entity – in fact it probably never existed as such, but it was convenient to assume that it did – in a situation of socio-political flux. Yet while powerful currents have been flooding and changing the landscape, large tracts of lethargy and conservatism have been little touched. Thus 'Soviet education' has never been such a problematic concept as it is today. Apart from purely historical works, therefore, this book may be the last one justifiably to include the notion in its title, in that sense marking the end of one era and the beginning of another.

Progressive innovatory ideas and practices have had a long but chequered history in Soviet education, though one must remember that formally similar means may differ in their aims and content. In Chapter 1 John Dunstan and Avril Suddaby trace this 'progressive tradition' in Soviet schooling, alongside general developments, as far as the early stages of educational perestroika. Six chapters (2 to 7) continue to deal primarily with children and young people of general school age. Jeanne Sutherland uses very recent Soviet sources and personal impressions to bring the story of educational policy and innovation in the schools into the 1990s. Jane Lommel, James Muckle and John Dunstan are concerned with different aspects of curriculum: with case-studies from the science and technology side, the humanities side, and also more particularly from the affective domain. Lommel focuses on computer studies to exemplify the enormous problems in introducing a new compulsory course with extensive demands in human and material resources. Muckle analyses the impact of recent change on a traditional area of curriculum which has acquired enhanced importance: music, art and literature. Whereas aesthetic education has been boosted, atheistic education is under attack, and Dunstan examines the partial transition from atheism to religion as a component of the upbringing programme.

In times of educational turbulence and rapid change, children with special educational and social needs may either be particularly vulnerable or receive new opportunities, depending on the prevailing economic and social climate. Avril Suddaby, who has made the study of slow learners in ordinary Soviet schools very much her own, considers the innovations in this area from the early 1980s and assesses the impact of perestroika upon them. Moving into the domain of educational initiatives outside the state system, Landon Pearson describes and discusses the Lenin Children's Fund and the help which it provides for 'special children'.

Friedrich Kuebart next examines vocational education, that controversial sector which has seen several divergent policies over a short space of time (Chapter 8). It has had to adjust from being an integrated component of the economy to adopting the role of producer of qualifications for sale on the labour market. The restructuring of higher education, which had its own reform in 1986–7, is analysed in two complementary approaches by Stephen Kerr and Harley Balzer (Chapters 9 and 10). Kerr concentrates on policy development and implementation and the constraints upon them, including latterly the partial shift of emphasis from economic to social considerations. Balzer evaluates the progress and inadequacies of higher education on the basis of newly available statistical materials, some of them recently declassified.

The nationalities have lately been more fully recognized as a crucial centrifugal force in Soviet society. In Chapter 11 Youn-Cha Shin Chey presents a view in the round, past and present, of the education and culture of Soviet Koreans, a group lacking their own national territory. This people, much neglected both by Soviet power and by scholarly studies, is shown to conform only in part to current wisdom on nationality trends. Finally, Detlef Glowka (Chapter 12) considers the conceptual and methodological challenges issued by Soviet educational perestroika to comparative education research both in the USSR and in the West; this is a tailpiece intended to provoke reflection and action.

There is one other aspect of the book that I want to highlight. Recent years have seen other collaborative works on Soviet education from British publishers, but this is the first in which women scholars have provided virtually half of the contributions. This is a source of considerable satisfaction. Another is that the great majority of the contributors are members – or 'corresponding members' – of the UK Study Group on Soviet Education. This association has softly but surely come a long way since its inception at a pioneering conference organized by Janusz Tomiak in 1982. The German presence was already strong then, and an American one has since developed, in the field as in the group and among my contributors. To a great extent this book can be seen as a product of the UK Study Group as well as that of the larger body, the International Council for Soviet and East European Studies (ICSEES).

There are several people who merit my thanks. Stephen White (Glasgow), General Editor for ICSEES, who also deserves my forgiveness for twisting my arm in the first place, set up all the initial arrangements with the publisher. Helen Fairlie of Routledge has been a pleasure to work with. The publisher's reader's helpful and detailed scrutiny of the original papers went far beyond the call of convention. And all of my contributors have been very patient with an editor who on occasion may well have seemed excessively interventionist and pernickety. Given the frequency of visits to and visitors from the USSR these days, all demanding time, they have also been remarkably prompt to reply to my queries.

Finally, I am grateful to my colleagues at the Centre for Russian and East European Studies, University of Birmingham. Editing this book has caused me at last to cut my teeth on computer technology; while not actually being a latent Luddite, I had suffered from the 'too old to change' syndrome. So my thanks go to Julian Cooper, Director of CREES, for providing a word processor for my use; to Nancy Moore for putting some of the material on to disk and for assistance at the final stage; and to Marea Arries, Betty Bennett, Trish Carr and Hugh Jenkins for repeatedly bailing me out of bondage to the machine. Mike Berry and Hugh have helped me in various ways to check sources, facts and interpretations.

John Dunstan
Birmingham, July 1991

Note The conventions to denote year dates in this book are these: 1988–9 is used to signify successive calendar years and 1988/9 the academic or school year.

1

THE PROGRESSIVE TRADITION IN SOVIET SCHOOLING TO 1988

John Dunstan and Avril Suddaby

INTRODUCTION

The purpose of this opening chapter, which is written partly with the non-specialist reader in mind, is first to give a concise account of the origins and growth of Soviet general education up to the eve of perestroika or restructuring (Dunstan), and next to review its early dawn in 1986–8 in the sphere of education and particularly the school (Suddaby). We shall dwell on what might be paradoxically called the progressive tradition, those features which both prefigured and typified Soviet schooling under perestroika. This is intended to set the scene for the ensuing contributions on the later course of events, on particular aspects of the school curriculum or groups in the school population, on other major sectors of education which follow general schooling, and on wider problems of Soviet educational development and its scholarly study.

DEVELOPMENT OF THE SOVIET GENERAL SCHOOL TO THE MID-1980s

The progressive period

It is singularly appropriate to focus on the earliest period of Soviet school history, because many of its ideas and practices were to reappear in the second half of the 1980s. From the start the Soviet school has been compre-hensive, coeducational and free, and over the years these principles have been slightly eroded from time to time but never seriously so. From 1918 to the early 1930s, however, educational policy-makers, headed initially by N.K. Krupskaya and A.V. Lunacharsky, were also much concerned about children and young people as individuals, proceeding from their felt needs to prepare them for their part in the community. The education of this period has often been labelled 'child-centred'. Its hallmarks were – or were supposed to have been – freedom, activeness and enjoyment, as Soviet

1

educationists and teachers sought to adapt and apply to their own country the principles and experience of progressive educators such as John Dewey, W.H. Kilpatrick (the project method) and Helen Parkhurst (the Dalton Plan). In the literature on Soviet education these three are frequently cited but their approaches are seldom explained.

For John Dewey, the school was potentially one of the main instruments of social reconstruction.[1] He worked out his ideas and their applications at his Laboratory School, attached to the University of Chicago, from 1896 to 1903. In his own words: 'The school's ultimate social ideal was the transformation of society through a new, socially-minded individualism.'[2] To this end the school pursued social and individual goals simultaneously, building a cooperative community, developing each child's abilities and satisfying his or her needs. Activeness was central: the pupil's perceived needs should stimulate action, and problem situations should be set up bringing the mind to bear on the activity and evoking the best choice of solution. The curriculum started with the child too, based on activities springing from the 'four impulses': to share and communicate with others, to construct, to inquire and experiment, and to express oneself artistically. This combination of activity and reflective or scientific thinking, Dewey later emphasized, would help to form a new, more equitable, humane and democratic social order. Had he been a Russian, he might well have used the term 'perestroika'.

Dewey's ideas were espoused by Russia's own leading progressive educator, S.T. Shatsky (1878–1934),[3] whose Cheerful Life Colony, founded in 1911 with origins dating back to 1905, expanded into a vast educational laboratory by 1923. Shatsky was something of a Tolstoyan too, and basically accepted Tolstoy's insistence on freedom and joy in education. Yet he never took this to extremes; for example, he did not echo Tolstoy's abhorrence of moral education or 'training' (vospitanie) because of its allegedly coercive implications.[4] And if in his earlier career Shatsky inclined towards individualism, in the 1920s he saw his task as that of bringing up a 'Soviet citizen, competent to build socialism',[5] which was a long way from Tolstoy's conviction that education had no final aim at all.[6] Like Dewey, Shatsky endeavoured to form an educational community, on the basis of shared interests expressed in productive labour, self-government and artistic activities. Productive work as an 'organizing social force' was particularly emphasized. The content of the activity-based school curriculum should be selected for its social function and social significance.[7] Indeed, community education in a wider sense, as developed by the forward-looking pre-revolutionary local government bodies known as the zemstva, was for Shatsky and others the subject of lasting two-way communication with the international progressive education movement.

The centrality of work in Shatsky's schools is manifest in a description, by the American educationist Thomas Woody, of the 'complex method' devised by Shatsky, Krupskaya and others. This was a kind of integrated subject teaching focused vertically on the concepts of nature, labour and society, labour being the central one around which everything else hung. Horizontally the complex approach concentrated on the family as the child's immediate environment in the first school year, widening the horizons in successive years to cover the village or town, the region, and the USSR and other countries. It was officially introduced in the Russian Republic in 1923, with course outlines for the first nine classes. Visiting Shatsky's schools in November 1929, Woody recorded:

> The complexes are broad projects, themes to be stressed, and are all interrelated. Nine themes occupy the first year: first steps in school; autumn work in the family; care of health; . . . preparation for winter and winter work; life and work of winter; . . . approach of spring and preparation for its labours; spring work and children's share in it; participation in the holiday, the First of May; and participation in an exhibit of school work. All subject matter is interwoven in these nine themes.[8]

Woody also noted that this organization of materials had been developed partly from the project method.

The project method had been first propagated in 1918 by William Heard Kilpatrick, an associate of Dewey, whose ideas it was designed to apply. Projects were meant to be cooperatively planned, problem-oriented, productive and purposeful activities, whereby youngsters broadened their experience and felt they had learned something worthwhile. This might be through creative achievement, enjoyment of an artistic work or performance, solution of a problem or acquisition of a skill, or some combination of these.[9]

The third principal American influence on the new Soviet education was that of Helen Parkhurst. In 1920 she devised a method of teaching – though she denied it was a method, preferring to see it as 'a way of educational reorganization which reconciles the twin activities of teaching and learning'[10] – which she called the Dalton Laboratory Plan after the Massachusetts town where it originated. It was intended to give children freedom to organize their own studies and liberate them from the slavery of the timetable. For each school-year a maximum and minimum curriculum was drawn up and divided into four-week blocks of twenty units covering all the major subjects. Each block represented a 'contract-job' which the child undertook to complete, at his or her own pace within the overall limit, so that more time could be devoted to weaker subjects. This was reckoned to improve the efficiency of the educational process. Classrooms became 'laboratories' and teachers 'specialists' or 'advisers', and the pupil moved from one to the next when ready to do so. The desks were arranged in clusters so that the children could sit with others from the same year.[11]

In the USSR, the Dalton Plan was adopted in 1922 and became quite widespread at post-primary level, tending to replace the complex system after the primary stage. One reason for this may have been its retention of traditional subject divisions. In its original form, however, it was soon found to be too individualistic, and the children's semi-autonomous work in the 'laboratories' was officially put on to a group basis. The problem then arose that the weaker or lazier pupils were content to let the others do most of the work, and as the 1920s drew on the Dalton Plan too was gradually eroded. At the end of the decade the complex approach was increasingly superseded by the project method,[12] which had the merit of being applicable alongside the subject-based curriculum with its more systematic teaching of literacy and numeracy.

The reader will have noted that the pivotal concept of the complex approach was physical work, and the project method also lent itself to this emphasis. Productive labour, which was of course the cornerstone of social development for Marx and Lenin, was placed at the centre of the educational process by P.P. Blonsky in his book *Trudovaya shkola* (*The Labour School*) published in 1919. This worked out a pedagogical basis for the 'unified labour school' (state comprehensive school) set up in 1918 and modified in 1923. The present writer will not give labour education the pride of place here which it would rightfully claim in a general history of the Soviet school of the 1920s and 1940s onwards, simply because he does not sense that it has played much part in the educational debates of the later 1980s, except in a slightly negative way. Suffice it to say that there were many schemes and experiments in the organization of labour activity in the early Soviet period. They ranged from V.N. Soroka-Rosinsky's Dostoevsky School Commune in downtown Leningrad, where the total absence of conventional opportunities for labour education caused it to be conceived as creative literary work,[13] to the working commune visualized as the standard institution for the education of the young in the Ukraine of the early 1920s. Indeed, there was a brief policy episode about 1930 when some schools virtually dissolved into farms and factories.

Summing up on the progressive period in Soviet education, we may say that attempts were made to break down traditional subject barriers, to gear curriculum content more closely to the children's life experience, to afford them possibilities of choice and to give them opportunities of self-government in a community. It was an honest endeavour to provide a new type of public education in which the individual, far from being subordinated to systemic demands, was to be helped to develop his or her personal qualities and abilities and thus to contribute to the building of the new society. But although many of its features would recur in the era of perestroika, so would some of the constraints upon it. For the tragedy of it was that the wider context could hardly have been less appropriate. The disruption caused by the Revolution was sustained by the Civil War. Food, shelter and funds were in short supply. Some schools were reduced to anarchy or to impotence when pupil self-government was taken to extremes, while others assumed new names but otherwise carried on as if the events of 1917 had never been. Teachers generally tend to be suspicious of fundamental change.[14] In addition to this, the ideal of maximum general education plus a diversity of labour skills for every child was steadily eroded through the 1920s by the necessity of specific vocational training. As we shall see, however, this trend was to be the subject of repeated policy reversals, most recently in 1988.

From Stalin to Gorbachev

The beginning of the end of the early period of official progressive education in Russia was signalled by the issue of a compulsory timetable and syllabuses in 1927, although the situation was to remain extremely unstable for another four years. Between 1931 and 1936, conforming to the state's demand for the shaping of a disciplined workforce, the school reverted to a highly system-centred authoritarian pattern, with formal lessons, compulsory textbooks, homework, examinations and the teacher firmly in charge. Purposeful up-bringing was to be effected through the children's collective, led at first but increasingly leading itself. The practice-based theories of A.S. Makarenko gradually emerged as appropriate underpinning for this desired pedagogical style. Although the aims of communist education had in effect become very different from the ideals of the progressive educators, the principle of the centrality of upbringing nevertheless furnished a number of shared charac-teristics, as will be seen.

Meanwhile, except for varying interpretations of polytechnical education, this model of general schooling was to remain in place for half a century. But physical work, largely ousted in 1937 because of the trend towards the academic, came back to the school thanks to the exigencies of the Great Patriotic War; subjects such as mathematics and biology acquired a more practical orientation, and various forms of labour training entered the timetable, where they stayed until 1946. If this may be seen as an enforced, though limited, return to one of the principles of the new education, it is offset by the partial switch to single-sex education (except for primary schools) from 1943 to 1954. Under perestroika there has been a modest move to reintroduce separate schooling for boys. This has had very little impact, but it nevertheless suggests that the only fixed connotation of 'progressive' is 'unconventional'.

The era of Khrushchev has gone down in school history for three main reasons: his 'polytechnical experiment' (legislated in 1958, effective from 1959 to 1964 or 1966), whereby a massive dose of vocational training and manual work was injected into general education in order to turn out more and better motivated young skilled workers; the establishment of a system of boarding schools as 'beacons of the future' and in response to social need;

5

and the beginnings of diversification of the curricular structure by the creation of a limited number of schools and classes for special academic purposes. All three, in different ways, produced resonances of the progressive education period (e.g. the emphasis on physical activity, the school's social function, and the realization of individual potential) though certainly all could be interpreted just as means to strengthen the state. Overloading, inefficiency and superficiality largely put paid to the first; the second was soon downgraded by lack of resources and by public antipathy. The third, however, gained some ground, though economic and ideological brakes on the schools' expansion produced in 1966 a shift of policy towards optional studies or electives as the principal means of catering for particular interests and abilities. Somewhat muted during the Brezhnev years, discussion of the potentially divisive issue of curriculum differentiation would resurface in the 1980s[15] and become one of the chief features of the movement for educational renewal.

The overall reaction to the Khrushchev experiment was to make general education much more conceptually demanding, which did not consort well with a simultaneous drive to involve *all* youngsters of 15-plus in it at the senior stage. Some 60 per cent of them were to be at secondary general schools; the post-15 'specialized secondary' (i.e. technical) schools also had general-education classes; and in 1971 secondary general teaching began to be extended to some of the vocational schools, creating the term SPTU, *srednie* (secondary) *professional'no-tekhnicheskie uchilishcha*, to distinguish them from the ordinary PTU. It was also hoped that this would upgrade them in public consciousness.

By 1977, when full 'secondary education for all' was enshrined in the new Constitution, its vocational aspect was again being stressed. It was decreed that general school completers 'should have come near to mastering a specific occupation' – an intricate formulation hinting at divergence of views – and that labour training in the two senior forms would be doubled to four weekly periods. But to some this seemed to be mere tinkering with the problem of the expected slowdown in growth of the working-age population, itself due to the falling birthrate in the 1960s and to increasing retirements. Their counsels prevailed in the education reform of 1984. The most dramatic of its provisions was the long-term doubling of the SPTU intake at age 15, which would have to be at the expense of the secondary general schools in the absence of any intention to expand the specialized secondary sector. In the general schools, the overall time allocation for labour training and socially useful productive work went up by 100 per cent, enough at the senior stage to train people in low-grade skills but making a very awkward fit with the function of preparing for higher education. Attempts to loosen up the curriculum in other respects made little progress; references to differentiation were largely tokenist, and those to modernization prescriptive.[16] There was, however, a markedly innovative feature in the new compulsory senior-level course on information science and computer technology (see Chapter 3).

The 1984 reform rang bells with those who recalled Krushchev's innovations, let alone the late 1920s. The reinforcement of labour training presaged the eventual merger of general and vocational education. The lowering of the compulsory school starting-age from seven to six, while keeping the leaving-age steady, might be seen as a move by the state not only to make schooling more efficient and to lighten the burden of working mothers but also to extend a more systematic sway over childrearing, in the same way as the boarding education experiment and the earlier school-communes had been regarded. On the other hand, reduction of maximum class size by about 15 to 30 per cent, while also serving the cause of efficiency, must needs be directly beneficial to the individual pupil. It has also been pointed out that the reform expressly sought to involve parents in organizing children's domestic responsibilities at home, frequently a place of stark contradiction between official goals and actual behaviour.[17] Though the principle was nothing new, it is worth remembering that parent education is an important feature of the progressive tradition and thus has its roots going back beyond the Stalin era with which it is conventionally associated. Khrushchev's residential schools, on the other hand, were more often construed as an attack on the family.

Despite the optimism that we observed on a visit to the USSR in September 1984, when educationists felt that at last the state authorities were listening to them rather than to the scientists who had shaped the over-ambitious post-Khrushchev curriculum, the new reform did not live up to expectations. In April 1985 a plenum of the Central Committee of the Communist Party of the Soviet Union (CC CPSU) inaugurated the era of perestroika under M.S. Gorbachev. Some ten months later the XXVII CPSU Congress criticized the speed and depth of perestroika in the schools; in April 1987 Gorbachev himself declared that the school reform was 'slipping'; and the February 1988 Central Committee plenum did a stocktaking and set the CPSU line for educational perestroika. The 1984 reform was excoriated on three grounds: it had been evolutionary and piecemeal, not revolutionary and comprehensive; it had been extensive instead of intensive (the contradiction of mass training of general-school seniors in the simplest trades was specifically cited); and it had not been supported by democratic mechanisms for change involving all the parties concerned. In a nutshell, it had predated April 1985. The plenum gave the green light for divesting the general school of its mass training function and for encouraging differentiation and innovation. As will shortly be seen, an innovatory movement was already well under way.

As we consider the reform and restructuring of education in the USSR, a point to grapple with is this: throughout its history, Soviet schooling has manifested in some respects a striking (if sometimes superficial) concurrence of means with progressive education; it is the ends served by the means and determining their content that have in practice diverged so widely. Some, mindful of the stereotype of the formal classroom and austere teaching style, may question the first part of that statement, and certainly the correspondence has shown up in much higher relief in some periods than others. Yet even in the most authoritarian days, common features can be found. An essentially system-centred approach has not managed to monopolize the teacher's terrain. Teacher involvement in extracurricular and out-of-school activities and careers guidance, for example, has been characterized as child-centred, as has concern about equal opportunities.[18] Indeed, teacher accountability, the extension of the social functions of schooling, and participation by teachers in school governance along with parents and pupils and in local leadership may be more appropriately described as community-centred.[19] A distinction must be drawn, however, between these general features and specific ways of conceptualizing and realizing them. Moving on now to the beginnings of educational perestroika in the later 1980s, we shall detect the emergence or recurrence of facets of the progressive tradition, the means of teaching and upbringing and learning; but what will be of primary importance is the identification of the qualitatively new ends which ought to imbue the content of those means. And what difference are they making?

PRELUDE TO PERESTROIKA

In education as in other aspects of Soviet life, perestroika has involved a questioning of, if not an attack on, old values which have been found to be inadequate. It has also raised the question as to what should replace the old values and the social structures based upon them. Naturally there has been resistance from conservative forces for a mixture of reasons, including tenacious ideological conviction, suspicion of change, fear of instability and concern about loss of privilege.

What had been fermenting in Soviet education while party leaders had been expressing more and more dissatisfaction with the progress of the school reform? The teachers' newspaper *Uchitel'skaya gazeta* had played an important role in educational change by providing a forum for educationists to air their views, by publishing subsequent debate, and by organizing meetings and conferences where progressive teachers could discuss their theories. At the start of the 1986 school year, for example, the newspaper invited a small group of the best-known progressive teachers – Sh.A. Amonashvili, V.F. Shatalov, S.N. Lysenkova, I.P. Volkov, V.A. Karakovsky, E.N. Il'in and M.P. Shchetinin – to a two-day meeting in Peredelkino, near Moscow, for an exchange of ideas. The aim was to find ways and means of educating all children successfully since the participants considered themselves to be 'the first generation of educators whose task is to teach all children without any selection or dropouts'.[20]

The results of this meeting were published under the title 'Pedagogy of

8

cooperation'. This eighteen-point statement was the first manifesto of the teacher-innovators, as they came to be called, and it represented a challenge to the accepted educational theory and practice recommended by the USSR Academy of Pedagogical Sciences (*Akademiya pedagogicheskikh nauk* or APN). Publication of the manifesto immediately caused heated debate, with an avalanche of readers' letters, most of them in favour of the innovators' proposals.[21]

To understand why this manifesto was so revolutionary, we must consider the role of the APN, which places Soviet teachers in a somewhat different position from that of their colleagues elsewhere. The APN coordinates all educational research in the USSR. On the basis of the work of its research institutes, it advises on teaching methods and influences policy and decision-making. There has been in theory a clear-cut division of roles, with the Academy engaging in psychological and pedagogical research, and the educational practitioners, the teachers, implementing its recommendations. The advantage of this division of labour, from the viewpoint of the APN, is that: 'Research into new methods . . . frees teachers from repeated trial and error, from discovering what is already known to science, and from applying ideas that are unrealistic for the ordinary school'.[22]

The average Soviet teacher was therefore not concerned with the generation or interpretation of educational theory, at least before the advent of glasnost and perestroika. It was inevitable, however, that teachers would have their own views on educational theory which did not always coincide with those of the APN. The uneasy relationship between the APN, backed by the central and republic Ministries of Education (some of whom, however, would later show that they had minds of their own), and the more independent rank-and-file teachers can be seen in the cases of the Ukrainian teachers V.F. Shatalov[23] and M.P. Shchetinin.[24] Both came into conflict with the local Ministry of Education because of their independence of thinking and readiness to put their own ideas into practice.

The innovators' first manifesto – to be followed by three others[25] – was a more than implicit challenge to the APN. Rather than accept the Academy's recommendations, the innovators were devising and proposing not only their own teaching methods but also a new educational theory. The substance of the pedagogy of cooperation was that Soviet education needed new methods and relationships based on cooperation and trust between all participants – teachers, pupils and parents. Instead of the old methods based on compulsion, pupils should be freed from the fear of failure, and conditions should be created whereby successful learning would be assured. Of far greater importance than the methods recommended by the innovators, however, was their educational philosophy. As they claimed in their third manifesto: 'the pedagogy of cooperation is not a particular methodology but the pedagogical thinking of the epoch of perestroika'.[26]

This was not likely to meet with the approval of the APN, which sees the

9

creation of educational theory as its own domain. At first the Academy maintained an aloof silence about the pedagogy of cooperation; but criticisms from readers became more and more direct until eventually it was forced into making a response. Rather ambiguously, this took the form of an open letter to *Uchitel'skaya gazeta*, above the signatures of eight leading APN members.[27] The fact that the letter was signed by only eight people, rather than the Academy as a body, suggested a lack of unanimity within the APN. Indeed, other prominent APN academics subsequently made plain their support for many of the innovators' ideas.

Dissatisfaction on the part of certain academics with the conservatism of the Soviet educational establishment was shown in the founding of a new type of research base known as VNIK 'Shkola' (*vremennyi nauchno-issledovatel'skii kollektiv 'Shkola'* or Provisional Research Group on the School). This was set up in June 1988 after the CC CPSU plenum of February appeared to give its approval to creative educational experiment. To answer the question as to what sort of an institution VNIK 'Shkola' was, one needs to consider the normal Soviet research institution. The established centres for educational research are the APN institutes specializing in particular aspects of education; there are, for example, the Institute of Pre-school Education, the Institute of General Secondary Education (until 1990 Curriculum and Method), and the Institute of Defectology (for the education of the handi-capped). It was felt by some that this rather ossified framework was not meeting the requirements of contemporary educational research, and that more *ad hoc* structures might be better for tackling urgent educational problems which did not necessarily fit neatly into the divisions imposed by existing educational arrangements. Hence came the proposal for the Provisional Research Group. VNIK 'Shkola' was set up initially for six months. Although it was led by academic progressives, participation was not restricted to academics, and many ordinary teachers contributed to its work. The trial period was extended and eventually VNIK 'Shkola' acquired permanent status, as the Centre for Educational Innovation, in what is now the Institute of the Theory and History of Pedagogy (formerly General Pedagogy).

Since publication of the manifesto of October 1986, the world of Soviet education has been in a state of turmoil, with continual debates about the direction to be taken. Certainly the innovators' proposal for a new edu-cational philosophy and teaching approach shook the very foundations of the USSR's educational establishment. In August 1988 a commission was created to investigate the APN and to make recommendations for its reform, with reports of the commission subjected to examination and criticism in the press.[28] (For the outcome, see the opening section of Chapter 2.)

Taking a somewhat simplified view of the debate, one may discern two broad lines or directions: the essentially traditional line proposed by the APN and the progressive direction advanced by the innovators and their followers.[29] Other manifestations of the progressive line are the Eureka Clubs of Creative Pedagogy and the Author School movement. Eureka Clubs first appeared about 1986. They were in no way restricted to teachers. Such is the interest in education in the Soviet Union that membership of Eureka Clubs snowballed, and soon there were over 500 of them throughout the country. Their educational philosophy derives from the pedagogy of cooperation. The Author School movement evolved from Eureka sessions, when it was realized that a basis was needed to work out some of the more valuable educational ideas which had originated on these occasions. Collectives were formed, based on a school with a progressive director, or on a group of teachers from various schools meeting to develop their projects.[30] (Comments on the Eureka movement and on an Author School at a later stage will be found in Chapter 2.)

MORNING BRIGHT, OUTLOOK UNCERTAIN

In the 1980s it was still possible to speak of 'Soviet education'. By the early 1990s the concept had become fraught with difficulty. The school system was beginning in some respects to fragment and in others to fray at the edges. The underpinning ideology was no longer sacrosanct. School curricula were being partly decentralized and rethought, and new types of school created. Teachers and lecturers were officially encouraged to adopt a more individualized approach to their pupils and students and a more open-ended style in presenting their subjects. In educational administration too, democratization was the new watchword.

At the same time, however, the inherent conservatism of the teaching profession at all levels and that of bureaucratic organizations in general acted as a powerful brake on change. The USSR's colossal economic problems had the effect of constraining resources for innovation. And, especially in the vast republic of Russia, Moscow's radical writ might be slow to penetrate as a result of sheer distance and the mind-set conditioned by it. In a representative survey of urban residents in seven Union republics in October 1989, over 60 per cent of the respondents felt either that there had been no change in the educational sphere during the previous two or three years or that it was difficult to say how the situation had changed (which suggests that the changes were perceived to have cancelled one another out). Of the remainder, more thought that things had got worse (22 per cent) than better (17 per cent).[31] This depressing view must be set against the ebullience that was still spilling from the pages of sections of the educational press. We now move on, therefore, to consider such complex and countervailing tendencies in various areas of education, on from the early dawn of educational perestroika to its bright morning and its less luminous noontide.

NOTES AND REFERENCES

1 For an excellent summary of Dewey's educational philosophy see W.F. Connell, *A History of Education in the Twentieth Century World*, Canberra, Curriculum Development Centre, 1980, pp. 71–89.

2 J. Dewey, *The School and Society*, revised edn, Chicago, University of Chicago Press, 1915, p. 32, quoted in Connell, op. cit., p. 75.

3 W.W. Brickman (ed.), *John Dewey's Impressions of Soviet Russia and the Revolutionary World*, New York, Teacher's College, 1964, pp. 16–17.

4 See Tolstoy's essay, 'Training and education', in A. Pinch and M. Armstrong (eds), *Tolstoy on Education*, London, Athlone Press, 1982, pp. 290–325, especially p. 319.

5 O. Anweiler, 'Leben und Wirksamkeit des russischen Pädagogen Stanislaw Teofilowitsch Schazki', in O. Anweiler (ed.), *Die Sowjetpädagogik in der Welt von heute*, Heidelberg, Quelle & Meyer, 1968, p. 25.

6 Pinch and Armstrong (eds), op. cit., p. 85.

7 Anweiler, op. cit., p. 27.

8 T. Woody, *New Minds: New Men?*, New York, Macmillan, 1932, pp. 52–3.

9 Connell, op. cit., p. 283.

10 H. Parkhurst, *Education on the Dalton Plan*, London, Bell, 1922, p. 28.

11 ibid., pp. 28–36.

12 Connell, op. cit., pp. 205, 279.

13 J. Dunstan, *V.N. Soroka-Rosinsky, Soviet Teacher, in Fact and Fiction*, Lewiston, NY, Queenston, Ont. and Lampeter, UK, Edwin Mellen Press, 1991.

14 Glowing reports by foreign visitors can be contrasted on the one hand with the turbulence at Kostya Ryabtsev's school, where the students burned an effigy of 'bourgeois Lord Dalton' – originator, according to school lore, of the hated Plan (see N. Ognyov, *The Diary of a Communist Schoolboy*, London, Gollancz, 1928, or the modern translation, N. Ognev, *Kostya Ryabtsev's Diary*, Moscow, Progress, 1978), and, on the other, with allusions to the survival or reinstatement of traditional schooling (S. Fitzpatrick, *Education and Social Mobility in the Soviet Union, 1921–1934*, Cambridge, Cambridge University Press, 1979, pp. 43, 47, 141–2).

15 J. Dunstan, *Paths to Excellence and the Soviet School*, Windsor, NFER, 1978, *passim*; J. Dunstan, 'Gifted youngsters and special schools', in J. Riordan (ed.), *Soviet Education: the Gifted and the Handicapped*, London and New York, Routledge, 1988, pp. 29–69.

16 The 1984 reform is analysed in detail in J. Dunstan, 'Soviet education beyond 1984: a commentary on the reform guidelines', *Compare*, 1985, vol. 15, no. 2, pp. 161–87, and B.B. Szekely, 'The new Soviet educational reform', *Comparative Education Review*, 1986, vol. 30, no. 3, pp. 321–43.

17 M. Krüger-Potratz, 'Bildungspolitik: Bildungssystem und die aktuelle Bildungsreform', in C. Ferenczi and B. Löhr (eds), *Aufbruch mit Gorbatschow?*, Frankfurt am Main, Fischer Taschenbuch Verlag, 1987, p. 151.

18 J. Lynch and H.D. Plunkett, *Teacher Education and Cultural Change*, London, Allen & Unwin, 1973, pp. 80–1.

19 ibid., pp. 85–7.

20 'Pedagogika sotrudnichestva', *Uchitel'skaya gazeta* (hereafter *UG*), 18 October 1986, p. 2.

21 'My – za sotrudnichestvo', *UG*, 4 November 1986, p. 3.

22 P.R. Atutov, Yu.K. Babansky, A.A. Bodalev, I.D. Zverev, M.R. L'vov, Z.A. Mal'kova, M.N. Skatkin and G.N. Filonov, 'Soyuz nauki i praktiki', *UG*, 18 December 1986, p. 2.

23 A. Suddaby, 'V.F. Shatalov – the new Makarenko?', *Soviet Education Study Bulletin*, 1985, vol. 3, no. 1, pp. 11–17; A. Suddaby, 'V.F. Shatalov and the Makarenko tradition in Soviet education today', *Soviet Education Study Bulletin*, 1988, vol. 6, no. 1, pp. 1–11.

24 W. Mitter, 'The teacher and the bureaucracy: some considerations concluded from a Soviet case', *Compare*, 1987, vol. 17, no. 1, pp. 47–60.

25 'Demokratizatsiya lichnosti', *UG*, 17 October 1987, p. 3; 'Metodika obnovleniya', *UG*, 19 March 1988, pp. 2–3; 'Voidem v novuyu shkolu', *UG*, 18 October 1988, p. 2.

26 'Metodika obnovleniya', op. cit.

27 Atutov *et al.*, op. cit.

28 See, for example, 'Restavratsiya vmesto reorganizatsii', *UG*, 3 November 1988, p. 3.

29 'Ideas' (*kontseptsii*) or statements of their positions are compared in J. Muckle, *Portrait of a Soviet School under Glasnost*, Basingstoke and London, Macmillan, 1990, pp. 76–81.

30 A. Suddaby, 'Perestroika in Soviet education', *Soviet Education Study Bulletin*, 1989, vol. 7, no. 1, pp. 14–21; J. Sutherland, 'Soviet education since 1984: the school reform, the innovators and the APN', *Soviet Education Study Bulletin*, 1989, vol. 7, no. 1, pp. 21–33.

31 V. Rutgaizer, A. Grazhdankin, V. Kosmarsky, L. Khakhulina and S. Shpil'ko, 'Otnoshenie naseleniya k ekonomicheskoi reforme', *Voprosy ekonomiki*, 1990, no. 4, p. 38. Total respondents, 1148 (in large, medium and small towns in the RSFSR, Ukraine, Belorussia, Latvia, Moldavia, Georgia and Tadzhikistan). We owe this reference to Matthew Wyman.

2

PERESTROIKA IN THE SOVIET GENERAL SCHOOL: FROM INNOVATION TO INDEPENDENCE?

Jeanne Sutherland

The path to real diversity and pluralism . . . in the system of education is likely to be long. We took the first step a year ago when the mouldering monolith of state schooling finally collapsed, and from its remains there began to rise the first gymnasia and lycées . . . The next step, as far as one can judge from information from the schools, will be the introduction of fee-paid teaching. Are we ready for this?

(*Uchitel'skaya gazeta*, 1990, no. 38, p. 3)

INTRODUCTION:
PERESTROIKA AND THE CONGRESS OF WORKERS IN EDUCATION

Since 1984, when the school reform was introduced, many changes have taken place in Soviet education. Gradually the 1984 reform was discredited and supplanted by a call for complete perestroika. The February 1988 plenum of the Central Committee gave official approval to various movements for change and experimentation, some of which had been tried out for a considerable time by individual teachers or groups. The greater political and personal freedom of the last few years has enabled full publicity to be given to the most radical proposals, demanding the complete renewal of Soviet education. These included the need for much greater individuality, creativity and cooperation between teachers and pupils.

This chapter attempts to assess what happened in secondary schooling over some two years from the end of 1988. In December the long-postponed Congress of Workers in Education took place. The chairman of the State Committee for Education, G.A. Yagodin, spoke for humanization and democratization. He said that he proposed to carry out serious revolutionary changes in both the structure and the content of secondary education. The present system aimed to create a 'normal' child, extinguishing inquisitiveness, liveliness and unconventionality. This suppressed creativity, initiative and boldness of thought and deed. Yagodin stressed the need for instruction in the child's national language and free choice of the language of education. Youth organizations should be made more attractive, conditions for handicapped children improved, and legislation on juvenile crime revised. Above all, teachers' conditions demanded attention. There were still 300,000 teachers waiting for housing. Teachers suffered from lack of prestige, lack of holiday accommodation, lack of books and difficulty in buying food. Although their wages had been increased they were still below the national average. 'We talk', he said, 'of the individualization of the teaching process. What good is that when there are no computers, no piped water or sewage arrangements?'[1]

There was lively debate. Some delegates called for the retention of the old traditional authoritarian methods. A delegate from the Chelyabinsk province and director of School No. 1 in Kopeisk, A. Baronenko, decried the 'pedagogy of cooperation' (see Chapter 1), and was opposed to the election of school directors. He believed that it was impossible to give up coercion; the restructuring of education must begin not with the pedagogy of cooperation but with the solution of the fundamental problems of universal education. In reply Shalva Amonashvili, head of educational research in Georgia and himself a leading teacher-innovator, claimed that if Baronenko visited his school he would be helping in two weeks. Amonashvili believed that children suffered from teachers' lack of creativity because for sixty years teachers had been afraid of the inspectors.[2]

It was interesting that such frank and open debate was possible and that the innovators were able to speak freely. But their innovative work and the methods which had emerged at the first meeting in Peredelkino in October 1986, and subsequently throughout 1987 and 1988, received very little discussion. The Congress produced no startling conclusions and resolutions were bland and unspecific, leaving no clear decisions – a cause of considerable dissatisfaction for those who had hoped that more radical steps would be taken.

An article published in *Izvestiya* in December 1988, just before the Congress opened, entitled 'Two points of view', demonstrates the dichotomy between the innovators and the traditionalists in the APN (*Akademiya pedagogicheskikh nauk*, Academy of Pedagogical Sciences). In this article, E.D. Dneprov, head of the then VNIK 'Shkola' (*vremennyi nauchno-issledovatel'skii kollektiv 'Shkola'*), the Provisional Research Group on the School, and A. Petrovsky supported the greater freedom of choice of school subjects in conjunction with the development of the child's personal abilities and interests. Their opponents, V. Likhachev and L. Gordin, continued to favour the more traditional system, characterized since the 1920s by such notions as the 'all-round development of the child' and 'polytechnical education'. From the 1930s it developed into the more rigid and authoritarian form of general secondary education, where all children were taught the same subjects in the same way. Dneprov and Petrovsky saw the aim of teaching every child everything as unrealistic and idealistic.[3]

Perestroika in education, as in most aspects of Soviet life, has seldom gone smoothly. Also – as in most aspects – there has often been more talk than action. The State Committee for Education and its chairman, Yagodin, gave verbal support for the new look in Soviet education. But in practice this support was sometimes lacking, as it was for example at the All-Union Congress when they did not speak up for the teacher-innovators. Again, backing was absent at the January 1989 elections for the new officers of the APN, when many people with no pedagogical experience were elected. The Committee did not always speak out when these matters were being discussed. The Academy, the traditional arbiter of educational theory, has come under severe criticism since 1988 for its conservatism and pedagogical incompetence, and it was to have been completely reorganized under a commission set up by the State Committee. Instead they merely filled the vacancies. Although many good people were chosen, such as I. Ivanov, a founder of the Commune group (see below), Sh. Amonashvili, I. Kon, the philosopher and sociologist, I. Antonova, director of the Pushkin Museum in Moscow, I. Zyazyun, rector of the Poltava Pedagogical Institute, and E. Manyushin, innovator and specialist in higher education, many others were left out, such as E. Dneprov, V. Zinchenko, the learned psychologist, M. Shchetinin from the Ukraine, E.N. Il'in, teacher of literature from Leningrad, S. Ryabtsev, and others who had given constant support to the aims of humanism and democracy in educational perestroika. The 'complete reorganization' was postponed not for two or three months but for two or three years. The late V. Matveev, formerly chief editor of *Uchitel'skaya gazeta* (Teachers' Gazette), said that the government commission for the reorganization of the APN had taken the easy way out. 'Is this a step towards renewal or stagnation?', Matveev asked.[4]

MOVEMENTS FOR CHANGE

So what happened to the innovators, to the Creative Union of Teachers, to the Eureka and Commune movements and to the Author Schools, the groups who most strongly campaigned for a renewal of education? It is not always clear exactly how the various groups and individuals operate and overlap. Some, such as Sh. Amonashvili, V.F. Shatalov, teacher of physics in Donetsk, where he has his experimental laboratory, and S.N. Lysenkova, teacher at School No. 587 in Moscow, would appear to continue to work in their own particular style, opting for a freer and more democratic form of teaching within the general system of education. Lysenkova, whom I met during a visit to the Soviet Union in April 1990, had just returned from a meeting of the teacher-innovators in Bukhara, which was attended by many of the same people as the original gathering in October 1986, when the pedagogy of cooperation was proclaimed. At a seminar of the Commune groups held in Zvenigorod, just outside Moscow, in April 1990, part of which I attended, there were representatives from Amonashvili's school in Tbilisi, from the Eureka clubs and from the Creative Union of Teachers. The aims of the various groups were largely synonymous and there was certainly much overlapping in their activities; they will be more fully described below.

By mid-1990 the individual innovators seemed to have the support of the chairman of the State Committee for Education and, to a large extent, the educational establishment. In January 1989, however, when Lysenkova's latest book, *Metodom operezhayushchego obucheniya*, was published, she complained in an article in *Uchitel'skaya gazeta* that things were still not easy for innovators and that her work had been waiting for a decision for eight months.[5]

THE CREATIVE UNION OF TEACHERS

The Creative Union of Teachers was set up in 1988 under the auspices of *Uchitel'skaya gazeta*, through whose columns the voting for the organizing committee took place. It was gradually broadened to encompass all groups of innovators and workers in education, parents and teachers. During the early part of 1989 the newspaper contained reports of the formation of branches in the Far East, in Siberia and throughout the Soviet Union.[6] Its first full conference, at which its constitution was laid down, was held in Sochi in May. Also, a resolution was passed to the effect that the Union's aim was to participate in solving not only specific questions of schooling but also – and this was its major task – the principal problems of educational policy, on which the success of the renewal of society depended. This included the radical renewal of education, increase in the prestige of teachers, the development, widening and defence of pedagogical creativity, and the uniting of the efforts of a wide selection of the community in the task of educational perestroika.

The conference passed a special resolution that Shatalov and Lysenkova should be nominated for the award of People's Teacher of the USSR. It maintained that their work was so well known that nowadays if one wished to praise a person, one would say that he or she worked like Shatalov or Lysenkova. It set up a programme divided into basic subject areas: the Union and society, the Union and culture, the Union and the protection of children, the Union and school, the Union and the teacher, the Union and socio-pedagogical initiatives and the Union and science. Also part of the future programme was to be close cooperation with the State Committee and the Komsomol on problems of the content of education, new curricula and syllabuses and discussions on the priority direction of the development of public education. A data bank was to be set up so that teachers might have details of new ideas and research in progress.

A Central Council of twenty-seven members was elected, among whom were E. Dneprov, E. Grechkino, S. Soloveichik, educational journalist, O.

17

Gazman, leader of the Commune movement, and V. Davydov, deputy president of the APN. Sh. Amonashvili was elected president, with V. Matveev (now deceased) and A. Adamsky as his deputies. Before being elected to this office, Amonashvili wrote an article in *Uchitel'skaya gazeta* calling for closer collaboration between the APN and the Union. He stressed that without the cooperation of the various official bodies – the Party, the Komsomol, the State Committee for Education and the APN – with the Union, the full force of perestroika in education could not be implemented. The APN and the Union must join together in the search for new ideas and new practice. On the one hand, the APN must involve itself in actual pedagogical activity and, on the other, the Union must widen its experience of real scientific concepts.[7]

During the rest of 1989 the Union was not much mentioned in the teaching press. *Uchitel'skaya gazeta* changed its format at the beginning of 1990, becoming a weekly instead of thrice-weekly paper and losing much of the bite which it had had under its former chief editor and strong supporter of the innovators, V. Matveev. In February 1990 the new deputy president of the Union Central Council, Ya.A. Beregovoi, spoke of the need for official recognition. The Union's funds were based on the sale of its publication, *Peremena* (*Change*), and on payments from various enterprises, cooperatives and private individuals, both Soviet and foreign. He suggested that its greatest strength would lie in the setting up of school councils and that its biggest task was to mobilize teachers, schoolchildren and all like-minded persons so as to make these really democratic.[8] (The establishment of school councils had been confirmed by G.A. Yagodin, chairman of the State Committee for Education, by a decree of August 1989.[9] They are discussed later in this chapter.)

In the next issue of the paper, a report of a meeting of the Union in the Pushkino area of Moscow regretted that the first few months in the life of the Union had been more a chain of mistakes and mishaps than of victories. After wide discussion, various decisions were taken. Beregovoi was to leave his job in Kiev to take up full-time work for the Union, and the first general programme would be known as the 'Launch of the Union' (*Zapusk Soyuza*). Two main fields of activity were to be set up, with V. Novichkov having overall responsibility for a programme of development, experimental platforms, Author Schools and an open university, and A. Adamsky in charge of Eureka and Change Clubs. The Union also decided to back various initiatives, such as: the development of pedagogical activity, under A. Tubelsky; the setting up of the Centre for Educational Innovation (*Tsentr pedagogicheskikh innovatsii*), in place of VNIK 'Shkola', under E. Dneprov; the open university, under B. Bim-Bad; a school of innovators, under S. Lysenkova; a programme for the all-round development of the child, under L. Nikitina; the development of the Commune method as the means of democratization of education, under O. Gazman. Programmes of particular interest would be presented at the conference planned for May 1990 in Sverdlovsk.[10]

THE EUREKA PROGRAMME

According to the same article, not all of the clubs had died while waiting for orders from the centre. Some were lively. This seemed to be true from my meeting in Moscow in April 1990 with A. Adamsky. The Eureka movement under the leadership of Adamsky and R. Seltzer has set up the Eureka Professional Education Programme. To quote from its English-language leaflet 'The Eureka Professional Education Program': 'It has established a cooperative Centre Eureka to gather together teachers and administrators of a school or district or city to develop educational experiments in individual schools and city, district and regional school systems.' The movement's aims are differentiation, development and cooperation. The teacher and student must work out their problems together. Adamsky, a former physics teacher and correspondent of *Uchitel'skaya gazeta* under Matveev, and his colleagues felt that to wait for a new generation of teachers to be trained would be too slow, and they hoped to set up alternative schools of their own, the first planned for Krasnodar in September 1990.

THE COMMUNE MOVEMENT

The Commune movement, which held its seminar in Zvenigorod in April 1990, originated in Leningrad in the late 1950s under the aegis of I. Ivanov, and is based on the theories of 1920s educators such as Krupskaya, Makarenko and Shatsky. The fundamental ideas are the development of personality and creativity, humour and sincerity, and the needs of the child. The teacher should perform the role not of an actor holding forth on the stage, a lecturer haranguing from a podium or an all-knowing tutor giving an edifying monologue but of an older friend who provides cooperation and understanding.

These ideas were developed in the late 1950s and early 1960s, but ran into difficulties in 1964 with the general re-freeze of personal freedom and opposition to democratization and creativity in education. The ideas continued to circulate but only in seminars and among senior pupils who sometimes managed to pass them on. Gazman called this the period of 'conservation' when the Commune theories had had to be put on ice.[11]

After 1986, with the support of the teacher-innovators and journalists such as Soloveichik and the late Matveev in Moscow, the Commune ideas were taken up again. At the April 1990 seminar over 200 people came together under the leadership of Gazman to discuss the main aims of the Commune theories of education: humanism, creativity and citizenship. Morning lectures were followed by afternoon workshops discussing among other subjects the problems of the freedom of the individual for both the teacher and student, and particularly what is known as the rehabilitation of individuality.

19

NEW TYPES OF SCHOOLS

Organizations such as the Commune and Eureka movements wanted to change the whole basis of the system of education. Other individuals worked within the system but with many of the same aims. A. Tubelsky abandoned his dissertation at the APN to set up one of the first Author Schools in Moscow at School No. 734, Izmailov District. His aim was to make children want to learn, by discovering the ways of learning themselves. During a visit to his school in April 1990, children in a sixth-year Russian class were being encouraged to write, and to read out, poems on what they thought and felt about themselves. In a music class the teacher played the currently popular Latin American dance music, Lombada, and the children sang songs by Vysotsky and Okudzhava.

Not only have new methods of teaching been approved but also new types of schools have been freely discussed and promoted. Differentiation has been an approved word for some time. The development of the 'lycée' and the 'gymnasium' had already begun in 1989. By autumn 1989 and spring 1990 there were reports of gymnasia set up in areas as far-ranging as Leningrad, Volgograd, Tbilisi and Kazakhstan. One of the points in common was the teaching of a more liberal curriculum including history of local culture and art, the study of the theatre and cinema, and world culture.[12]

Gymnasium No. 13 in Moscow was reported as teaching – besides German and English – Latin, philosophy, elementary economics, sociology, logic, psychology and world artistic culture. A lycée for talented boys, known as the Andrei Rublev International Lycée, was planned to open in September 1990 under the auspices of the *Russkaya entsiklopediya* All-Union Cultural Centre. L. Bystrov, director of the Centre, said that it was élitist only in the sense that entrants would be required to show profound knowledge of and an interest in the humanities. Entry, based on examination, would be open to 13 to 14-year-olds from any part of the country and from among Russian speakers abroad. Ties had been established with foreign teachers such as Dr R. Stichel from Munich and D. Billington of the Library of Congress in Washington who had proposed a link with the international St Sebastian College in the USA. The boys would study the history of Russian culture and Russian language, the history and literature of the Middle Ages, world religions, ethnography, and so on.[13]

The April 1990 issue of *Narodnoe obrazovanie*, the journal of the State Committee for Education, included details and photographs of two competing projects for 'lycée schools', one from Kiev and one from Moscow. The designs provided for classrooms, sports halls, swimming pools and a computer centre, as well as a school for the arts and one for industrial production, all with the most up-to-date equipment. A decision was made to divide the prize between both groups and to combine the best of both projects in the final construction.[14]

It would take too long to mention all of the different schools that have emerged. There were reports of the first fee-paying general school at work in Riga in September 1990;[15] an Orthodox gymnasium opening at School No. 1106, Moscow, on 2 September[16] (see Chapter 5); and seven alternative schools starting in Moscow, also in September. In the Bashkir Republic, self-financing schools, lycées, studios, courses and clubs were reported.[17]

THE PROBLEM OF FINANCE

Against the background of discussion and argument, and of innovation versus traditionalism, is the disturbing truth concerning the lack of funds available for education in the USSR. The chairman of the State Committee for Public Education, speaking at the XXVIII Party Congress in July 1990, commented on Gorbachev's assessment of the situation. That the establishment of new schools had increased by 38 per cent was true, but it did not take into account the number of schools which had been destroyed and the number which had deteriorated to the extent that they were no longer usable. This meant that the 38 per cent was quite unrepresentative of the situation. Only 50 per cent of the children who should be in kindergarten were there, and in schools 20 per cent of pupils still had to go to the second shift, that is every fifth child. Although teachers' salaries had been raised, they were still below the national average and well below the average for the production industries. Yagodin considered teachers to be productive people and thought that they should be paid on the same scale as those in the production industries. In Sweden, he said, they spent 1,000 dollars a year on a child's education. In the Soviet Union they spent 295 roubles. One could not underprice education.[18]

The director of Moscow School No. 855, G. Frish, also spoke at the Congress. He warned that the crisis in education was taking place at that very moment. It was happening to their children and their grandchildren. About one million minors in 1988 ended up committing criminal offences and about 80,000 14- to 17-year-olds were sent to penal colonies. There were now 67,000 youngsters in children's homes as well as 64,000 orphans in boarding schools. In 1960 the USSR was adjudged by UNESCO to be second in the world in the intellectualization of youth, and in 1990 it was lower than fiftieth. Their country was in need of everything: bread, flats and clothes. Teachers were paid little more than cleaners and the prestige of schools was lower than that of any other institution. At his school he was short of six teachers and it was impossible to find them anywhere. His friends from Volgograd were in the same situation. They were on the verge of a national catastrophe.[19]

Many others have criticized the amount to be spent on education. In June 1989 Rolan Bykov, the film director, spoke at the Congress of People's Deputies, comparing the 80,000 dollars spent in capitalist countries to train a specialist in a higher education establishment with the 12,000 roubles spent in the USSR, and even three times less in a teacher training institute.[20] Comparisons were constantly made between the amounts expended in Western countries and in the Soviet Union. V. Shukshunov, deputy chairman of the State Committee for Public Education, compared the 178,800m dollars spent on education in the USA in 1985 with the 37,900m roubles in the USSR.[21] The prognosis was not good either. Whereas 35 per cent of the non-industrial budget went to education in the 1960s, only 27.6 per cent was planned for 1990 and 35 per cent again in 1995. Many deputies at the December 1989 meeting voiced their anxieties and many tried to speak and failed. One teacher who spoke during a break in the proceedings was reported as saying that the shortage of teachers could cause a catastrophe and no young teachers wanted to teach in present conditions.[22] Many others felt that the Government's programme was devoid of interest in the development of education.[23]

At a discussion in the Supreme Soviet Committee for Science, Education, Culture and Upbringing, reported on 14 October 1989, Amonashvili expressed dismay that there were to be no funds for new teachers or buildings for 6-year-olds, and said that they might as well give up all of the aims that they had worked for and hand everything over to the military budget.[24]

Not even everything in education that was budgeted for was expected to come from the state. A proportion was to come from such organizations as the social development fund, state farms and other sources.[25] Schools were being encouraged to look around for private funding. At the IV World Congress for Soviet and East European Studies in July 1990, the then newly appointed Minister of Education of the RSFSR, E. Dneprov, spoke of the need for the economic independence of schools. Although Yagodin has supported this concept, little seems to have been achieved. In March 1990 a director of a secondary school in the Irkutsk Region referred to the independent funding of schools as a myth. The *rono* (district education authority), as before, holds the purse strings.[26]

DIFFICULTIES OF RURAL SCHOOLS

Lack of funds has led to shortages in most areas of education. Anyone who knows the Soviet secondary school scene in general must be aware that schools were never generously equipped. The bitterest complaints during the eighteen months to December 1990, however, were about rural schools, and particularly about teachers' conditions. The State Committee for Public Education set up a programme on the village school and together with *Uchitel'skaya gazeta* produced a questionnaire for rural teachers to indicate the circumstances in which they had to live and work.[27] By 23 February the paper reported having received 12,000 letters and gave examples, such as lack of cooperation with school councils by local party officials in the Sakhalin Region and bad conditions in a school in the Yurtov District of the Chechen-Ingush Autonomous Republic; a new school had been promised there in 1984, had been started but never completed and was now crumbling. Many of these letters contained horror stories: for example, in Yakutsk, there were outside toilets in weather of –15° C; there was nowhere to buy clothes or make-up, and no hairdressers; there were no men to meet; there was nothing to eat except horsemeat and sausage, and never any milk. From the Alma-Ata Region there were thirty letters about unpleasant conditions.[28] One teacher from Alupka wrote: 'I am in despair. In my room the temperature is below zero. I am freezing, almost dying and constantly ill. There is fungus growing on the walls and water under the floor. I am not the only one, but nobody cares.'[29]

On 20 April 1989 an article in *Uchitel'skaya gazeta* published statistics on village schools: 90,000 were without piped water, 1,353 without sewerage, 68,000 without heating and 6,000 without electricity. The campaign continued throughout 1989. December brought more statistics at the Conference of Education Workers in Moscow. While 40–45,000m roubles were needed for rural schools, so far only 12 million had been provided. Although help was expected under a new programme, '*Sel'skaya shkola*', in less than a year, how were they to survive until then, since 6.8 per cent of school buildings, accommodating over a million children, were being pulled down, while 18 per cent were under major repair?[30] There was little mention of village schools in the new and changed form of *Uchitel'skaya gazeta*, perhaps a sign of its less investigative style.

UNREST IN THE PRE-SCHOOL SECTOR

The year 1990 saw an attempt by workers in pre-school institutions to organize a strike over their poor working conditions and bad pay. The movement started in Moscow but spread to other areas and republics, where strike committees were set up in sympathy with the workers in the capital. Mention was made of such committees in Belorussia and in Sverdlovsk. A conference of pre-school workers was held in Moscow in April. Among the 1,200 participants were workers from many towns in the RSFSR and the Ukraine who complained that only Moscow was discussed.[31] The strike was finally cancelled after reassurances that the improvements in budgeting and administration which had been set out in Order No. 45 of January 1990 would be implemented.[32]

CHILDREN'S HEALTH AND ATTITUDINAL PROBLEMS

There has been much concern about the health of school children. On 25 November 1989, at a meeting of the State Committee which was called to consider problems of public education and children's health care, Yagodin was reported as saying that only one-quarter of school children could be considered completely healthy. More than 50 per cent of pre-school children had some kind of health problem. Up to 30 per cent of primary school children had speech problems, and 15-20 per cent suffered from nervous or psychological disorders.[33] Unfortunately, the children's standard of health did not improve as they went up the school but in fact became worse during the first eight years of their education. Of those leaving school, 45 per cent had chronic disorders and every fifth student in higher education was in need of medical care. Much of this, Yagodin said, was due to poor health care in the pre-school period.

When Yagodin's opponents attacked his educational changes, he charged them with such problems as the poor relationship between teachers and students and the lack of interest in education and study. Among the older students in secondary schools only 9 per cent had any real interest. While 30 per cent wished to attain a profession, 20 per cent thought study unnecessary for this purpose and 15 per cent considered that there was no point in education. It is not surprising therefore that only 19 per cent studied systematically, while 18 per cent did not study at all and 63 per cent merely studied from time to time.[34] Nor is it surprising that a teacher to whom I talked at School No. 587 in Moscow, where teacher-innovator Lysenkova works, shook her head sadly as she remarked that children did not want to learn. One of Tubelsky's main aims at his Author's School was to make children want to do so.[35]

THE SCHOOL COUNCIL

Attempts have been made to improve matters. In August 1989 Yagodin signed an order to set up school councils in secondary general schools. The intention was to give schools more autonomy in the choice of directors, to develop initiative in the work of the school collective, to create greater independence in the teaching process and in financial affairs, and to generate more democratic forms of administrative and self-governing bodies such as the school conference and the school council itself. The council was to be elected by the conference which in turn was elected by those members of the school collective with the right of a deciding vote. These were to consist equally of members from the three following categories: teachers and other school workers, pupils at the second and third stages (i.e. from class 5 onwards), and parents and members of the local community.

The role of the council was to be wide and varied, covering most aspects of the administration. It was intended to have authority over what subjects were taught in the school, the timetabling of school work (within the basic parameters of the curriculum), the age of the first-year pupils (whether 6 or 7), the numbers in the classes and the length of holidays. It was also intended to exercise control over budgetary expenditure, to hear reports from the teachers and the director, and to liaise with the work of local cooperative, experimental and charitable organizations. The council was to meet at least four times a year and, in order for its decisions to be binding, two-thirds of its membership had to be present.[36]

It is not surprising that with such a diversified role the councils came in for criticism. In certain areas they were said to exist in 30–40 per cent of schools. In others they existed to a lesser extent and, in some, attempts were being made to get rid of them. In many schools they were carrying out duties which should be performed by class parent associations, by organizers of extra-curricular activities or by the administration. Sometimes the director did not cooperate with the council, with a resultant lowering of the council's prestige. Generally speaking, the terms of reference of the councils were considered to be too vague, and there was a need for a clearer definition of the councils' role as well as of the rights and obligations of teachers and pupils. There were complaints that discipline was on the wane and that children were becoming more difficult to work with. Pupils were demanding their rights, rights which the APN journal *Sovetskaya pedagogika* considered were not always appropriate. This was said to reflect the complex socio-political situation in the country as a whole.[37]

VNIK 'SHKOLA-MIKRORAION'

Perhaps as an antidote to some of the social problems facing Soviet youth, an organization known as *VNIK 'Shkola-mikroraion'* (Provisional Research Group on the School and Catchment Area) was set up. Its aim was to find a new model of social upbringing for children and adults. The head of the organization, V. Bocharova, believed that the social changes that had occurred and the fact that the child was no longer part of a unified state machine where school, Pioneer camp and Komsomol were the centres of attention meant that there was a need for something to take their place. The family should now become a micro-centre. As there was nobody capable of making the link between school and family, a system of social educators was being constructed to provide contacts between the individual, family and society. The social educators would work in all teaching establishments and would be trained specially for the job in teacher training institutions. By summer 1990 there were already 1,000 of them at work. At the spring session of VNIK an Association of Social Educators was set up, headed by D. Fel'dshtein of the Institute of General and Pedagogical Psychology of the APN.[38] The scheme is presumably meant to bridge the Soviet version of the generation gap and to try to provide an alternative for the lost ideology of Marxism-Leninism among disillusioned and disorientated youth, who seem to have nothing to look forward to except increasing unemployment and a continually low standard of living.

NEW MODEL CURRICULUM

On 22 September 1989 the State Committee for Public Education approved a new model curriculum (Table 2.1). Its purpose was to reduce the standardization of the old curriculum and provide greater flexibility, to lighten the workload, and to lay a more humanitarian basis for schooling. It was intended to fulfil the aims of society and state with regard to educational and cultural needs at national, regional and local levels. It had three components, designated those of the Union and republic, the republic and the school. The humanization of teaching meant showing respect for the child and his or her individuality, skills and interests. To this end there was to be a cutback in the study load, which would result in a reduction of homework and a five-day week. There was to be a shift to the humanities, from 41 to 50 per cent of the curriculum.[39] (For further comment, see the introductory section of Chapter 4.)

DIFFERENTIATION: THE FUTURE PATTERN?

The emergence of radical reform and the independent initiatives of the Commune and Eureka groups and the Author Schools was supported by G. Yagodin. His confirmation of the need for many different kinds of schools was encouraging to their advocates. During 1989 and 1990 one read of gymnasia and lycées, and of school cooperatives where the children earned some of the much-needed money by selling goods or services.

During the World Congress on Soviet and East European Studies in Harrogate in July 1990, E. Dneprov was asked about private schools. In his answer he made it clear that such schools, which in the Soviet Union were called alternative or cooperative schools, 'because the word "private" causes allergic reactions in the USSR', were already on the way to being generally recognized. The legalization of cooperative schools was then being considered by the Supreme Soviet. There were already private day nurseries and nursery schools and tentative moves towards private schools.

On the question of finance the Soviet approach was different from other countries. The aim, according to Dneprov, was to establish a basic minimum education provided by the state and a statutory minimum spending per capita to achieve it. This was to be the foundation of the new system of financing. For any school, including private schools, the government was obliged to pay the per capita minimum. Above this there could be payments by parents. Dneprov said that opinion had been prepared for the change in the last two years, and provision was being made for supplementary payments in the new school statutes. A draft of these had been published in April 1990.[40]

All this is a long way from the universal, free, compulsory, secular and undifferentiated school of the 1917 Revolution. The new differentiated

Table 2.1 Outline curriculum for Soviet secondary general schools, lesson periods per week, 1989[a]

	Stages and classes											Total
	I				II					III		
	1	2	3	4	5	6	7	8	9	10	11	
UNION AND REPUBLIC COMPONENT												
Russian language	–	2	3	3	3	3	3	2	2	2	–	23
USSR peoples' literature	–	–	–	–	–	–	–	–	–	2	2	4
Mathematics	4	4	5	5	5	5	5	5	5	4	4	51
Natural science[b]	1	1	1	1	2	3	4	6	6	4	4	33
Social science[b]	1	1	1	1	2	2	2	4	4	4	4	26
Total (A)	6	8	10	10	12	13	14	17	17	16	14	137
REPUBLIC COMPONENT[c] (B)	14	14	14	14	14	15	14	11	11	8	10	139
SCHOOL COMPONENT												
Compulsory-choice courses and special studies (C)	–	–	–	–	–	–	–	2	2	6	6	16
Options and supplementary studies (D)	2	2	2	2	4	4	4	4	4	6	6	40
Total (C + D)	2	2	2	2	4	4	4	6	6	12	12	56
TOTAL LESSON PERIODS excluding options (A+B+C)	20	22	24	24	26	28	28	30	30	30	30	292
Permitted study load including options (A+B+C+D)	22	24	26	26	30	32	32	34	34	36	36	332

[a] Approved 22 September 1989, i.e. after start of school year; no firm date for introduction.
[b] 'Natural science' includes geography; 'social science' includes history.
[c] 'Republic component' includes national language and literature, foreign language, history and geography of the republic, music, art, labour training and physical education/military training.

Source: Byulleten' Gosudarstvennogo komiteta SSSR po narodnomu obrazovaniyu. Seriya: Doshkol'noe vospitanie i obshchee srednee obrazovanie, 1990, no. 1, pp. 17–18. Layout slightly simplified; notes based on accompanying commentary, pp. 18–20. Cited in 'Outline curriculum for Soviet general schools', *Soviet Education Study Bulletin,* 1991, vol. 9, no. 2, p. 76.

system is likely to percolate slowly through a country the size of the Soviet Union. Much of the experimentation and innovation is contained in small areas of independent initiative and will probably remain there for some time.

Dneprov mentioned some of the difficulties involved in combating the bureaucratic system. He said that they were working with the IMTEC[41] system for educational innovation set up by the OECD in the 1960s, in order to hasten the spread of innovatory methods throughout the country, but that there were still difficulties with state organizations and with others who wanted to cash in on the problems.[42]

The possibilities of differentiation, however, will mean that those who wish something other than the basic minimum, who can afford it and who are in reach of it, will be able to benefit by it. How widespread it becomes and how quickly it develops will obviously depend on the future political and economic development of the Soviet Union, which is as unpredictable now as it ever was. The growing independence of the various regions makes the situation even more unpredictable. It heightens the possibility of the gradual replacement of *Soviet* education by increasingly more autonomous local and regional versions.

NOTES AND REFERENCES

1 'Through humanization and democratization toward a new quality of education', *Current Digest of the Soviet Press*, 1989, vol. 40, no. 52, p. 1 (translated from *Pravda*, 21 December 1988, p. 3).

2 'The mission of the teacher and the instructor is noble and responsible', *Current Digest of the Soviet Press*, 1989, vol. 40, no. 52, p. 4 (translated from *Uchitel'skaya gazeta* [hereafter *UG*], 24 December 1988, pp. 1–8).

3 'Dve tochki zreniya – obyazatel'no li obshchee srednee?', *Izvestiya*, 15 December 1988, p. 3.

4 V. Matveev, 'Sdelat' shag, kuda?', *UG*, 4 February 1989, p. 2.

5 S.N. Lysenkova, 'Terpite, vy novatory', *UG*, 12 January 1989, p. 2.

6 A. Adamsky, 'Soyuz soyuznikov – Vstretitsya na teplokhode', *UG*, 15 April 1989, p. 1.

7 Sh. Amonashvili, 'Soyuz soyuznikov – Uspekh tebe uchreditel'nyi', *UG*, 11 May 1989, p. 1.

8 'Kogda v tovarishchakh soglas'e est'' (interview with Ya.A. Beregovoi), *UG*, 1990, no. 7, p. 3. The style of reference to *UG* is changed in accordance with its new frequency of publication from 1990.

9 'Shkol'nyi sovet: prava i obyazannosti. Polozhenie o sovete srednei obshche-obrazovatel'noi shkole', *UG*, 24 August 1989, p. 2.

10 T. Miledina, 'Soyuz soyuznikov – Programma: zapusk', *UG*, 1990, no. 8, p. 5. The Nikitins' methods of rearing their own children received much publicity in the West from the 1970s; see in particular B. and L. Nikitin, *Die Nikitin-Kinder: ein Modell frühkindlicher Erziehung* and *Aufbauende Spiele* (M. Butenschön, ed.), Cologne, Kiepenheuer & Witsch, 1978 and 1980 respectively (Ed.).

11 O. Gazman, 'Kollektivnoe tvorcheskoe', *UG*, 17 December 1987, p.2.

12 'Ideya v rabote – vozvrashchenie gimnazii', *UG*, 5 October 1989, p. 1.

13 P. Fil', 'V litsee tol'ko mal'chiki', *Moskovskaya Pravda*, 7 January 1990, p. 2. German name retransliterated.

14 'Proekt utverzhden', *Narodnoe obrazovanie*, 1990, no. 4, p. 68.

15 S. Alferenko, 'Ideya v rabote – Imei sto rublei!', *UG*, 1990, no. 36, p. 3. Interview with one of the teachers of the proposed new-style school, to be called at first

'experimental classes of Author humanitarian fee-paying schooling', based on School No. 70.
16 'Moskva, 2 sentyabrya', *UG*, 1990, no. 36, p. 2 (caption to picture).
17 'Al'ternativa 2', *UG*, 1990, no. 38, p. 3.
18 G. Yagodin, 'Obrazovanie pervichno!', *UG*, 1990, no. 28, p. 2.
19 G. Frish, 'Kogda partii postuchatsya v shkoly', *UG*, 1990, no. 28, p. 2.
20 R. Bykov, 'Slova i tribuny – ekonomika nashego detstva', *UG*, 13 June 1989, p. 1.
21 V. Shukshunov, 'Vuz – eto sozvezdie lichnostei', *UG*, 7 September 1989, p. 1.
22 T. Skorobogatko, 'Opyat' ne do shkoly – pochemu golos uchitelei po-prezhnemu ne slyshen na s"ezde?', *UG*, 19 December 1989, p. 1.
23 V. Zhukov, 'Razgovory v pol'zu bednykh', *UG*, 21 December 1989, p. 1.
24 'U kogo klyuchi ot seifov', *UG*, 14 October 1989, pp. 1–2.
25 'Mery chrezvychainye. Rezul'tat tot zhe?', *UG*, 30 September 1989, p. 2.
26 V. Nikiforov, 'Chto dumayu – pryach'te kotel'ki ot rono', *UG*, 1990, no. 11, p. 7.
27 'Sel'skaya shkola zhdet peremen', *UG*, 16 February 1989, p. 1.
28 'Pis'mo v nomer – gde-to tam daleko', *UG*, 21 February 1989, p. 1; 'Rukhnuvshii podarok', *UG*, 23 February 1989, p. 2.
29 'Kvadratnye metry – lyubvi i boli', *UG*, 28 March 1989, p. 3.
30 'Klass v yurte, pochemu by net?', *UG*, 2 December 1989, p. 2.
31 'O detskikh sadakh vserez', and 'A chto v Moskve? Poiski konstruktivnykh reshenii', *UG*, 1990, no. 18, p. 2.
32 'Zabastovku ne provodit', *UG*, 1990, no. 20, p. 2.
33 'Absolyutno zdorov tol'ko kazhdyi chetvertyi', *UG*, 25 November 1989, p. 1.
34 G. Yagodin, 'Kakoe zhe vse-taki u nas obrazovanie?', *UG*, 23 December 1989, p. 1.
35 S.N. Lysenkova and A. Tubelsky, personal communications, April 1990.
36 'Shkol'nyi sovet: prava i obyazannosti. Polozhenie o sovete srednei obshche-obrazovatel'noi shkoly', *UG*, 24 August 1989, p. 2.
37 'Shkol'nyi sovet: kakim byt'?', *Sovetskaya pedagogika*, 1990, no. 9, pp. 113–17.
38 V. Bocharova, 'Eksperimental'nye ploshchadki – put' k novoi shkole – zona doveriya', *Narodnoe obrazovanie*, 1990, no. 9, p. 41.
39 'Ob utverzhdenii gosudarstvennogo bazisnogo uchebnogo plana srednei obshcheobrazovatel'noi shkoly', *Byulleten' Gosudarstvennogo komiteta SSSR po narodnomu obrazovaniyu. Seriya: Doshkol'noe vospitanie i obshchee srednee obrazovanie*, 1990, no. 1, pp. 17–23.
40 'Osnovy zakonodatel'stva Soyuza SSR i soyuznykh respublik o narodnom obrazovanii', *UG*, 1990, no. 15, pp. 9–10.
41 International Movement towards Educational Change (now known as the International Learning Cooperative on Educational Reform), located in Oslo, Norway, and coordinated by Per Dalin.
42 E. Dneprov, address to education researchers at IV World Congress on Soviet and East European Studies, Harrogate, UK, 23 July 1990.

3

THE COMING OF COMPUTER AGE IN SOVIET GENERAL EDUCATION, 1985–90

Jane M. Lommel

INTRODUCTION

Compared to its growth in the United States, Japan and Western Europe, a popular computer culture has been slow to take off in the Soviet Union. The reasons for this are numerous. Some observers have argued that Soviet citizens have little use for computers and therefore little interest in them. Graham[1] and Shanor[2] conjectured that Soviet leaders were deeply suspicious of computers because they perceived them and the information revolution as a threat to the state's control of information and its uses.

One of the main reasons for the stunted Soviet computer culture has been nothing more mysterious than the general unavailability of appropriate hardware and software. Although there has been significant improvement in Soviet mainframe and mini-computer technology, personal computers have remained extremely scarce and of dubious quality. This situation led E.P. Velikhov, a prominent Soviet computer expert, to complain that a vicious circle is at work, that is, the demand for personal computers is weak because few are available, while few are produced because the demand is weak.[3]

Whatever the reasons for the computer literacy gap, the Soviet leadership under Gorbachev was determined to try to close it shortly after he came to power in 1985. 'Microelectronics, computer technology, instrument making and the entire information science industry', said the General Secretary in *Pravda* on 12 June 1985, 'are the catalysts of progress.' Other Soviet writers saw this technology as decisive in the great contest between the USSR and the West. For example, Vinokurov and Zuev, writing in the party journal *Kommunist*, argued: 'The progress of modern electronic, computer and robot technology is not only an essential part of the scientific and technical revolution but also an arena of fundamental competition between the two socio-economic systems.'[4]

The Soviet leadership understood that it would be futile to produce more and better microprocessors and computers without also training and educating its workforce to make best use of the new technology. To make up for lost time and to develop a level of popular computer culture appropriate to the demands of a new age, the leadership launched a major campaign to spur computer literacy in its schools, beginning in 1985.

Gorbachev's strong personal support for this particular aspect of the campaign was manifest from the start. The Commission on the Reform of General and Vocational Schools, which he had chaired under Chernenko and which oversaw the introduction of a comprehensive reorganization of Soviet secondary education, went on record with its concern that school students should attain computer literacy and that computers should be widely used in the teaching process.[5] Although much of the school reform was later to be repudiated, this principle retained its validity.

Early in 1985, with Chernenko near death, the Politburo of the CPSU Central Committee met under Gorbachev's gavel to adopt a resolution providing for the introduction of a new course called 'Fundamentals of Information Science and Computer Technology' in all Soviet secondary schools. The same resolution also provided for an intensive experiment in computer-assisted teaching, for conducting training courses for teachers of the subject, for creating computer laboratories in the schools, and for the development of appropriate software and teaching methods.[6]

SOME HISTORICAL PERSPECTIVES

Computers have not always been at the top of the Politburo's priority list. Indeed, in the early 1950s the subject of cybernetics was considered by Soviet ideologists to be a 'bourgeois false science' and 'idealistic obscurantism'.[7] After Stalin's death, the subject was habilitated – it could hardly have been 'rehabilitated' since it had enjoyed no previous Soviet existence – and cybernetics became the Russian rage. But it was what A.A. Dorodnitsyn, a prominent Soviet computer scientist, called 'cybernetics talkative' as opposed to 'cybernetics active'.[8] In other words, it was mostly empty abstraction.

In recent years, the term 'cybernetics' has rather fallen from fashion and given way in Russian to the term *informatika*, which translates as the French *informatique* and in English as 'computer science' or 'information science'. With the name change has come a significant rise in the subject's intellectual content. In 1984 the prestigious Academy of Sciences established a new Section of Information Sciences, Computers and Automation to foster research and development in the field. All of this has been accompanied by an overall improvement in the quantity and quality of Soviet computer technology.

Kerr gave American readers a very useful picture of Soviet educational technology.[9] Subsequently he described some of the considerable activity that has characterized Soviet efforts in educational computing. He also accurately noted that American readers would never guess that such activity exists if their reading were confined to the 'generally condescending news accounts about Soviet capabilities in the area of high technology'.[10] Soviet educators in 1985 were at considerable pains to counter the condescension noted by Kerr. They pointed out that the new schools literacy campaign did not start from square one. An increasing number of academic computer centres are equipped with machines of the ES or SM families of computers. The ES (*Edinaya sistema* or 'Unified System', more widely known as the *Ryad*) mainframe computers are program-compatible with the IBM 360/370 family. The SM (*Sistema malaya*) series of mini-computers is less homogeneous, but many of them are program-compatible with machines manufactured by the Digital Equipment Corporation and Hewlett Packard.[11]

In the last few years, microcomputers of various descriptions have appeared in the Soviet academic computer environment. Computer specialists in increasing numbers are graduating from post-secondary institutions. At the middle stage of the secondary level, the Class 8 algebra syllabus contains an introduction to algorithms. Some schools have offered computer science or programming as an enrichment subject. Most if not all of such schools are fortunate to have close ties with more senior educational or research organizations. Evening courses and summer schools or 'camps' have been available in certain places, especially in Novosibirsk which was an early hotbed of interest in educational computing. Pereslavl'-Zalesskii also offers a summer camp for exceptional Soviet teenagers to improve their programming skills.[12]

In recent years another group of schools has joined the set of élite institutions that provide computer instruction and/or computer-assisted learning. The programs here are experimental in nature and designed to give educators and researchers an opportunity to develop the role that computers should play in mass education. Novosibirsk was the epicentre of this activity. At School No. 166, children in the lowest years partake of computer-assisted pedagogy under the gaze of researchers from the Siberian Section of the Academy of Sciences. In Pereslavl' the Academy's Software Development Institute works out ideas for educational software with young people. The direction and focus that the youngsters give to this software assists researchers to produce quality materials for the mass education market.

More than 300 schools were said to be giving instruction in computer programming before the new course began to be introduced in September 1985. These comprised about one-half of 1 per cent of the nearly 61,000 secondary schools in the USSR.[13] The great majority of these privileged schools shared two features. First, they were physically or organizationally close to senior institutions of education, research or industry and were able to make some use of the latter's facilities and staff. Second, instruction in computers was focused on programming and was considered to be an enrichment for selected pupils taking the regular mathematics, physics and chemistry courses. This is in contrast to the pattern in US schools where competence in computer usage is understood by many *not* to include programming languages and skills, and where computers at the secondary level are more heavily used in the language arts for word processing and in many other subject areas outside mathematics and the physical sciences.

The current drive for computer literacy goes far beyond any previous effort to introduce computers into Soviet schools. Its zealots have likened it to the great campaign to stamp out illiteracy that was undertaken in the years immediately following the Bolshevik Revolution. That famous campaign was but one of the first of a long list of forced drives to achieve goals posited as imperatives by the party leadership. In this respect, however it may be in others, Gorbachev's drive to achieve universal computer literacy is well within the Soviet tradition.

AIMS AND OBJECTIVES OF THE NEW COMPUTER COURSE

The new course was designed by a team of eminent Soviet computer scientists and educators. Captain of the team was the late Academician A.P. Ershov, an internationally respected computer scientist from the Computing Centre of the Siberian Section of the USSR Academy of Sciences in Novosibirsk. In addition to Ershov, the design group included V.M. Monakhov, director of the then Institute of Curriculum and Method of the APN (*Akademiya pedagogicheskikh nauk*, Academy of Pedagogical Sciences), as well as other prominent representatives of the two academies. Both Ershov and Monakhov became Soviet media celebrities in connection with their leadership of the computer literacy campaign.

From their earlier work with in-school computing, the course designers developed some definite ideas of what computer literacy in the Soviet schools should be. This is exemplified by the contents of the syllabus[14] and the first experimental textbook (to be reviewed below) and the teacher's handbook, all published under the direction of Ershov and Monakhov.[15]

It is instructive to examine the Soviet definition of the term 'information science'. According to Monakhov:

> Information science is that field of science which studies the structure and general attributes of scientific information and also questions connected with the collection, storage, retrieval, processing, transformation, and use of information in the most diverse spheres of human activity.[16]

The definition is a little vague but one well within the mainstream of international computer science thinking.

No secret is made of the ultimate goal to be furthered by bringing computer literacy instruction to the schools. It is to equip young people with the skills and knowledge of computers that will make them productive workers in the new information age. This will be an age in which microprocessors, computers and other information processing devices are to be commonplace from the shop floor to Gosplan (the State Planning Commission) and from cars to missiles.

In the United States and the Western world, the microprocessor is most famous for being the brains of the personal computer. In the Soviet vision, that role is not totally ignored but its importance is far behind the microprocessor's place as the controller of programmable machine tools, production processes and robotics. A second major role in which Soviet thinkers cast the computer is that of CAD/CAM (computer-assisted design and manufacturing). Third in importance would be the use of microcomputers in research development. Ershov gave us a clue to what 'personal computing' means in the Soviet lexicon: 'The computer will become the personal tool of an ever greater number of people: engineers, designers, dispatchers, librarians, cashiers, operators of program-controlled machine tools, production controllers, and workers in dozens of occupations'.[17]

To cope successfully in a robotic world, the future Soviet worker must feel at ease with and be able to use a wide range of devices containing embedded microprocessors. That implies a level of technical familiarity with computer components and functions, a kind of nitty-gritty knowledge, beyond that encompassed by the usual American and Western understanding of computer literacy. When spurning technical details of computers or programming languages, the typical American secondary student is wont to draw a parallel between computers and automobiles by saying, 'I don't need to be a mechanic to drive a car'. For those to whom computing means using Microsoft Works, electronic mail and Hypermedia, the analogy is not altogether misplaced. But an information age predominantly defined by their personal use of word processing, desktop publishing and electronic bulletin boards is not what Gorbachev and his colleagues have in mind. Their vision is one of ubiquitous robotics and the professional use of desktop computers by designers, project planners, engineers, researchers and technologists. The importance of this difference in Soviet and Western visions of the information age would be hard to exaggerate.

The new course was pulled by a troika of basic concepts: information, the algorithm and the computer. All three are said to be equal, but in fact one is more equal than the others. Ershov defined an algorithm as 'an intelligible and precise set of instructions to an executor to fulfil a sequence of actions aimed to achieve a specified goal or to solve a predetermined task'.[18] Ershov, Monakhov and their colleagues understood an algorithm as not only a structured, sequential method of problem-solving but also a way of thinking, a culture, a way of life. Once again, Ershov:

> the students' interaction with the computer will develop in them a unique mode of cognition. It will include certain skills of mental activity that are especially essential to the modern Soviet person irrespective of

his or her line of work . . . It is hard to exaggerate the value of being able to think algorithmically.[19]

As important and challenging as the new course was, it was regarded as only one skirmish in the battle to achieve broad computer literacy among Soviet secondary school students. Computer literacy is seen as a basic component of the content of all secondary education. That means eventually using the computer as a learning tool in geography, history and the social sciences. Computer-assisted learning systems and colourful, graphic and animated educational software are visualized on the horizon in Soviet education.

There was no shortage of dreams among the leaders of the educational computer literacy campaign. Dreams, however, are cheap, while computers are not. By concentrating first on the daunting but relatively more tractable task of introducing the new course and deferring the more ambitious computer applications to another day, Ershov and his colleagues were practising their own preaching about solving big problems as a sequence of smaller, more manageable ones.

COURSE CONTENT

Greater insight into the nature of the new course can be gained by studying the original outline syllabus and the preliminary textbook. As indicated earlier, the new course was designed as a broadening of the normal mathematical instruction provided to senior (Classes 9 and 10) students in all Soviet secondary general schools. As such, it accompanies four to five hours per week of other mathematics in those years. ('Hour' [chas] signifies a 50-minute lesson period.)

The course has both theoretical and applied components. Local availability of computers and teacher preferences dictated and still dictate the proportions of each in the course as it is actually delivered; this point will be further addressed below. On the theoretical level, the course was designed to provide knowledge of the following: how to analyse phenomena with a view to modelling them mathematically; how to build mathematical models of phenomena; the various types of algorithms; how to construct algorithms; the elements and syntax of an algorithm; one computer language; and the concept of software and applications programs. At the practical level, the aim of the course was to give students practice in choosing and developing algorithms, writing computer programs and solving problems through programming.

The ninth-year portion was designed to occupy one hour per week of class time or 34 hours in total. The specific parts of the course broke down as follows:

1 Introduction (2 hours). Definitions. Basic computer components and their functions. The relation between computers and information science. (The

hand calculator was to be the main device used to acquaint students with computer concepts.)

2 Algorithms and an algorithmic language (6 hours). The concept of an algorithm. Examples and attributes. Executors of algorithms, human and machine. Writing algorithms. Instructions. Looping and branching. Practical examples. Automatic execution.

3 Algorithms that work with variables (10 hours). Variables, their types, names and values. Arguments in algorithms. Assignment. Conditions, testing and branching. Arrays. Sub-procedures. Top-down specifications.

4 Building algorithms for problem solution (16 hours). The steps of problem solution. Formulating the problem. Determining arguments and results. Building the mathematical model. The micro-calculator as a computing unit. Constructing algorithms and solution of problems from courses in mathematics, physics and chemistry.[20]

In Class 10, the emphasis moved towards computers. In schools blessed with computers, the course was designed to occupy two hours per week of classroom time or 68 hours in total. Students in schools without computers, the vast majority since 1985, were budgeted to spend half as much time in class. The course continued thus:

5 The basics of computer design and operation (12 hours). Number systems. Data and text representation in computers. Computer memory, the various types and functions. Computer arithmetic. Registers, accumulators, arithmetic and logical unit. Control principles: machine instructions and their structure. The control unit. Automatic program execution. Input/output; functions and units. Computer generations. Integrated circuits and microprocessors; their technology and production.

6 Introduction to programming (16 hours). The program as implemented algorithm. Features of the computer as an executor of algorithms. Comparisons of algorithmic languages and their features. Programming languages. Data. Variables. Basic instructions of input and output, assignment, control. Sub-programs and functions. Writing a program. Prepared programs and software packages.

7 The role of computers in modern society. Perspectives for further development of the technology (2 hours). Computer applications: engineering and economic calculations, mathematical modelling, automatic control systems, information retrieval systems, automated work stations. The changing workplace. Computers and the future of the Soviet economy.

8 Excursion to a computer centre (4 hours).[21]

An alternative syllabus, intended for schools which actually possessed a computer laboratory, was issued in the spring of 1986.[22]

RESOURCES FOR THE NEW COURSE

The Soviet handbook of educational statistics records over 63,000 day secondary general schools in the Soviet Union for the 1987/8 school year. Senior-stage students numbered approximately 5.9m.[23] Of these, nearly 98 per cent were reported to have studied the computing course. Only 13.7 per cent of the schools, however, had computer laboratories (Table 3.1). These privileged 8,600 schools had nearly 62,000 computer workstations (Table 3.2). This compares favourably to the situation only a year earlier when only 9.9 per cent of Soviet secondary schools had computer laboratories, with 38,300 computers.[24] When one breaks down the 1987/8 statistics into data by republic, there are striking contrasts. The Russian Republic had 15 per cent of its schools with 33,900 computers, while Tadzhikistan and Turkmenia

Table 3.1 Provision of Soviet secondary general schools[a] (SGS) with laboratories for Information Science and Computer Technology, 1986–8 (day schools, start of school year)

	Number of SGS with computer laboratories and percentage of all SGS					
	1986	*%*	*1987*[b]	*%*	*1988*	*%*
USSR	6111	9.9	8636	13.7	7438	11.5
RSFSR	3341	11.5	4452	15.0	4035	13.2
Ukraine	1464	16.2	1991	21.6	949	10.0
Belorussia	56	2.3	97	3.9	193	7.6
Uzbekistan	774	12.8	519	8.4	590	9.3
Kazakhstan	202	4.9	717	17.1	758	17.8
Georgia	38	2.1	162	8.7	136	7.2
Azerbaidzhan	21	0.9	195	8.2	114	4.7
Lithuania	21	3.3	60	9.4	95	14.7
Moldavia	52	5.9	137	15.4	48	5.3
Latvia	23	6.8	65	18.9	115	32.7
Kirgizia	17	1.4	63	5.1	85	6.7
Tadzhikistan	40	2.5	10	0.6	37	2.2
Armenia	48	4.7	138	13.3	217	20.6
Turkmenia	–	–	8	0.6	34	2.7
Estonia	14	6.8	22	10.7	32	15.4

[a] Secondary general schools are those which include the senior stage.
[b] Derived from percentages, so approximate.

Sources: Vestnik statistiki, 1988, no. 8, p. 67; *Narodnoe obrazovanie i kul'tura v SSSR*, Moscow, Finansy i statistika, 1989, pp. 48–63, 104.

Table 3.2 Provision of computer workstations at Soviet secondary general schools, 1986–8 (day schools, start of school year)

	1986	1987 [a]	*1988*
USSR	38290	61800	69196
RSFSR	22706	33900	39371
Ukraine	6598	9200	7500
Belorussia	401	900	1918
Uzbekistan	3931	4500	5956
Kazakhstan	770	2800	1851
Georgia	332	2400	1726
Azerbaidzhan	316	2500	2075
Lithuania	279	600	1115
Moldavia	815	1300	570
Latvia	280	800	1487
Kirgizia	227	800	1386
Tadzhikistan	790	100	483
Armenia	683	1600	2606
Turkmenia	–	100	565
Estonia	162	300	587

[a] Rounded in original.

Sources: Vestnik statistiki, 1988, no. 8, p. 67; *Narodnoe obrazovanie i kul'tura v SSSR,* Moscow, Finansy i statistika, 1989, p. 104.

shared the dubious distinction of each having only 0.6 per cent of their schools with a combined total of 200 computers. Belorussia and Kirgizia had respectively 3.9 per cent and 5.1 per cent of their schools equipped. Azerbaidzhan (8.2 per cent), Uzbekistan (8.4 per cent), Georgia (8.7 per cent) and Lithuania (9.4 per cent) had a somewhat higher share of their schools covered. Along with the RSFSR, the 10 per cent level was exceeded only by Estonia with 10.7 per cent, Armenia with 13.3 per cent, Moldavia with 15.4 per cent, Kazakhstan with 17.1 per cent, Latvia with 18.9 per cent and the Ukraine with 21.6 per cent.[25] These figures starkly outline the magnitude of the task of providing the resources to deliver the computer literacy course.

The resources for the new course fall into three categories: the course materials which had to be prepared and published, the teachers whose knowledge had to be created or upgraded, and the computer hardware and software to be used. The provision of these resources was in no case a simple matter.

Course materials

The course materials consisted initially of a textbook, a student workbook and a teacher's handbook. All were under the editorship of Ershov and Monakhov. Some 3.3m copies of the student workbook and enough copies of the teacher's handbook to supply each school with three or four were reportedly published by early September 1985. The textbook was also made available to the schools.

Although the books may have been off the presses by the opening day of the 1985/6 school year, many teachers and students had not received them. The editors of *Uchitel'skaya gazeta*, the teachers' newspaper, were receiving letters daily during the autumn of 1985 asking questions such as: 'How do we teach information systems without textbooks?' and 'Where is the promised teacher's handbook?' Every other letter asked for help and for any kind of material that could be used in lesson preparation.

Responding to such requests, *Uchitel'skaya gazeta* began in September 1985 to print a series of articles on the principles of computers. These articles, designed to fill the void left by the tardy course materials and to supplement them after they arrived, appeared at approximately weekly intervals throughout the 1985/6 school year. They paralleled the syllabus and probably helped the teachers to stay a few days ahead of their students.[26]

Initial developments in teacher training

The job of teaching information science and computers fell mainly to teachers of mathematics and physics. According to Ershov, there were about 50,000 of these teachers during the 1985/6 school year[27] – which would have left at least 10,000 schools without a teacher of the subject. If Soviet statistics are to be taken seriously, teachers must have been very taxed. Given that they were already working long hours with relatively large classes, the prospect of the additional teaching load must have aroused some consternation in their ranks.

The challenge of the staffing problem lies not only in the number of teachers but also in their qualifications or lack thereof. Fewer than 10 per cent of Soviet mathematics and physics teachers were likely to have had any previous experience with computers. Whatever the precise figures, it is clear that a teacher training task of impressive proportions loomed, and continues to do so if the new course is to be taught satisfactorily.

The first response was to mount a crash course in information systems and computers for thousands of mathematics and physics teachers. Assignments to conduct summer teacher training courses went out from Moscow in early 1985 to scores of post-secondary institutions. No staff member with training or experience in computers was safe from the call to become an instructor on this new course. The dragnet reached also into industrial enterprises, research institutes and other organizations. Anyone with computer expertise was a candidate.

In April 1985 hundreds of summer instructors-to-be attended a national conference at Moscow State University to hear from Ershov and his colleagues about how teacher training was to be conducted. The most important hurdle to overcome was taken to be that of the teachers' 'computer phobia'. Their confidence had to be buttressed. Ershov admonished this new army of instructors as follows:

> The most important task, by far, of these training courses is to convince the teacher of his or her ability to cope fully and successfully with the challenge of teaching information science and computer technology. This conviction will not come automatically. Impressive displays of computer capabilities that the teacher may see at the training centre may only reinforce his or her fear of the computer, and evoke the image of an unbridgeable chasm between his or her familiar world and the imposing surroundings of the training institution or computer centre.[28]

Ershov was clearly concerned that the instructors might intimidate the teachers with their computer expertise. Instructors were told to take a sensitive and interactive approach to their summer students. They were warned not to try to impress teachers with their own erudition or with awesome displays of computer prowess. The first thing to do was 'to get to know the teachers personally, to understand their attitudes, to try to gauge the extent of their previous preparation, to assess their psychological state and to learn the conditions under which they work and the capabilities of their students'.[29]

Didactic lectures were to be kept to a minimum. The goal was not to try to stuff the teachers' heads with a mass of technological knowledge. The whole summer course was to be structured around the student workbook. 'For the overwhelming majority of teachers', wrote Ershov, 'the workbook will be the main resource available to influence their students.' It was vital that the teachers should understand thoroughly every assignment and know how to solve every problem. 'Every phrase must be read together (i.e. by the instructor and trainees), every problem solved. Every possible submerged shoal must be marked and its circumnavigation charted.'[30]

In the interests of good pedagogy, it undoubtedly made plenty of sense to structure tightly the summer training programme. A more fundamental factor, however, was at stake. The Soviet school is hardly an egalitarian environment. By its tradition, teachers impart knowledge; students receive it. Thus any situation in which students were on their own, out ahead of their teachers, could be quite disconcerting to the teachers who might find their status as authority figures threatened. Even so, Ershov warned teachers that they should not even try to disguise from students the fact that they were learning the new subject simultaneously with their students. To do otherwise would soon be exposed as fraudulent by the students and the loss of face would be even greater. He continued:

> The teacher remains as before the senior comrade with a reservoir of experience and authority. At the same time, an atmosphere of equality before the subject, as all the experience of giving information science lessons in the schools convincingly shows, strengthens the creative situation in the classroom, bolsters the students' confidence in the teacher, and reduces the likelihood of pompous parroting or silent sabotage in this important matter.[31]

By the time that the 1985 summer school for secondary teachers actually began, neither the textbook nor the student workbook nor the teacher's handbook was off the press. However great the chagrin of Ershov must have been, he kept a stiff upper lip, at least in print, and he advised his instructors to keep one too. Instructors were not to let the absence of the workbook daunt them even though it had been stated to be their main teaching tool. If the official publishers could not meet the schedule, the instructors were recommended to turn to that famous (or infamous) Soviet publishing house Samizdat. In Samizdat, carbon paper and duplicating machines do the work of presses. So manuscripts of the semi-final version of the workbook were duplicated and sent to each of the institutions offering the summer sessions. 'It won't take more than two weeks to retype the manuscript on to a duplicator stencil and then to run off a copy for each trainee,' encouraged Ershov.[32]

Despite these and other travails, the summer sessions went forward. It seems reasonable to suppose that they were successful at some institutions. Elsewhere the scene was one of *shturmovshchina* (this translates literally as 'storming' and is used pejoratively to describe situations in which too much ground must be covered in too little time), as recorded in Irkutsk:

> The situation is ridiculous . . . People are dropping with exhaustion from overtime work in organizing the flood of teachers. Meanwhile the equipment in the computer laboratory consists of twenty MKSh-2 calculators. Even these are on temporary loan from Irkutsk School No. 42. Nevertheless, 1,500 teachers must be trained – 500 of them in the fundamentals of information science and 1,000 in the use of computers in the schools.[33]

Computer hardware

However bothersome may have been the problems encountered in preparing course materials and retraining the teachers, they were likely to be solved or greatly ameliorated in a relatively short time. They pale alongside the problem of providing the proper quantity and quality of computer equipment to the schools.

First of all, a consensus on which type of computers should be supplied to the schools has been hard to develop. Several candidate models have been in the running. Perhaps the best known of these outside the Soviet Union is the Agat. This machine is software compatible with the American Apple II family and can read the Apple's familiar floppy disks. The Agat, dubbed by some Westerners the 'Yabloko' (the Russian word for 'apple'), is an eight bit personal computer with memory size from 32K to 128K bytes. According to N.B. Mozhaeva, it is capable of up to 300,000 simple operations per second.[34] It accommodates a medium resolution black and white monitor or a low resolution colour monitor. Like the Apple II, the architecture of the Agat is open with seven expansion slots. It also has parallel and serial ports for communicating with peripherals such as printers and modems. Soviet opinion has been sharply divided on the Agat. Its proponents include the influential Novosibirsk group who have developed some interesting educational software for it. Also on record in favour of the Agat have been I. Makarov, formerly Deputy Minister of Higher and Specialized Secondary Education, and Academician E.P. Velikhov, chief of the newly formed Information Sciences Section of the Academy of Sciences.

The anti-Agat forces have based their public arguments on the 'technical deficiencies' of that machine. Little specific criticism has been made of the Agat, but legitimate objections may relate to its inadequate reliability and to the fact that its design reflects the Apple II at a technically early stage of the latter's evolution. Objectionable too are the scarcity of domestically manufactured peripheral equipment (e.g. disk drives, memory expansion modules and printers) and the languid rate of production.

Bremmer[35] and other writers in the popular Western computer press have reported the demise of the Agat. Its fate indeed has been shrouded in a fog of uncertainty but such reports may be exaggerated. Given the great library of educational software and array of peripheral equipment for the Apple II family, a Soviet instructional computer that is compatible with the Apple has much in its favour. Second, the argument that the Apple II is beyond the ability of Soviet or East European computer designers and manufacturers lacks force. Neither the Apple II nor the Agat is a particularly complicated design. As the people from the Ministry of Radio Technology have already succeeded in cloning IBM mainframes for Soviet industries, doing the same for the Apple II should not exceed their design capabilities.

Another reason that the Agat has attracted criticism is that competing personal computer designs have their own strong institutional proponents and the opposing forces have been locked in contention. A machine that has been pictured frequently in Soviet press accounts of instructional and personal computing is the Elektronika NTs-80-20, a PDP-11 compatible microcomputer fitted with floppy disks, a monitor and a thermal printer. A third contender is the Iskra-250, an IBM-PC compatible computer based on a Soviet version of the Intel-8086 microprocessor with an optional version of the Intel-8087 maths co-processor available. This machine has been plagued by design and manufacturing problems with its keyboard, the read-write heads of its floppy disk drives, and its hard disk.

Standardization is a Soviet byword. Concentration on a few models of a product has been a goal of Soviet manufacturing. The computer industry is no exception. Keeping to this strategy, the Soviet educational authorities would prefer to standardize on one basic design of personal computer for use in the schools. They are quite aware of the economies of scale in hardware manufacture, software design and production and human learning. But they also have not wished to standardize on an unsatisfactory design or to select a manufacturer who cannot or will not cope with the production and support assignments. An educational computer design contest was announced in late 1984 and the search for the most appropriate system continued throughout the late 1980s.

The East European countries represent possible sources of personal computers for Soviet schools. Several of these countries have moved more aggressively into educational computing than has the Soviet Union and they have produced a variety of microcomputers.[36] A lively trade in mainframe and mini-computers has continued between these countries and the USSR. Broadening that trade to include educational computers could be the next logical step.

Soviet educators and computer specialists have visited Great Britain, France, Japan and the United States under a variety of exchange programmes. Western and Japanese computer firms have eyed the Soviet school market with interest. After a flurry of activity in the summer of 1985, during which foreign firms sought to demonstrate the superiority of their products, the Soviets ordered 4,000 Yamaha microcomputers that were equipped with printers from Star Micronics, another Japanese firm. Some additional machines were purchased from British firms. There were also reports in the Western press that IBM had arranged to sell 15,000 personal computers with 286 microprocessors over a three-year period for use in schools.[37]

Whether the Soviets eventually purchase any significant numbers of computers from Western or Japanese manufacturers will be decided after a debate of which foreigners are likely to know little. That debate will consider factors such as foreign exchange availabilities, the willingness of Soviet or East European computer makers to commit to an output and support plan, the funds that the State Committee for Education is willing to assign to computer purchases, Soviet technological protectionism, and notions of national pride and national defence, all mixed with arcane bureaucratic manoeuvres.

The decision to 'make or buy' or to do some of each continues to be made at the highest levels of the Soviet leadership. Forced to conjecture the outcome, one would be on solid ground to anticipate victory for a coalition of forces favouring a domestic solution with a bone tossed to the opposition in the form of an approval to buy a strictly limited quantity of foreign computers as cheaply as possible. If Gorbachev sustains his enthusiasm for computer literacy, the winning coalition will try to parley that enthusiasm into a greater sense of urgency to solve the question of computers in the schools. The perceived urgency will in turn be used as a lever to try to prize more resources from the State Planning Commission for the domestic computer industry.

After deciding which computers to place in the schools comes the tougher job of actually obtaining them. One is impressed by the sheer magnitude of the task. Ershov wrote of creating no fewer than 50,000 computer laboratories with more than 1m computers to support the course; more would be required in the longer run.[38] At the prevailing price of Soviet computers, that would entail a sum of between 2,000m and 3,000m roubles. When one considers that the total Soviet school budget amounts to about 10,000m roubles, the magnitude of the problem emerges in full form. And even zealous advocates of the new computer literacy course do not expect an early solution. Ershov dramatically understated it in 1985 as follows: 'It is unreasonable to think that all schools will be supplied with the required quantities of microprocessor technology in the forthcoming year.'[39]

The lack of computers compelled a major slowdown in the campaign to introduce the new course. In late August 1985 the then Minister of Education stated that only the class 9 portion (i.e. the more theoretical part on information systems) of the course would be given in the 1985/6 school year. The class 10 portion, that dealing more heavily with computers, would be deferred until 1986/7. He optimistically continued:

> By that time, computer laboratories in the schools will be supplied with equipment. It will not be easy to organize this, of course. But the task is of such great national economic importance that we must make every effort to accomplish it.[40]

The only way that 'hundreds of thousands' of microcomputers could be in place by 1986/7 was through massive importation. Imports in modest quantities undoubtedly have occurred. But it is highly unlikely, for reasons discussed earlier, that sufficient hard currency will be available to buy educational computers in great numbers. The political explosions in the Soviet Union, the incredible budget deficit and the crushing basic economic needs have seriously reduced the willingness of the Soviet leadership to allocate this very scarce resource to pay for large imports of educational computers. Reliance mainly upon domestic suppliers is likely to shift into the year 2000 at least, the date by which all Soviet schools receive an adequate number of computers.

If very few computers are now available in the schools and the outlook for the future looks even more bleak, what hardware will play the role of computing device in the computer literacy course? In the non-computer equipped schools, which will be the vast majority for several years, that role will be played by desk and hand calculators. And in most schools, students do not have access to any electronic device. The course syllabus makes valiant efforts to turn to good account the unfortunate fact that the vast majority of students have no hands-on experience with a calculator or computer. The student workbook was revised in 1988 to give numerical examples of algorithms that can be executed without calculators. Teachers are told to make a virtue of necessity by stressing to the students that they, while using the pencil and a piece of paper, are fulfilling the control function that would be performed automatically if a computer or calculator were used.

Educational software

The outlook for educational software is even more obscure than that for hardware. Those schools following a strictly computerless option have no problem, of course, since they have no computers anyway. Students can stay with an algorithmic pseudocode with some limited exposure, on paper, to machine code or a low-level algorithmic language.

Schools that must rely on other institutions for their computer support will take what is available at those installations in the way of programming languages and other software. Most modern Soviet mainframes and mini-computers support languages such as FORTRAN, COBOL and PL/1. Several also offer BASIC and/or Pascal. Whatever else may be said about the suitability of any of these as beginners' languages, they share one major disadvantage: the syntax of each is in English. It is one thing for a professional Soviet programmer or engineer to be constrained to write programs in an English–Russian pidgin language. It is quite another to ask a senior school student to do the same. Learning to program is sufficiently intimidating for most people without simultaneously having to juggle two natural languages and two alphabets.

Those schools fortunate enough to have their own computers face a somewhat richer set of choices. For the Agat computer, the energetic and innovative group at Novosibirsk have produced a package of interesting educational software collectively called *Shkol'nitsa* (Schoolgirl).[41] The Schoolgirl package offers two programming languages, Robik (Little Robot) and Rapira (Rapier), suitable respectively for learning to program and for a broader range of educational uses. Both languages employ Russian syntax and Cyrillic characters. Robik is based on Logo, the children's visual programming language that was designed by Seymour Papert at Massachusetts Institute of Technology, and offers many of its advantages.[42] Rapira preserves the same user interface as Robik but offers an enhanced set of features including graphics, animation and sound, as well as text and tabular processing. Schoolgirl also contains a facility for authoring courseware, allowing teachers to prepare individualized lessons. Several pieces of educational software have been created using Schoolgirl, mostly from the fields of mathematics, physics and chemistry. Examples include simulations of nuclear and chemical reactions, aerodynamic processes and internal combustion engines.

Schoolgirl appears to have friends in high places. On 1 December 1986 *Izvestiya* editorially took the Ministry of Education to task for failing to go beyond the experimental stage with the package. The criticism may have had its effect: six months later, a Soviet governmental commission reviewed Schoolgirl, officially certified it, and cited it as model software for the schools.

Yet, more than official certification is required to get Schoolgirl or any other educational software into the schools. Major problems of testing, documentation, production, copyright protection for the authors, distribution and end-user support must be solved if Schoolgirl or any other educational software is to move from being an interesting academic research exercise to being a robust product of commercial quality. Such software, because it is destined to be used by the technically unsophisticated, offers challenges far beyond the ordinary. Little evidence is available to suggest that Soviet educational authorities yet appreciate the seriousness of these problems.

Apart from BASIC, no educational software specifically designed for the Elektronika NTs-80-20 or other Soviet microcomputers has surfaced. A Russian-language version of ALGOL called ALMIR-65, written several years ago, has its advocates. O.P. L'vov, among other purists, has voiced the argument long silent in the United States that students should cut their programming teeth on machine language because only then 'do they really know what the machine is doing'.[43]

PROBLEMS AND PROSPECTS FOR THE 1990S

Over the past quarter-century, Soviet leaders have frequently paid homage to computers and their use. Actions, however, give better clues than words to true priorities. It is hard to avoid the conclusion that recognition of the information revolution has dawned slowly and even reluctantly in their minds. Perhaps the low priority traditionally assigned to computers and information systems by Soviet leaders reflects a subliminal awareness of some fundamental contradiction between the information society and the closed society. Perhaps, on some level of consciousness, they agree with Graham[44] and others who have suggested that such a contradiction exists.

The matter may, however, be explained more simply. Perhaps it was mainly a matter of generations. The old leadership understood little about computers and their potential. For them, as for many around the world, computers were an 'enigma wrapped in a mystery'. Information at the propaganda level was concrete; at the level of the bit, byte and baud it became an unreal abstraction. It took a new generation, men such as M.S. Gorbachev and N.V. Ogarkov, to recognize that a new age had dawned and that the USSR had better arouse herself; perhaps it took the spectacle of the advanced capitalist countries bounding ahead with miocroprocessor applications in every corner of their economic and military systems.

Whichever, if any, of these conjectures is true, a change of mind and of priorities indisputably has occurred. Information systems, microprocessors and computers have taken over top billing from steel mills, coal mines and tractors. Novosibirsk has become the Soviet silicon steppe. In the schools, the new course in Fundamentals of Information Science and Computer Technology and its descendants raise several interesting points and arouse speculation about future developments.

The new course as institutionalized reform

One of the most striking features of the computer literacy campaign is its crash nature. After waiting for a quarter-century, the Soviet leadership proposed to leapfrog in a few years to a level of computer awareness that took the West fully those twenty-five years to reach. Storming is an old tradition. Russian and Soviet history abounds with stories of crash programmes; some have been successful, others were dismal failures. In a centrally directed society, such as that traditionally of the Soviet Union, reform must be institutionalized if it is to be successful.

Whether the computer literacy drive, conceived in its broadest social sense, fails or accomplishes its impressive goals will depend upon many factors. For a start, it relies on a strong continuous commitment and resources from the top. This, however, has not been and will not be enough. Top-down pressure, while a necessary condition for effecting change in the Soviet system, is insufficient. There have been too many campaigns already since Gorbachev came to power and too many top priorities for them all to be regarded as truly of paramount importance. Furthermore it is increasingly difficult for the top leadership to sustain the pressure. After the first displacement of a crash campaign by other more immediate new pressures, the system tends naturally to return to equilibrium and to the status quo ante.

Means must be found to institutionalize the drive for computer literacy in the Soviet popular consciousness if it is to become more than a passing enthusiasm. The introduction of the revised course in Fundamentals of Information Science and Computer Technology can be interpreted as such a means. Placing this course in the schools is not quite like etching it on to stone tablets, but it is the next best thing to it. It will stay there until it is removed by a force equal to the one that put it there. Meanwhile each new generation of secondary school students will be exposed to the subject, at least to some degree. Thoughts of this kind were expressed in a revealing comment by Ershov:

I'm sometimes asked, 'Why was the school course in information systems begun in the absence of computers?' I understand why the question is asked. But a decisive first step was needed to move computer studies off dead centre. And indeed to do that, everybody had to move immediately and together. That's why, in my opinion, the only correct decision was taken.[45]

Resistance in the schools

The Soviet educational establishment is conservative, although it is only fair to admit that it is not unique in this respect. The teachers may be the most significant inertial force. The training and retraining problem is huge, both numerically and psychologically. Many teachers still feel threatened by and suspicious of the computer. It is no great pleasure for most to be asked to learn a totally new subject while trying simultaneously to teach it to students whose young minds seem to grasp it faster than older ones.

Letters received from many teachers by the editors of the educational press show their writers to be dubious about the new course. Many posed the question, 'Why must we teach information science?' Numerous teachers have written to warn of a suspected health threat to children working with computers. Some have voiced concern that a harmful and antisocial computer mania might grip their students. Others have complained about the lack of textbooks, teacher's handbooks and student workbooks several years after the course began.

In-service and initial teacher training: problems and requirements

As we have seen, a major part of the 1985 and subsequent summer teacher-training courses was given over to winning the hearts and minds of the teachers. The importance of the new subject had to be impressed upon them. Their computer phobia was to be overcome by gentle persuasion, and they were to be supported wherever possible by outside expertise.

According to A. Uvarov, the training of teachers is the determining factor in making progress with information science in Soviet schools. At present (1991), the great majority of teachers of this subject also teach physics and mathematics and have undergone a short course of preparation. Occasionally the course is taught by computer specialists and programmers who have no pedagogical education themselves. This has been a real disaster. The short courses that these teachers attended did not give them enough knowledge or experience with computers themselves. As a consequence, many were limited to a simplistic repetition of the contents of the textbook, and the problems to be solved on the computer were the most simple programming examples.[46]

Experience in the West indicates that a teacher retraining programme must be continuous if it is to be successful. A summer course can be only the beginning. Repeated in-service and short courses of carefully graduated levels of sophistication and difficulty are necessary. Not least important, the teachers must be given ample opportunity to learn at a computer keyboard. No number of handbooks or handouts, calculators or excursions to computer centres can substitute for hours of hands-on experience. The Soviet case shows significant weakening at this level of continued resources and support. Paradoxically, the successful early training of teachers may have some unintended consequences. Some Soviet teachers who have acquired computer proficiency in the past few years have left the teaching profession for the more lucrative field of professional programming.

The process of putting together courses for the preparation of teachers of information science in teacher-training institutions has not been completed. To quote Uvarov:

> We experienced a deficit of teachers with higher education for the conduct of this work. In other words, there were not enough educationists to train students to teach information science. There is an acute shortage of educational computers for the teachers themselves. The course in information science provides a quite remarkable opportunity for developing new forms and methods in working with students. The computer, as we well know, is a remarkable instrument for individualized instruction. In practice, however, this potential is seldom fully realized. The necessary methodological preparation is almost totally absent.[47]

At the II Plenum of the All-Union Scientific-Methodological Council for the Informatization of Education, held in October 1989, participants noted that the level of preparation of the majority of teachers was unsatisfactory and insufficient to permit them to teach information science. Every teacher of this subject should have experience of the program in which students would be working, together with an adequately equipped computer laboratory. The Council made recommendations to the State Committee for Education on the content of initial teacher training in information science. This should include:

1 Introduction to information science and the practical use of computers.
2 Theory of information science: elements of mathematical logic theory and algorithms; questions of theoretical programming; information systems and their place in society; documentation.
3 Applied programming: introduction to operating systems in computers; acquaintance with computer languages and modern technology programming; basics of computer mathematics and numerical methods for solving problems; introduction to machine graphics.

4 Computing practice: solution of individual computer program projects.
5 Use of information technology in the teaching process: methods of planning, evaluation, use of programming software; methodology of teaching information science.[48]

The critical role of computer hardware and software

The litmus test of Gorbachev's commitment to the computer literacy campaign is his continued willingness to do what is necessary to supply the schools with a sufficient stock of computer hardware and software. These resources are critical to the learning of both students and their teachers.

A rigorous algorithmic approach to the subject is legitimate and laudable. It is fair to say, however, that this approach has not proved to be an easy one for most American schools. Soviet observers regard the mathematical preparation of their students to be an order of magnitude better than that of most American high school students. If this assessment is correct, perhaps Soviet students will cope better with algorithmic rigour than their American counterparts.

S.D. Shenfield's review of previous attempts to reform mathematics education in Soviet schools gives grounds for scepticism about the feasibility of a lean and rigorous computerless approach in which students are given only algorithmic nourishment. In the late 1960s and early 1970s, Soviet school mathematics was rocked by a set of reforms based on Kolmogorov's axiomatic and Bourbaki's set-theoretic approaches. The attempt was made to introduce much greater rigour and abstraction. Soviet mathematics educators now concede that these reforms were flawed at their core. The level of abstraction was more than either teachers or students could take. Complicated symbolism was used for essentially simple ideas. A misleading impression was created of mathematics as a formal discipline removed from applications. These reforms were later themselves reformed. They were seen as the unfortunate results of putting the school mathematics curriculum too much under the power of prominent academic mathematicians whose research brilliance was not matched by their pedagogical insight.[49]

Might the same thing happen to Fundamentals of Information Science and Computer Technology? Even if Soviet students do have a higher tolerance for abstract rigour than Americans, theory without practical work on the computer is unlikely to accomplish much in the way of real computer competence. More fundamentally, nowhere in the Soviet literature is evidence to be found that someone has systematically thought about what computer knowledge and skills the citizens of a future Soviet infomation society might need.

Beyond algorithms lies the role of computers as learning tools. As such they are seen by Soviet educators as vital to exploiting the new technology's full potential and to developing greater computer sophistication on the part of teachers and students. If computers are to become one of the electronic learning tools with a role far broader than that of mere executors of student courses, the Western experience points up the necessity for a flowering and continuing educational software development. More than this, the software needs to be carefully integrated into the existing curriculum and the student's individual learning style. Few teachers have the time, talent or inclination to develop their own courseware or to integrate disparate pieces of software into their study plans. Substantial progress is evident on this front in the United States, mainly in the private sector with collaboration by the major hardware vendors such as IBM and Apple with independent software publishers. How will it happen, if it happens, in the Soviet Union?

Attitudes to the course

The introduction of computer studies was totally unexpected for the majority of both students and teachers. As a result of the efforts undertaken to roll out a set of preparatory courses, most teachers did have the necessary opportunity to learn the new course and begin to acquaint themselves with the computers. Soviet society at large basically supported the new course. People regarded it as a symbol of the reforms of the educational process that they hoped would be under way. According to Uvarov, students enthusiastically greeted the possibility of becoming acquainted with what had been up to then a practically inaccessible form of technology. After that initial enthusiasm, their attitude to the course began to change. What they encountered in their information science lessons was something very close, at least externally, to the traditional mathematical discipline. The actual introduction to computer hardware for a majority of students consisted at best in watching instructional television.[50]

The decline of interest together with other factors was reflected in the results of the coursework itself. According to data collected by the Research Institute of the Siberian Division of the Academy of Pedagogical Sciences, in 1988 only one in five students fully mastered the material in the information science course. In the schools where there were qualified teachers and where the students had adequate access to computer technology, their original positive attitude to the subject grew. In fact, many of these students were so inspired by the course that they expressed a desire to pursue careers in computer-related fields, as well as demonstrating a high level of mastery of the content of the course. The ability to solve problems through the use of a computer was an equally high-prestige capability among students as the winning of computer games.[51]

In summary, where there is a combination of highly trained and motivated teachers and a supply of computers, the information science course is a success. Accomplishments in computing are highly regarded by students in these privileged schools where the computer to student ratio averages one to thirteen or better. The arrival of school leavers who did have the opportunity to prepare themselves in the field of informatics has begun to cause embarrassment in the higher education institutions where they have enrolled.

The volume of student work for the information science course is not large but it demands a great deal of work by the teacher. Many difficulties are encountered in acquiring computers, keeping them operational and preparing course materials. More work is involved in trying to seek out and obtain educational software. The great labour requirements of this subject affect the attitudes of teachers towards it. The prestige of qualified teachers of information science is sufficiently high, however, and the shortage of them is slowly being overcome.

The longer-term outlook for Soviet educational computing

The present (1990) deployment of computers to Soviet schools comprises the first stage of a three-stage educational computing plan spanning the period 1986–2000. This plan was formulated in 1985 and early 1986, and its three quinquennia correspond to the XII, XIII and XIV Five-Year Plans. As indicated earlier, during stage one (1986–90), Soviet schools were supposed to receive some 400,000 personal computers or enough to equip 30–35,000 computer laboratories throughout the country. Soviet planners intend to increase the number of these laboratories to 100,000 by 1995 and to more than 120,000 by the year 2000. To fulfil these ambitious targets by the end of 1990, Soviet industry would have needed to increase the production of personal computers strictly for school use by an average annual rate of more than 50 per cent during the XII Five-Year Plan. By 1990, this annual number needed to be about 200,000. Assuming that Soviet school computers have useful lifetimes of five years, annual deliveries would have to increase gradually to about 270,000 by the end of the century to meet the targets for the next decade. According to the most recent statistics available, for the three years 1986–8, the production of school computers has been 88,900 units, against the targeted 106,000.[52]

Can the Soviets do it? To put the Soviet task into a Western perspective it is useful to note that Apple Computer Corporation produced more than 750,000 Macintosh computers in 1988. The crushing economic demands on the Soviet Union, its industries caught between centralized command control and little flexibility with regard to their own suppliers and to hiring and firing, as well as their poor record of producing highly reliable consumer electronic products, is hardly encouraging. Fragmentary evidence in continuing issues of *Uchitel'skaya gazeta* and *Informatika i obrazovanie* from 1987 to 1990 and eyewitness reports by Western educational computing experts indicate that the effort is continuing but at an increasingly lethargic snail's pace.

This impression is strengthened by a look at the September 1988 statistics, published at the end of the decade (Table 3.1, p. 37). Still only 7,438 (11.5

per cent) of all Soviet secondary general schools and 4,035 (13.2 per cent) of Russian ones had computer laboratories. Indeed, this signified a decrease from the previous year in the absolute number of such schools, although the number of workstations was slightly up. For reasons which await elucidation, there were actually fewer schools with laboratories than a year previously in the RSFSR (formerly 15 per cent of its secondary general schools), the Ukraine (from 21.6 to 10 per cent), Georgia (from 8.7 to 7.2 per cent), Azerbaidzhan (from 8.2 to 4.7 per cent) and Moldavia (from 15.4 to 5.3 per cent). True, the other republics all showed increases, so that the proportion of such schools with computer laboratories had come to range from 2.2 per cent in Tadzhikistan and 2.7 per cent in Turkmenia to 20.6 per cent in Armenia and 32.7 per cent in Latvia. As for workstations, they reflected the fortunes of the laboratories, except that they had increased in the RSFSR and decreased in Kazakhstan (Table 3.2, p. 38).[53] Overall, however, the tempo had slowed.

The Soviet educational software industry is universally retarded, owing to a general lack of incentives for developers. An underdeveloped system for protecting intellectual property rights, combined with impediments to private or cooperative software development, have stunted the Soviet software industry generally for many years. Educational software development has suffered even more than management or industrial software because there has been no market for it. The dilemma is familiar: no educational software is produced because nobody wants it, and nobody wants educational software because its paucity prevents people from developing a taste for it.

The Soviets have responded to the software shortage in a typical fashion. They have created institutions. One of the most notable is the Institute of Programming of the Academy of Sciences. This body, organized in 1985 and headed by A.K. Ailamazyan, is located in the ancient Russian town of Pereslavl'-Zalesskii. Among its tasks is that of developing software for Soviet schools. At the Institute's international summer computer camp, groups of Americans who attended confirmed that lack of original software. Most of it was current Western educational software that had been pirated from Western sources. The emphasis was on students learning to program in Pascal and Prolog, an artificial intelligence programming language.[54]

Controversy about the direction of educational computing

Earlier articles by Judy and Lommel[55] and by Kerr[56] described the narrow focus of the new Soviet course on the logic of developing algorithms. This narrowness stands in sharp contrast to educational computing as it is evolving in the United States. Kerr expressed it well:

There is little of the exploratory quality that characterizes most American courses in the subject; rather, there is a strong emphasis on learning how to think logically and how to make a computer do a very specific set of tasks that are seen as directly related to a student's future job. While Western enthusiasts extol the value of LOGO as a way to learn logic without being taught logic explicitly, Soviet students learn logic first – *without* computers – and then apply their learning in a very prescribed way to the use of computers as tools.[57]

This narrow focus of the information science course has become the subject of a major controversy in Soviet educational computing circles. The issue arose sharply in a public discussion surrounding a course syllabus that was published as a guide for prospective authors hoping to enter the competition for a design for a new textbook to replace the preliminary book edited by Ershov and Monakhov. What is interesting is that the new syllabus preserves all of the stress on algorithms and programming that characterized the original version of the course.

The mounting cry from Soviet teachers and educators is that the narrow focus on algorithms and programming is harmful. Uvarov, an editor of *Informatika i obrazovanie*, and his colleagues contend that the teaching of information science in the secondary general schools is undergoing a crisis. The 'non-machine' variant which 5m students are taking has outlived its usefulness. The revised version of the course also sadly neglects the fact that most Soviet students will be users of computer software, not developers of it. Therefore, the argument continues, the goal of the course should be to teach students how to use packaged software such as word processors, spreadsheets, database managers, desktop publishing and hypermedia. At best, the critics claim, the present course is creating dilettante programmers. At worst, they say, its dry and abstract subject matter is alienating students from computing, which is precisely the opposite of its intent.[58]

The late Academician Ershov and other proponents of the algorithmic approach to educational computing have countered that algorithms and programming should remain central features of the course. They fear that abandoning or diluting those features will rob the course of its rigour and turn it into the thin gruel that they perceive most American educational computing to be.

The war between these two camps of Soviet opinion continues at this writing. To foretell the outcome is difficult but we suspect that Ershov's allies will eventually lose. The American experience is that educational computing was initially the preserve of mathematicians and computer scientists cut from the same cloth as was Ershov. Early American school textbooks in computing effused no less algorithmic zeal than present Soviet ones. A good example was the comprehensive text prepared by the School Mathematics Study Group at Stanford University in 1965. As microcomputers have infiltrated American schools, homes and offices, most people quickly shifted their interests from learning how to program – few probably had much of an interest in the first place – to learning how to use the burgeoning supply of commercial software to accomplish things that they wanted to do in their personal and professional lives.

Many aspects of the Soviet educational computing environment are different from those in the United States. Soviets do not have an abundance of personal computers, nor are they likely to have such plenty in this century. As computers make their way on to desktops in offices and schools, however, we suspect that they will follow the American pattern of gradually being used as sophisticated and interactive teaching and learning devices.

The speed with which the mature development of Soviet educational computing takes place depends greatly on the Soviets' success in meeting and exceeding their present plans to supply computers to the schools. Equally important, it will depend on a satisfactory solution to the problem of producing, distributing and supporting educational software development in the USSR. It will also depend on how well teachers are trained in educational computing and upon the ingenuity with which curriculum designers weave software into the fabric of their current course offerings.

Despite all of the difficulties confronting it, educational computing in Soviet secondary schools is well launched. Its original champion, A.P. Ershov, kept the computer campaign charged with creative energy. If not all of its champions' hopes have been realized, its accomplishments have been greater than the sceptics expected. As it continues to unfold, by the end of the 1990s the educational computing campaign seems likely to make a significant impact on Soviet education and society.

NOTES AND REFERENCES

1 L. Graham, 'The Soviet Union is missing out on the computer revolution', *Washington Post*, 11 March 1984, pp. C1–C4.
2 D.R. Shanor, *Behind the Lines*, New York, St Martin's Press, 1985.
3 E.P. Velikhov, 'Personal'nye EVM – segodnyashnyaya praktika i perspektivy', *Vestnik Akademii Nauk SSSR*, 1984, no. 8, pp. 3–9.
4 V. Vinokurov and K. Zuev, 'Aktual'nye problemy razvitiya vychislitel'noi tekhniki', *Kommunist*, 1985, no. 5, pp. 18–29.
5 A.P. Ershov, 'EVM v klasse', *Pravda*, 2 February 1985, p. 3.
6 'V Politbyuro TsK KPSS', *Pravda*, 29 March 1985, p. 1.
7 L. Graham, *Science and Philosophy in the Soviet Union*, New York, Knopf, 1982; A.A. Dorodnitsyn, 'Informatika: predmet i zadachi', *Vestnik Akademii Nauk SSSR*, 1985, no. 2, pp. 85–9.
8 ibid.
9 S.T. Kerr, 'Innovation on command: instructional development and educational technology in the Soviet Union', *ECTJ: Educational Communications and Technology Journal*, 1982, vol. 30, no. 2, pp. 98–116.
10 S.T. Kerr, 'Instructional computing in the USSR', *Educational Media International*, 1985, vol. 3, pp. 17–21.
11 N.C. Davis and S.E. Goodman, 'The Soviet bloc's Unified System of computers', *Computing Surveys*, 1988, vol. 10, no. 2, pp. 93–112; R.W. Judy and J.M. Lommel,

'The new Soviet computer literacy campaign', *ECTJ: Educational Communications and Technology Journal*, 1986, vol. 34, no. 2, pp. 108–23.

12 S. Lando and O. Manakova, 'Komputer v letnem lagere', *Informatika i obrazovanie*, 1990, no. 4, pp. 194–7.

13 *Narodnoe obrazovanie i kul'tura v SSSR*, Moscow, Finansy i statistika, 1989, p. 48.

14 'Programma kursa "Osnovy informatiki i vychislitel'noi tekhniki"', *Matematika v shkole*, 1985, no. 3, pp. 4–7.

15 A.P. Ershov, V.M. Monakhov, A.A. Kuznetsov, M.P. Lapchik, I.N. Antipov, S.A. Beshenkov, Ya.N. Kobrinsky and D.O. Smekalin, 'K nachalu obucheniya osnovam informatiki i vychislitel'noi tekhniki', *Matematika v shkole*, 1985, no. 4, pp. 5–16, and no. 5, pp. 35–48 (extracts from handbook). The two-volume preliminary textbook (1985) was entitled *Osnovy informatiki i vychislitel'noi tekhniki*, after the course.

16 V.M. Monakhov, 'Kakim byt' novogo kursa?', *Uchitel'skaya gazeta* (hereafter *UG*), 5 February 1985, p. 2; V.M. Monakhov, 'O soderzhanii kursa "Osnovy informatiki i vychislitel'noi tekhniki"', *Matematika v shkole*, 1985, no. 3, p. 8.

17 A.P. Ershov, 'Chto takoe informatika?', *UG*, 5 March 1985, p. 2.

18 A.P. Ershov, 'Real'nost' epokhi', *UG*, 23 February 1985, p. 2.

19 ibid. For the case for the algorithmic approach, see also A.P. Ershov, 'Algoritmicheskii yazyk', *UG*, 30 May 1985, p. 2.

20 Preliminary textbook; 'Programma kursa', op. cit., pp. 4–6.

21 ibid., pp. 6–7.

22 'Programma kursa "Osnovy informatiki i vychislitel'noi tekhniki"', *Mikroprotsessornye sredstva i sistemy*, 1986, no. 2, pp. 86–9, and *Matematika v shkole*, 1986, no. 3, pp. 49–53.

23 *Narodnoe obrazovanie*..., op. cit., p. 48.

24 'Osnovnye pokazateli razvitiya narodnogo obrazovaniya v SSSR', *Vestnik statistiki*, 1988, no. 8, p. 67.

25 ibid.

26 *Uchitel'skaya gazeta* kept up the good work in 1986 and 1987. For 1986, see 4 March, p. 3; 8 April, p. 3; 17 April, p. 2; 17 June, p. 2; 7 August, p. 1; 12 August, p. 1; 22 August, p. 2; 2 September, p. 1; 8 September, p. 1; 25 September, p. 2; 30 October, p. 2. For 1987: 10 January, p. 3; 17 January, p. 4; 7 July, p. 2; 22 August, p. 2.

27 A.P. Ershov, 'EVM: osobenno neotlozhno!', *UG*, 17 April 1986, p. 4.

28 A.P. Ershov, 'Letnie kursy', *UG*, 6 June 1985, p. 2.

29 ibid.

30 ibid.

31 A.P. Ershov, 'EVM v klasse', *Pravda*, 6 February 1985, p. 3.

32 Ershov, 1985 (June), op. cit.

33 V. Galkina, 'Kabinet ... kotorogo net?', *UG*, 6 June 1985, p. 2.

34 N.B. Mozhaeva, 'Mikroprotsessory v narodnom khozyaistve', *Pribory i sistemy upravleniya*, 1983, no. 12, pp. 37–40.

35 B. Bremmer, 'Red PC book? Nyet yet!', *MIS Week*, 16 October 1988, pp. 1, 16.

36 B. Himmel, 'Computertechnik und Elektronik im tschechoslowakischen Bildungswesen', *Halbjahresbericht zur Bildungspolitik und pädagogischen Entwicklung in der DDR, der UdSSR, der VR Polen, der ČSSR und der VR China*, 1985, no. 1, pp. 72–5; W. Hörner, 'DDR: "Neue" Technologien in der allgemeinbildenden Schule', ibid., pp. 5–9; W. Hörner and B. Mucha, 'Volksrepublik Polen: Mikrocomputer im Unterricht', ibid., pp. 55–61; 'Mikroprotsessornoi tekhnike – nadezhnye kadry', *Ekonomicheskoe sotrudnichestvo stran-chlenov SEV*, 1984, no. 11, pp. 30–4.

37 The Times, 9 July 1985, pp. 23–4; *Wall Street Journal*, 19 July 1985, p. 18, and 26

July 1985, p. 33; personal communication, 1990.
38 Ershov, 1986, op. cit.
39 Ershov, 1985 (February), op. cit.
40 S.G. Shcherbakov, 'Reforma. God vtoroi', *UG*, 31 August 1985, p. 2.
41 G. Frolova, 'Uchenik V. Boshniak, Elenochka i "agat"', *UG*, 22 January 1985, p. 2.
42 S. Papert, *Mindstorms*, New York, Basic Books, 1980.
43 O.P. L'vov, 'Problemy bol'shogo dela', *Matematika v shkole*, 1985, no. 2, pp. 31–3.
44 L. Graham, 'Cyclical patterns in the history of Russian and Soviet technology', paper at the conference on 'Technology, Culture and Development: The Experience of the Soviet Model', Ohio State University, 30–31 October 1990.
45 Ershov, 1986, op. cit.
46 A. Uvarov, 'Informatika v shkole: vchera, segodnya, zavtra', *Informatika i obrazovanie*, 1990, no. 4, pp. 1–10.
47 ibid.
48 'Vtoroi plenum Obshchesoyuznogo nauchno-metodicheskogo soveta informatizatsii obrazovaniya', *Informatika i obrazovanie*, 1990, no. 4, pp. 120–1.
49 S.D. Shenfield, 'The reform of mathematics teaching in Soviet schools', *Soviet Education Study Bulletin*, 1984, vol. 2, no. 1, pp. 22–6.
50 Uvarov, op. cit.
51 ibid.
52 *Narodnoe obrazovanie . . .*, op. cit., p. 104. Production amounted to 10,500 units in 1986; 22,600 in 1987; and 55,800 in 1988.
53 ibid.; 'Osnovnye pokazateli . . .', op. cit.
54 B. Kaimin and S. Gregor'ev, 'Prolog v shkol'noi informatike', *Informatika i obrazovanie*, 1990, no. 2, pp. 25–31.
55 Judy and Lommel, op. cit.; R.W. Judy and J.M. Lommel, 'Soviet educational computing: an interim report', in R.F. Staar (ed.), *The Future Information Revolution in the USSR*, Stanford, CA, Hoover Institution Press, 1988, pp. 19–34.
56 S.T. Kerr, 'Soviet applications of microcomputers in education: developments in research and practice during the Gorbachev era', *Journal of Educational Computing Research*, 1987, vol. 3, no. 1, pp. 1–17.
57 ibid., p. 15.
58 Uvarov, op. cit.

4

BREAKING NEW GROUND IN ARTS TEACHING IN THE SOVIET GENERAL SCHOOL

James Muckle

And art made tongue-tied by authority
And folly, doctor-like, controlling skill,
. . . from these would I be gone.

Shakespeare, Sonnet LXVI

INTRODUCTION

The most striking change in Soviet attitudes to their education system as perestroika gets into its stride is the tendency towards abandonment of central control. This is true of the curriculum as of many other things; indeed the curriculum is perceived as the root of many of the weaknesses of the system.[1] As the notion of democratization gains ground, educators proclaim that the days when change could be imposed from above are gone; without the support and participation of workers in the field, reform will be impossible.[2] A newly appointed Education Minister, admittedly on a privileged private occasion when overstatement might have been made for effect,[3] stated that educational problems could only be solved locally, and a highly respected academician has recently reflected that when the need for change is so obvious, it is not surprising that people seek an about-turn so as to overthrow central control completely.[4] As Britain imposes a national curriculum in some considerable detail, as the Federal government in America seeks to raise the quality of education by placing certain requirements on schools and school boards, and as France cautiously relinquishes some of her much vaunted central control, the Soviet Union seems to some of its teachers to be rushing madly towards too high a degree of independence. This is surely something of an illusion; in any case they have a long way to go. While visiting England G.A. Yagodin, Chairman of the State Committee on Education, was reported in the following words:

> He made it plain that the Soviet Union was decentralizing and liberalizing its curriculum rapidly while the United Kingdom was moving in

58

the opposite direction. 'Maybe we will meet in the middle', he joked, although he thought the Soviet system would still be more centralized at the end of the day.[5]

Excessive centralization in the curriculum has, it is argued, led to a sameness in the schools, too many subjects, overloading of syllabuses and of pupils, fragmentation, and 'technocratic orientation' – that is, a failure to encourage and develop culture.[6] There is, it is strongly felt, a desperate need for new approaches to scientific subjects, for a whole new generation of syllabuses, textbooks and teaching aids, for the needs of national cultural groups in the Soviet Union to be satisfied, for differentiated instruction, and for the whole system to be brought up to a quality comparable with that in other developed countries.[7]

A proposal of 1989 is for the school curriculum to consist of a Union-republic component (Russian language, literature of the Soviet peoples, mathematics, science and social studies) decided at the centre in consultation with the republic education ministries, a republic component decided in consultation with educational organs within the individual republics, and a school component, to be decided by the individual school council (Table 2.1, p. 27).[8] All of this is intended to make the process of creating the school curriculum open and democratic. One wonders how far it can be allowed to go, and whether teachers, parents and pupils on the newly established school councils (see Chapter 2) will have the knowledge and awareness of curricular issues to make a good and consistent job of it. Progress by mid-1990 seems to suggest that much of their work at that time was to choose which subjects are to be compulsory at certain levels of education and which optional courses the school can offer; in other words to choose from a fairly restricted menu offered by the central authorities which appear to be relinquishing power.

Has the ideology behind the curriculum changed under glasnost? The spirit of it can perhaps best be illustrated by this passage from the project on the curriculum which has been set up by the State Committee:

The aim of the programme is to work out a new content for general secondary education which corresponds to the level of scientific and technical progress, socio-economic and cultural development which society has achieved and to the abilities of the pupils, and which is directed at providing every pupil with profound, sound knowledge, skills and the ability to put them into practice. The curriculum is required to ensure that every school leaver has the opportunity to receive knowledge about man, nature and society on the basis of a dialectical-materialist world view; orientation towards choice of a sphere of future practical activity; experience of intellectual communicative, physical and labour activity, facilitating the formation of basic intellectual, labour and organizational abilities and of habits leading to a healthy life-style and the improvement of his or her physical condition, which are necessary in everyday life, in social production, for the continuation of education and self-education; to receive experience of creative activity such as will lead to the opportunity to develop individual abilities and talents; experience of social and personal relationships, which should prepare young people for active participation in the life of the country, the creation of families and the construction of personal life on a basis of communist ideals and the ethical and aesthetic values of Soviet society.[9]

Previously standard Marxist-Leninist ideas are still present: the 'triad' of man, nature and society, the dialectical materialist world view and communist ideals. If perestroika and glasnost continue, it may be necessary to do some more rewriting here. There is, however, a hint that the needs of *individuals* are to be considered in such matters as how and what they are to be taught, which is new; 'experience of social and personal relationships' is a new formulation. There is the slightest suggestion that careers counselling means finding a role for the individual rather than directing or coaxing him or her into the vacancy that local industry needs to fill. Otherwise this paragraph alone does not exactly presage a revolution in philosophical attitudes. Relaxation of the central stranglehold may be a significant change, but it seems from this document as if the local powers are called upon to fill the curriculum according more or less to the same theoretical basis as before. That, at least, is the conclusion reached after studying some of the official papers. The feeling on the ground, in the better schools, may be somewhat different. Study of moves in arts education reveals a more liberal spirit at work.

The Soviet Union is a state in which traditionally science and technology are held in high esteem, and what has been at least until now the dominant ideology of Marxism-Leninism is described as 'scientific socialism'. Though the arts have never been excluded from the work of the Soviet school, the curriculum has been dominated by the natural sciences and mathematics and by technology and vocational education in the shape of labour training. Seven years of attempted reform of the school system have brought about an accentuated interest in the arts in education which is increasing rather than declining. Now why should this be? It certainly means infinitely more than the narrow ideological preparation of the workforce to serve 'communist construction', though practical benefits are claimed for the arts. Literature as a means to instil political orthodoxy is dying. The answer to the paradox lies in a desire for the 'humanization' of the curriculum and of the whole education system, and in the wish to combat the 'technocratic orientation' referred to above. Arts for the Soviet child are perceived as an answer to this problem.

The purpose of this study, therefore, is to examine what has been happening in the teaching of the arts in the general school and to assess what real change has taken place.

THE PRESENT STATE OF ARTS EDUCATION

Arts education is not an uncontroversial matter anywhere in the world. There is, for example, the question of the conflicting requirements of the future specialist – the professional writer, artist or musician – and the lay person with general interests, whose needs in terms of education are quite different. This chapter is not concerned principally with the training of future professionals. Even in connection with the general education of the lay person, approaches to arts education are the subject of animated or even acrimonious discussion. What should be the *subject matter* of arts lessons? Is it a 'body of knowledge' – facts about the great composers, novelists and painters and their work? Should it be confined to 'standard classics', so that, for example, works of modern popular music are excluded from music lessons, and literature lessons contain principally famous plays and poems of the past? Should children in school be taught only to *appreciate* the arts: to listen intelligently to musical works, to discuss paintings and literature in intellectual terms? To what extent, if at all, should schoolchildren learn to *write* poetry, *paint* pictures or *compose* music? What is the role of literacy and technical skills (such as reading standard musical notation)? Then there are the proponents of 'process' over 'product' in arts education, who, for instance, attach greater importance to what children might learn, for example, from the experience of putting on a dramatic performance rather than to any judgement of the quality of that performance.

It may be thought necessary too to ask some far-reaching questions with implications for the teaching of the arts. What are we doing when we listen to a piece of music or read a poem? In what ways is it different from hearing, say, noise from the street or consulting a cookery book? It is sometimes said that the arts help us to 'structure experience'. If that statement means anything, why and how do they do this? One thing is certain: all over the world the realization has now dawned that education in the arts is different from other forms of education. Studying art, music and literature at school is not purely an intellectual matter, as was once assumed, though an intellectual side it undoubtedly has. Experience of the arts is different from other types of experience, and educators recognize that it is concerned with the development of the feelings and emotions. This cannot be taught effectively by lecturing about the life and loves of Beethoven or tested adequately by questions about the chronology of Shakespeare's plays.

THE ARTS IN SOVIET SOCIETY

In discussing arts education in the ordinary school (by which is to be understood the regular 'mass' six or seven-to-seventeen comprehensive co-educational establishment), it is well to remember the peculiar role of the arts in Soviet society. 'High culture' is not meant to be a hobby for an élite.

Despite the desire of some of the revolutionaries of 1917 to sweep away the culture of the past, the ideal quickly became to make the formerly élite cultural heritage the property of the masses. There has been firm faith in the ability of the arts to enrich the lives of workers and intellectuals alike.

The arts in Russia have never been politically neutral. Students of nineteenth-century Russian literature know well that the works of Turgenev, Tolstoy, Dostoevsky and many minor figures were constantly scrutinized for their political message. Nikolai Leskov's literary career came close to ruin in 1861 when a series of his works gave offence to the political left. Turgenev left Russia when *Fathers and Children* raised a great furore, and he never returned for permanent residence. In the Soviet Union, political orthodoxy has been required of practitioners in all branches of the creative arts. Works of music, literature and art have been searched diligently for their political meaning. Reputations have been made and lost over the content of an opera, painting, novel or poem. But Russians have always appeared to be acutely sensitive to the purely artistic merit of those of the greatest creative figures whose works found their way into print, and have eagerly passed samizdat works from hand to hand.

This is one aspect of the background against which arts education in the USSR must be considered. Things are, of course, changing. It was common a few years ago to stand open-mouthed in admiration at the cultural awareness of the Soviet population: the way they read 'good' books in the metro, besieged theatres and opera houses for spare tickets and flocked to galleries, cinemas and symphony concerts. Some have, of course, argued that the non-availability of trashy literature or pornography and the difficulty of obtaining records of Western pop music led masses of people to the good stuff because there was simply nothing else. This, if true, would appear to be a very good thing, though if they now really are deserting high quality for rubbish, something must surely be wrong. Whatever the truth of this, the average Soviet citizen is still probably much closer to the arts in his or her society than the average Briton.

NEW ELEMENTS IN THE SITUATION

There are none the less several considerations likely to affect arts education in the USSR under glasnost and perestroika. Some of these are societal, others principally educational. They are: the invasion of Western pop culture, especially music, and a conservative reaction to it; openness to styles of art and music (especially perhaps the abstract and *avant-garde*) not previously admitted from abroad; the publication of literary works once banned, such as Pasternak's *Dr Zhivago* (so many other works by established as well as unknown writers are emerging from secret bottom drawers that it is claimed that the history of Soviet literature will have to be completely rewritten); the introduction of market forces in the theatre (and probably eventually in other forms of art too, such as publishing); the widespread questioning in the media of previous attitudes to the arts; an increased interest in the cultural history both of the recent and of the more distant past (church music, traditional architecture, and, significantly, biblical traditions in literature); the apparent demand from school pupils for a continuation of music and art instruction beyond the age of 12 or 13; and the consolidation of the position of the 'schools with a special profile', including some with musical or artistic bias.

It may be necessary to comment briefly on some of these phenomena, not all of which are relevant to the subject of this chapter. The all-pervasive pop music is an interesting one. Has its spread anything to do with musical matters, or is it, as some would assert, a sociological phenomenon, whereby young people identify themselves with a social group by expressing fanatical allegiance to one particular style of composition and performance, in the same way as they might support a football team? Are Soviet young people merely rebelling against their elders who do not want them to listen to such music? Is Western pop 'the people's music', or is it a means for commercial interests to make a great deal of money by marketing rubbish? Is it intellectually 'respectable'? The Soviet musical establishment has had difficulty in coming to terms with it, and many still regard pop as cultural pollution from which they would protect the youth of the USSR.[10] If so, they are having a rough time. Attendances at classical concerts are declining, and even such a leading musical body as the Leningrad Conservatoire claims to have noted a falling-off in interest in serious music by young people.[11] On the other hand, there is the paradoxical fact that school pupils are demanding musical education beyond the present compulsory limits. Stories abound that older schoolchildren are asking to attend voluntarily the music lessons held for junior classes, in order to experience again the pleasure they obtained from the exploration of music. The experimental introduction of the course in 'World Artistic Culture' (*mirovaya khudozhestvennaya kul'tura*, hereafter MKhK) is arousing enthusiasm, rather than the opposite. We shall return to this in due course.

TWO CROSS-CULTURAL MATTERS

Further light may be thrown on current moves in Soviet arts education by a brief comparative glance at thought on the subject in Britain (and other western countries to a greater or lesser extent). The word 'creative' has come to be regarded as good when applied to work done in schools; the same is true with the Russian word *tvorcheskii*. The difference is in the meaning attached to that word. In Britain it clearly refers to children writing their own stories, painting their own pictures and composing their own music; we shall see below in the discussion of literature teaching that some Russians use a new word, *kreativnyi*, to convey something of this meaning. The walls of

English schools are festooned with children's writing and painting; most of the displays in a Soviet school show a very limited contribution by the children. Musical composition by pupils is now *de rigueur* in the English secondary school, while in the Soviet Union there still persists a wariness of 'dilettantism' in this respect.[12] Children do, of course, draw and paint in Soviet art lessons. Their poems and stories are more likely to be composed in extracurricular activities than in the formal classroom. Creativity (*tvorchestvo*) is a word applied to an attitude, a quality of response, the ability to empathize, by Soviet educators.

Another possible contrast between British and Soviet arts education is the respect accorded to the cultural heritage in the two societies. As we have already seen, the Soviet arts educator has no doubt of the value of Mozart, Tolstoy or Rembrandt and sees it as a duty to present their works to the child. Some British teachers assert that the value or superiority of what they would term high-status art is not objectively demonstrable. Being unable in their own minds to prove that Beethoven's fifth symphony is a superior work of music to the latest pop single, and being influenced (one might say 'corrupted') by pseudo-sociological pronouncements about what constitutes working-class or middle-class culture, such teachers adopt a neutral stance towards works of art and avoid, as they would say, imposing their own standards on the pupils.[13] To what extent the teachers concerned really believe this, or are merely adopting an intellectual posture while in fact fostering the cause of 'high' culture or excusing their own ignorance of it, is another matter. Soviet educators, however, take the view that Beethoven *is* superior, and that even if he were once the property of the upper classes, the Revolution gave him to the workers. This point is made not to attack British arts teachers (many of whom do not subscribe to the view anyway) but to show that the idea of a cultural heritage which should be passed on to children is not under attack in the Soviet Union.

SOVIET ARTS EDUCATION IN THE RECENT PAST

In the national curriculum which has held sway hitherto the arts have figured in the following ways. The only musical education which all children once received was 'singing'. Changing the very title of this course in the primary and early secondary years (1 to 6) to 'music' was a political issue: for a while it was called 'music and singing'. Art was taught in years 1 to 6 only. Literature was taught throughout the whole compulsory period of education. A short technical drawing course in years 7 and 8 was related to labour training, despite the perfunctory obeisance that was paid in the syllabuses to aesthetic considerations. Film, dance and drama as separate activities did not appear in the curriculum.

In the proposed curriculum for the year 1990/1, which appeared in the wake of the 1984 reform of education,[14] there were slight changes: music and art each had two lessons per week in the very first year (the new class for 6-year-olds) and one in the succeeding years, but study of these subjects was to end in the new year 7, i.e. when pupils were the same age as in the old year 6. Things are changing quickly in Soviet education at present, and these proposals are now virtually superseded, though doubtless many schools will be operating in accordance with them for some time yet. The curricular proposals of 1989, however, recommend two lessons a week in both art and music for each of the first seven years and one lesson in years 8 and 9,[15] a doubling of the time allocated previously.

More important than the number of lessons or the syllabus outline is the spirit in which education is carried out. All too often in the past, as Soviet educators now freely admit, arts education has meant learning to recognize and repeat the political message of an art object. This has been particularly true of literary studies; literature, indeed, was habitually seen as a vital part of political and ideological education. Answers to examination questions were learned off by heart. In art, academic exercises held sway: children would draw 'two apples on a plate'. In music, importance was attached to vocal exercises and to technical information about musical notation and the like. Emotional response to music, painting or poetry was very much less regarded.

INNOVATION: MUSIC AND ART

This unsatisfactory position must have been obvious to any reasonably progressive teacher, and as long ago as the early 1970s highly significant steps were taken in the field of music education. The instigator of these was the composer Dmitrii Kabalevsky (1904–87), scarcely a young hothead, and rather, as a member of the Supreme Soviet and an academician, a well entrenched figure in the establishment. Kabalevsky's work is becoming better known abroad through the International Society for Music Education (ISME); until his death he was editor-in-chief of *Muzyka v shkole*, some of his writings have been translated into English,[16] and I have published a fairly substantial article on his system.[17]

What was new about his work was that it rejected standard Soviet ideas that music education was simply another manifestation of general pedagogy and the instilling of knowledge, skills and habits. Music has a nature of its own and makes special demands on the learner. The Kabalevsky system assumes that children should regard a feeling for music as something vital, and should be given a *love* of music. Motivation is essential, and teachers must set out to create it; boredom in lessons is to be avoided at all costs, and the stultifying, meaningless vocal exercises with which too many Soviet teachers have filled their lessons should be swept away. Children should be so inspired that they seek musical experiences outside of school. To place such a requirement on teachers – that they should create enjoyment – is likewise new (and shocking to some). Furthermore, the freedom of expression which teachers should encourage in their classes is feared by many, both inside the music teaching profession and in other areas of teaching. If the lessons are to foster emotional response to music and to encourage the 'development of mature musical thinking' through discussion and the free expression of the children's reactions to what they have heard, then this creates expectations in the pupils' minds as to what lessons in other subjects should be like. It is easy to imagine the effect of this on teachers of a more conservative disposition: 'Why can't the music teachers make the children sit still, keep quiet and do as they are told? They make life difficult for the rest of us by all this nonsense about forming and expressing their own opinions!'

A strong impression is received by the visitor that the cause of music education in the Kabalevsky mode is won. There is considerable enthusiasm among teachers about the changes in approach which the new syllabus has introduced. Reform in art education has not quite had the same impetus. Since 1975 it has been in the hands of the painter and educator Boris Nemensky. His experimental syllabuses[18] have not yet been adopted in their entirety. A published art syllabus dated 1988[19] contains certain conservative features. Nevertheless, his cause is not lost, and his work unquestionably influences the progress of art in Soviet schools.

Nemensky's programme bears more than a superficial resemblance to Kabalevsky's. He favours independence of working, discovery methods, the use of initiative and creative freedom within the classroom. Freedom of choice as regards the medium in which the pupils work is encouraged. Fantasy is fostered as a counterbalance to the depiction of reality and formal decorative art. As in the music lessons, the universality of art is emphasized, and multi-cultural education is served by study of the crafts and art of the people of the USSR and the world. There is less stress on 'academic' exercises in the drawing of groupings of cubes and cylinders. Collective discussion of each other's finished work is carried on as an aid to the discovery of strengths and weaknesses. The syllabus, like Kabalevsky's, is constructed thematically, and slides or reproductions of famous works by standard artists are studied in relation to topics such as 'art as protest'. In the same way as the last lesson in the music programme every term is a miniature concert open to parents and visitors, the final art lesson of the year becomes an exhibition and festival of art, at which at least one work by each pupil is displayed.

The 1988 art syllabus is constructed differently from Nemensky's. Whereas the latter is presented thematically, the former consists of lists of media, tasks, skills to be mastered, objects and scenes which the children might be called upon to draw and stories and scenes they might illustrate, and famous paintings (many of them revolutionary) they might look at. The emphasis would appear to be on the acquisition of technical skills, though it must be said that the variety of activities would be stimulating to any child if presented by an enlightened teacher. Nevertheless, this syllabus is anchored firmly in the past and it represents an updating of traditional approaches rather than a distinctly new concept.

LITERATURE AND RELATED ACTIVITIES

Music, pictures, words . . . We turn to the teaching of literature. It is probably in this area that art, in Shakespeare's words, has been most obviously 'made tongue-tied by authority'. To read the textbooks, accompanying literature, methodological advice and examination questions of recent years would be sufficient to conclude, correctly, that literature teaching was intended as a potent force in the political and moral education of youth. Huge numbers of teachers will have been trained in this tradition and have many years' experience of running lessons in this way; are they going to change now? At the same time, one meets many teachers in the schools with apparently a genuine and consuming love of Russian literature. One wonders how such people survived the long age when all that was required of them was to drill pupils to answer questions on 'Lenin and the party spirit in literature' or 'The next XXVII Congress of the Communist party on the role and aims of Soviet literature in the communist education of the working masses in the modern age'.[20]

If new ground is being broken in Soviet arts education in literature lessons, one might expect to find a number of innovations. Literature is not just a matter of reading, discussing, 'appreciating' and intellectualizing standard authors. Are pupils taught to write poetry or imaginative prose? Do drama or theatre skills play any part in education? Is the content and coverage of the literature syllabus changing in tune with the times? How are teaching methods and class organization being adapted? Are assessment methods changing? Is the primary aim of literature teaching to achieve intellectual discussion, or have the feelings a role in the modern lesson? Is discussion free, or are particular conclusions still expected by the teacher? It must surely be obvious that there can as yet be no simple answer to many of these questions, but indications can be sought in the educational press as to the direction of current thinking.

Creative writing does not necessarily mean the same thing as literary work, but even the sort of simple, personal composition that young children do can be seen as the start of insight into the work of a writer. The use of the word 'creative' opens a whole series of questions of educational importance, which it is not appropriate to discuss here; a somewhat sceptical, but none the less helpful, exploration of the concept of creativity is to be found (and read with caution) in R.G. Woods and R.St C. Barrow, *An Introduction to Philosophy of Education*, London, Methuen, 1975 (chapter 8: 'Creativity', pp. 142–57). There are, of course, those in Britain who sneer at the idea of children 'expressing themselves', as though self-expression were necessarily undisciplined and educationally worthless. British teachers on the whole, however, attach great importance to encouraging children of all ages to compose stories, poems and many other genres of writing. Events in the language class and in the literature lesson are not totally divorced from each other.

Soviet teachers of language are coming to the conclusion that even humdrum language tasks should be 'creative'. One writer in the journal *Russkii yazyk v shkole* urges teachers to motivate children by setting real-life relevant tasks (such as composing an advertisement to find a lost dog) or by helping them to learn to address a specific audience; she deprecates traditional essay subjects such as 'What I like to do in my spare time and why' as off-putting. She uses the word *kreativnyi* to name this approach, rather than *tvorcheskii*; *kreativnyi* is a new formation.[21] There is evidence in the pages of this journal during 1989 and 1990 of an interest in the use of music and painting to stimulate what Russian educators call 'the development of connected language' through the writing down of aesthetic response. This is not entirely new, and I saw lessons of this type ten or more years ago, but it would appear that Soviet education is still only in the early stages of exploiting the possibilities of imaginative composition by pupils. That is, unless it is considered 'imaginative' to produce the sort of whimsy, moralizing and socio-political reflection that is expected in public examinations: 'Heroes are born in labour', 'They fought for the fatherland', 'An unforgettable meeting', 'A good name depends on good deeds', or 'The person most dear to me'. These are five examples from nearly 200 essay titles set a few years ago; the titles are announced in advance of the examination and so essays can be – and often are – prepared beforehand. Not all children, it can safely be said, will find that writing on such topics gives adequate scope for their creative instincts! Out-of-school activities probably remain the focus for the writing of poetry and stories, and the class or school wall-newspaper offers opportunities for embryonic literary and journalistic writing.

At the beginning of this chapter mention was made of certain radical changes in the position of the arts in the Soviet Union, in particular of the relaxation of censorship and control of what is published. Not only are new works and new writers emerging but also previously unpublished books by established socialist-realist writers, some of them deceased, are seeing the light of day after decades in bottom drawers. The educational press shows that many Soviet teachers are responding with enthusiasm to this situation. Sholokhov among Soviet classics is being re-assessed, and is vigorously defended as well as questioned. Anna Akhmatova, Nikolai Gumilev, Alexander Solzhenitsyn, and Boris Pasternak are four of the major writers who are rehabilitated, and whom teachers are being urged to include in their lessons. Teachers are free, and are using the freedom, to introduce pupils to works not in the official textbooks and anthologies. In a perceptive article, one Moscow schoolteacher reflects on the way that she teaches Soviet literature in the light of this new situation. She deplores the tendency in the past to set the social message of a poem above its value as 'real poetry', and illustrates how, as she sees it, true feeling defeats artificiality, and how themes such as war and peace, man's relationship with history and the future, nature, love, humanity and cruelty can be explored through poetry.[22]

A contribution to a teachers' journal which would have been impossible a year or two ago was a substantial article by an Orthodox priest and scholar on the Bible and biblical teaching. This reflects concern on the part of educators that knowledge of the religious traditions of Christianity are unknown to many Russian children, and the purpose of publishing the article was, in the words of the editor, to illuminate 'a necessary part of our common spiritual and cultural values'; it is 'a shame' that so many children 'pass over beautiful works of religious art, remain indifferent to religious music or do not grasp the full meaning of works by literary masters'. The priest's article works through Christianity from Moses to St John's Gospel and the Apocalypse; however, it takes a traditional view of biblical studies, avoiding any controversy over the authorship of the gospels, for example.[23] (These matters are more fully explored in Chapter 5.)

No less refreshing than this innovation is the appearance of attacks on the former sacred cow of Soviet literature, the theory of socialist realism. An article by G. Mitin, 'What is Marxism responsible for? Retrospective comments on "socialist realism"', argues that the theory, when enunciated, prevented writers telling the truth until Khrushchev's denunciation of Stalin in 1956; after that socialist realism was moribund, suffering defeat after defeat at the hands of 'free realism'. Like the shell from the gunboat *Aurora*, which was the signal for the storming of the Winter Palace in 1917, it was a 'blank', disarmed by Stalin who would never have allowed socialist or any other realism to tear the mask off his anti-national, inhuman, criminal development. To require and define a creative method was a fatal mistake, and a Stalinist one. It is amazing, says Mitin, that some good literary works actually came out after 1933. He gives as examples Makarenko's books, Nekrasov's *In the Trenches of Stalingrad* and Grossman's *For the Just Cause*, saying that better works than these could not be achieved under Stalin.[24] It is indeed good news that this barren literary theory can now be forgotten by schoolchildren – and by the rest of us.

Even the person of Lenin is to be freed from taboo. D.N. Murin, in an article entitled 'Party literature and the party spirit in literature' (the title is a play on Lenin's own 'Party organization and the party spirit in literature'), analyses Lenin's article from the point of view of how it might be taught in the new circumstances. He declares that the great man's dicta should be considered in their historical context, not as absolute truth (though he cautiously admits that some of Lenin's statements are still not to be questioned); he envisages that pupils might discuss freely who was right, Lenin or Bryusov, in their controversy over whether the relationship between literature and society is the same, be that society proletarian or bourgeois.[25]

That particular issue might not thrill all adolescents, but the point is that Lenin's views might be dispassionately assessed.

Teaching methods and the conduct of classes figure in a number of contributions to the journals. Nothing here would be new to forward-looking Western teachers of literature. Soviet teachers have been discovering group work in the last few years, and new impetus is given to it in the journals *Literatura v shkole* and *Russkii yazyk v shkole*. Several practising teachers describe their methods:[26] one divides the class into groups of fourteen (presumably this means three groups in a class, as Soviet classes are rather large), another of seven. The groups select themselves entirely voluntarily, they are given tasks to work at and have to organize themselves and get on with it. At last teachers understand that collective working, which orthodox Soviet morality always saw as highly desirable, is fostered by group work; it also, they say, places responsibility on the individual, and motivates the shy to speak their mind in smaller groups when they have to take the initiative. Other active methods of achieving pupil involvement are under discussion. The dramatization of crucial episodes from books is becoming more common (and a teacher argues that it is worthwhile and efficient in the use of time if it clarifies a work for pupils and the effect rubs off on all of the other, subsequent lessons on the same book).[27] This has regularly been a part of foreign language lessons, but with a different purpose – language development – in mind. The use of debates and discussions, now that all sorts of matters can be discussed freely, seems worthwhile to many teachers. Sometimes questionnaires are distributed to pupils to discover their reactions to books and stories; this is not to test children but to serve as a basis for the teacher's planning of a series of lessons.

Literature teachers writing in the educational press include some who are uneasy about certain aspects of modern Soviet society. These are not necessarily conservatives in every sense of the word. A Moscow teacher called Alla Kosenkova writes in *Literatura v shkole* that she deplores the decline in public morals and standards of discourse, but she sees Russian literature as a great force counteracting obscenity and irresponsibility in society. She sees it as her mission to present to children noble literary figures who have been in the past vilified and persecuted by party stalwarts. Russian literature is 'the expression of the conscience of society, its traditions, needs and hopes'. The patriotic spirit has saved Russia at difficult times in the past. When she writes of uniting all nationalities, 'all the peoples of Russia', under the banner of the love of literature,[28] the impression is given of the re-emergence of a type of Russian messianism in some ways not unlike that which existed in the nineteenth century. Or is it perhaps a genuine attempt to rescue something from what she perceives as the ruins of Russian society?

New material, new aims, new methods . . . If the methods by which literature courses are assessed were not changing, teachers would still have to cram their pupils with guaranteed ways of passing the old exams. Reform is under way, however. Literature will still be tested orally by the 'ticket' method: candidates pick up a ticket lying face down on the table and answer the question, after due preparation. What is on the ticket is changing. Although official tickets are published and sold in advance of the examination date, various bodies are issuing alternatives for use by teachers who prefer them. Teachers are even free to make up their own. *Literatura v shkole* publishes a set drawn up by the Leningrad In-service Training Institute. Although political issues are still there ('Lenin on literature and art', 'Policy of the Communist party of the USSR in literature today [with reference to Gorbachev's meeting with people active in the fields of science and culture on 6 January 1989]'), they are often phrased in a way which invites personal response: 'What have Shatrov's plays revealed to me about Lenin, in his time and today?' (Shatrov's plays contain daring re-assessments of Stalin, Trotsky and even Lenin himself); 'Subjects and themes in Soviet literature of the 1980s (2 to 3 examples)'; 'Basic themes and social fears in contemporary Soviet publicistics'; '"I am your poet!" Is Mayakovsky *your* poet?' The once ubiquitous Maxim Gorky still figures prominently, but those who set the topics are easing off on him somewhat. Blok particularly and also Esenin and Tvardovsky make appearances, and some lively answers may be expected to questions on the search for the meaning of life in *War and Peace* and the generation gap in Turgenev.[29]

The overall impression is that literature, or in the main the reading and appreciation of literature, is a subject which has at last come to life and which may soon, if it is not doing so already, make the massive contribution to the education of Soviet young people that it is well able to do.

HOW SOVIET EDUCATORS SEE ARTS EDUCATION TODAY

Arts educators in many parts of the world complain of the disregard in which their subjects are held, and this is true in the Soviet Union too. However, the outside observer may well think that Soviet educators have less cause for complaint than in some other countries. There, the officially expressed views of those who make policy give considerable support to the arts in education. Even the Reform Guidelines of 1984 declared how important it was to 'develop a sense of the beautiful' and to 'form good aesthetic taste'.[30] The reasons for this faith in the importance of aesthetic education are various. One is a general belief that it is good for children to know and appreciate their cultural heritage. Another is the oft-expressed need to give children protection against 'social corrosion' and 'ideologically cheap and banal works which might reach young people' (presumably from the capitalist West, though perhaps not only from outside the borders of the Soviet Union).[31] Third is the firm belief in the psychological and intellectual benefits of studying the arts (what a British writer has termed 'the intelligence of feeling', perhaps);[32] Vygotsky is quoted to the effect that full development of

71

the child cannot take place without contact with the arts. Fourth is the development of this into a firm conviction that artistic experience leads to imaginative ways of working and higher productivity in industry. The poet Yevtushenko, in rejecting narrow vocationalism in education, goes so far as to say that 'only people of high and many-sided culture can achieve qualitative revolutionary changes in their own work and in history as a whole'.[33]

Such claims could scarcely be termed modest; some might consider the productivity argument breathtakingly audacious. Some arts educators in the West take exception to such justifications on the grounds that they undervalue the arts. Connoisseurs of Soviet schooling will have noticed that there is nothing here about developing a Marxist-Leninist world view or producing convinced communists, until very recently staple expressed aims of the education system. Belief in the importance of education through the arts is gaining ground. Traditional reverence for the scientific has not been allowed to detract from this renewed interest in the arts. The draft curricula of 1989 for the general school, as we have seen, double the time allocated to art and music. In classes 5–11 literature is listed separately from language and is allocated an average of three weekly lessons in each year. But what of the *integration* of the arts in the Soviet school? Some steps in this direction are being taken through the course in World Artistic Culture, one lesson a week in years 9–11, which has been the subject of an experiment for several years now.[34] We shall next examine this recent innovation in the Russian Republic's curriculum after making an important preliminary point.

ART AND THE SOVIET CHILD

One feature of the Soviet school which has struck me forcibly as an observer is the willingness and ability of youngsters to discuss works of art in class. They seem to have the vocabulary and conceptual apparatus with which to talk about paintings, music and literature, and to have been given some elementary insight into what an artist's work is about. Moreover, most or all of the senior pupils in classes in (admittedly) good schools will contribute to such discussions and show themselves to be far from tongue-tied: they do not leave it to one or two highly articulate fellow-pupils to make the running. This could be explained in various ways. Perhaps their parents are more inclined than in some other countries to take them to exhibitions or concerts and, more important, to talk to them about the experience afterwards. Excursions to museums and galleries are a frequent feature of school life, and doubtless teachers exploit such trips afterwards in discussions.

Two examples may illustrate this; both are taken from English lessons, it may be interesting to note. In the first lesson a class of 15-year-olds used a set of reproductions of abstract paintings for an activity in which one half of the class had to guess which painting in particular the other half were talking about. The discussion revolved around the shapes, colours and also the emotions aroused when looking at the paintings. Considering that no abstract paintings had been widely exhibited in the Soviet Union until a relatively short time before the lesson took place (1988), the achievement was considerable. The lesson was a demonstration on a day of in-service training, so it may be thought that the pupils had rehearsed the lesson. I can, however, vouch for the fact that my second example was unprepared, because it took place in a tenth-class lesson which I taught myself. I had brought a set of art postcards from England which the teenage pupils had certainly never seen before and which I sprang on them without warning. They had few problems (other than linguistic ones) in expressing their reactions, which covered the colour, composition, mood, feelings aroused, and search for hidden meanings.[35]

WORLD ARTISTIC CULTURE

It would therefore not be too improbable to assume that Soviet educators, when they say that school pupils have actually demanded instruction in the arts, are telling the truth. The course in World Artistic Culture (*mirovaya khudozhestvennaya kul'tura* or MKhK)[36] may be seen as a response to this demand. It has been in experimental existence since the 1977/8 school year in certain schools in the RSFSR; interest has been shown in other republics, though it is a Russian initiative. Freedom has been given to individual teachers to experiment with subject matter until official syllabuses are issued. Orders for the extension of the experiment were published in 1989.[37]

The person at the head of the subject and the author of several published articles on the content and teaching of MKhK is L. Predtechenskaya, Senior Scientific Worker at the Research Institute of the Ministry of Education of the RSFSR. The subject has at least one influential ally: a report of a meeting on 23 June 1989 praises G.A. Yagodin, that dominant figure in education under perestroika, for being the only member of the State Committee on Education to take MKhK seriously.[38]

The Soviet curriculum has been based until now on traditional disciplines, separate subjects rather than an integrated programme. It is a feature of the so-called progressive teacher in the West to integrate. The traditional Soviet answer to this, since about 1930, has been to insist on 'systematic' instruction in established disciplines, but to stress the importance of 'inter-subject links'. Yagodin, at the meeting referred to above, declared that he believed in integrated classes for labour, music, art and Russian from the primary years upwards. (He demonstrated current Soviet interest in continuing education by remarking also that MKhK is or should be for the whole population, not just the schools.) MKhK is an attempt to integrate all of the arts with intellectual history. It is clearly seen as an opportunity to allow teachers to synthesize and give pupils an overall picture, and as related to all subjects in the humanities. It is even envisaged that science lessons should be influenced, for example, by the use of impressionist painting when the subject of optics is introduced in physics, or the depiction of plants and animals in biology.[39] The subject seeks to teach pupils to generalize, to exercise logical thought, and to go in for problem-solving and evaluative activities.[40] Moreover, like music and art in the junior classes, it has an element of multi-culturalism in it. A recent directive requires those responsible for the syllabus to see that the cultural heritage of all of the peoples in the RSFSR is represented and that national trends in the arts should lead to appreciation of the culture of *all* peoples.[41]

There is little expression of overt political aims in relation to this course. Predtechenskaya writes, in the introduction to some draft extracts from a proposed textbook, that the aims of MKhK are,

> through various arts and the combined strength of their influence, to shape the spiritual world of the senior school pupil. How can we achieve the result that such pupils receive the necessary knowledge about the arts through a direct relationship with art, 'from inside' art and with the support of its principles?[42]

The subject is, therefore, not a lecture course on highlights from the great masters, but, in theory at least, an attempt to make pupils engage with the arts and experience them directly. An author of a section from the proposed textbook writes of her aim to involve the pupil fully with the arts, to make this involvement enjoyable and to make the pupil 'reflect on himself and the world in which he lives'. Predtechenskaya, in an earlier article, writes: 'The clarification of one's attitude to the world and the choice of a way of life is one of the main spiritual tasks which a person decides in youth. Art is capable of suggesting a decision.'[43]

What does the MKhK course consist of in terms of actual content?[44] It is based on a number of topics such as: 'Leading ideas of the revolutionary epoch and romanticism in foreign musical art', 'Romanticism in foreign literature: Victor Hugo's novel *Notre Dame de Paris*', 'The ideas of the Enlightenment in foreign graphic art: Jacques Louis David', 'The ideas of the Enlightenment in foreign literature: J.W. von Goethe's *Sturm und Drang* works'. Some ideas of the more detailed content of lessons may be had by a study of extracts from the proposed textbook with its skeleton teaching notes. The biographical approach to the artist, in this case David, is present, though it is not his life story for its own sake but rather in order to illustrate David's work. Much use is made of the artist's own statements about his painting. There is a good deal about technical aspects of the paintings, their colour, composition and rhythm. Some of this would need very expert handling by the teacher and a multiplicity of visual aids to make it accessible to the average pupil. David's work is related to its historical context; the furore surrounding the exhibition of the *Oath of the Horatii* is recounted. Stress is placed on the message, the effect on the public, the historical

74

relevance of this particular painting, and the changes in the artist's ideological position.

The Goethe topic begins with a statement presenting the writer as a great polymath: writer, painter, scientist, statesman, actor and stage director. Opinions of Goethe are quoted from a constituency as broad as Engels, Karamzin, Thomas Mann, Kuchelbecker and Mazzini (the punchline of the whole section is the opinion of Pasternak's hero, Yury Zhivago: 'I read Goethe and my mind is in turmoil'). Goethe's work on the uncompleted 'Prometheus' is recounted; the story moves on to *Die Leiden des jungen Werther.* The theme suggested by this work is adolescence, and there is a brief reference to J.D. Salinger's *Catcher in the Rye.* Very much more attention, however, is accorded to Ulrich Plenzdorf's novel, *Die neuen Leiden des jungen W.,* which became almost a cult in the German Democratic Republic, and which the author of the extract obviously feels to be of the greatest interest to Soviet young people. *Faust* is referred to briefly, since pupils will have become acquainted with it from the tenth-class literature syllabus.

As to what teaching materials are available for the course, it will be remembered that the textbook did not exist in 1990, and that even the materials discussed above were presented to teachers as a basis for discussion. Suggestions were invited for a title for the book, and, more importantly, a competition was announced for two further chapters on the Enlightenment 'in foreign music' and 'in the musical culture of Russia'. A course such as this requires more than a textbook. The publication of sets of gramophone records and colour slides was announced in early 1990.[45] However, the planned numbers of copies, 6,500 of each of the sets of records and 3,000 for the slide collections, seem to suggest either that not a very large proportion of Russian schools is teaching MKhK as yet or that there will be much borrowing between schools and complaints about the non-availability of visual and audio aids. The educational technology available to the teacher in the average Russian school could scarcely be described as lavish and the success of the course will depend to some extent on the resourcefulness of teachers in overcoming the inevitable practical difficulties.

The teaching methods to be used are, it is scarcely necessary to say, crucial in deciding whether or not new ground is being broken in arts education in the Soviet school. We have seen that content-dominated methods, assessed by factual recall questions, are at last on the way out, and that the Kabalevsky system along with a new spirit in art and literature teaching has been received with enthusiasm in many, if not all, quarters.

Predtechenskaya, in her article of 1984,[46] suggested visualizing the lessons as something akin to a dramatic performance. An atmosphere, like that at a concert or play, should be created. This would aid the specific methodological feature of a lesson in the arts: experiential learning rather than the development of cognitive abilities, which is the function of other curriculum areas. The Ancient Greeks saw the theatre as a 'school' for adults; but its effect was greatest when the educative aspect was unperceived by the spectator. The same applies even in a real school; if the pupils perceive that they are indeed in school – if, in other words, they see that they are being preached to – they will switch off. The teacher must give great thought to the presentation of the lesson; it should be constructed like a drama and have a scenario. Pupils should be involved in problem-solving; important questions should be posed; the pupils should leave the room 'aroused' and in a mood to provide their own answers, which might have been suggested but not imposed by the teacher. The problems should be made relevant to the pupils and to the present age. In class, discussion should be open, and may take directions not anticipated by the teacher (which, in Predtechenskaya's opinion, is 'very desirable'). The teacher is not required to manipulate discussion in order to demonstrate the superiority of the Marxist-Leninist world view. 'The aim . . . is to form the personality of the senior pupil, his ideological and moral convictions'.[47] Predtechenskaya does not specify the nature of these convictions.

If the policy outlined in the previous paragraph were put into practice, the result would be enlightened and fascinating lessons. It is no criticism of the Soviet educators who advocate it to say that it all depends on the individual teacher whether or not the spirit of the lesson reflects the educational philosophy of the designers of the course in World Artistic Culture. Many teachers sometimes find it hard to allow their students to have their heads in the way that they believe, intellectually, that they should. It would scarcely be surprising if Soviet teachers who have been brought up to believe in the authority of the teacher, the syllabus and the textbook found it difficult to allow schoolchildren, even senior pupils, to participate actively.

When we study the text that Predtechenskaya presents as her lesson notes for a session on Schubert and his treatment of the common man, the difficulties are illustrated. The teacher is given advice on how to create an atmosphere by the use of musical performance and the reading of poetry and critical extracts. He or she is given a cunning plan, based on a series of quite interesting questions: what does Schubert tell us about his contemporaries and about each of us? What is new about his contribution to our view of life? How did he present the common man? Under each of these headings suggestions are made as to how the pupils' likely knowledge of Schubert and of other music and literature could be built upon to work towards answers to the questions. It is recognized that the answers are difficult to find and likely to be only partly appreciated by the children. It must be said that the line of argument underlying the teachers' notes is extremely interesting, but is predestined to lead to certain conclusions. On the one hand, one wonders how many teachers will be able to let their pupils indulge in the open discussion which is regarded as desirable, or how many pupils will have the knowledge or maturity to come to conclusions which are not 'suggested by the teacher'. On the other hand it would be unreasonable to expect this to happen in every lesson, or even, perhaps, in most lessons; something may be gained if some pupils have been moved by the music and have followed the teacher's argument to its conclusion. At best the lesson may lead to fruitful and enlightening discussions, at worst (and some may think this not a bad result) it may be a well-prepared lecture on an interesting subject including some splendid music.

CONCLUSION

It will perhaps be helpful to sum up this account of Soviet arts education from two points of view. First, what has the international educational community to learn from these reforms? Soviet arts education has been behind that in many other countries for a long time, and it represents a conservative strain in world tradition. A slow rate of progress may make the whole process look over-cautious and unadventurous. A strength of the Soviet system, however, is its liking for carefully worked out theory; if the theory is sound, the result is likely to be more effective in the long run than if it had been based on intuition alone. In the case of music education, the theory and its practical application were worked out by a leading composer – perhaps not a great one, but a prominent, respected figure. The parallels which suggest themselves in other countries are the work of Carl Orff in Germany and Kodaly in Hungary. The activity of Peter Maxwell Davies in Britain is another example of a composer with a real flair for education, but his work never had, indeed never was intended to have, the overarching construction and coherence of a syllabus for every child in every school. Until recently the educational system in England and Wales could not conceivably have given any one person or agency the coverage which Kabalevsky had in the USSR. The Kabalevsky syllabus (and that of Nemensky in art, as yet unadopted) is devised as one seamless garment; it is thematic and fundamentally progressive, not in the political sense but in that it involves progression as the child develops.

Is it a strength or a weakness of the Soviet system that whatever syllabus is compiled should be applicable to all children? Modern Soviet syllabuses are allowing ever more discretion to the individual republic, area, school and particularly teacher, but they are doing so within the limits of a coherently structured framework. A Soviet syllabus is, in its experimental stage, presented to the teaching profession for discussion, but sooner or later its supporters and opponents struggle to establish it or topple it as an entity acceptable to all children. The underlying assumption about children as essentially similar beings is too obvious to require comment. This remains true even in the light of recent statements by Soviet educators that the curriculum in the senior classes should be 'profoundly differentiated', since Soviet belief in a basic large curricular core appears to remain unshaken. Nevertheless, Soviet educators believe firmly in the ability of all schoolchildren to benefit from courses of demanding and worthwhile content both in the younger classes and in the senior years of secondary education. It may be added that they remain refreshingly uninhibited and unashamed on a number of other points: the importance and quality of the culture of the past, the need to inculcate 'good taste' and, more controversially, the practical benefits in a person's working life of experience of the arts. We all surely have a good deal to learn from this positive and courageous approach to education.

The importance of the changes for Soviet education itself is easier to pinpoint. First, there is a real and striking transfer of emphasis from the teacher to the pupils. Child-centred education as a concept has been increasingly mocked in recent years, since the novelty of the idea has worn off, but there can be few people with a serious claim to expertise in education who would not think that Soviet schools are ripe for some little recognition of its claims. Second, Soviet teachers have realized that the arts, especially music, are primarily a matter of feeling rather than cognitive activity, and that they have special characteristics affecting the way in which they should be taught in schools. Third, integration of subject matter, exemplified primarily in the MKhK course, is a direction in which the system has been poised to move for some while, but is now only beginning to do so. Fourth, stress on enjoyment in the arts lesson, an open-endedness and free discussion are all new and represent an important new spirit. The implications of this are the most significant for the understanding of change not in education but in Soviet society: pupils in many schools are actually being encouraged to think for themselves; in classes where this is denied to them, they are protesting; and the formerly automatic rider that the lessons should produce convinced communists is being gradually forgotten. Of course, changes in received wisdom might lead to nothing more exciting than pupils being drilled to produce pat answers according to the new orthodoxy. We must wait to see whether this will be the result, but present signs are that it will be impossible to enforce conformity by the old methods. The arts are leading the field in reforming Soviet pedagogy. They are both contributing to and reinforcing change in society outside the school.

NOTES AND REFERENCES

1 'Ob utverzhdenii gosudarstvennogo bazisnogo uchebnogo plana srednei obshcheobrazovatel'noi shkoly', *Byulleten' Gosudarstvennogo komiteta SSSR po narodnomu obrazovaniyu. Seriya: Doshkol'noe vospitanie i obshchee srednee obrazovanie,* (hereafter *BGKNO/DVOSO*), 1990, no. 1, pp. 17–23, especially p. 18.
2 B. Mitin, 'Tochka zreniya', *Uchitel'skaya gazeta,* 1990, no. 1, p. 1.
3 E. Dneprov, at the IV World Congress of ICSEES, July 1990.
4 N.D. Nikandrov, 'What to compare, when and why: a Soviet perspective', *Comparative Education,* 1989, vol. 25, no. 3, pp. 275–82, especially p. 280.

5 'Problema [sic] net', *Education*, 1990, vol. 175, no. 17, p. 421. Readers will be relieved in view of the elementary error in the title that the article was in English. Nikandrov (op. cit., p. 280) also comments that the curricula of England and the Soviet Union may 'meet in the middle'.
6 'Ob utverzhdenii . . . ', op. cit., p. 18.
7 'O tselevoi kompleksnoi programme "soderzhanie obshchego srednego obrazovaniya"', *BGKNO/DVOSO*, 1990, no. 5, pp. 2–11, especially pp. 2–3.
8 'Ob utverzhdenii . . . ', op. cit., p. 18.
9 'O tselevoi kompleksnoi programme . . . ', op. cit., p. 3.
10 See C. Rice, 'Soviet music in the era of *perestroika*', in J. Graffy and G.A. Hosking (eds), *Culture and the Media in the USSR Today*, London, Macmillan, 1989, especially pp. 100–3.
11 Private communication, as are several of the statements in this paragraph.
12 D. Kabalevsky, 'The basic principles and methods of the music curriculum for the general education school', *Soviet Education*, 1988, vol. 30, no. 1, pp. 53–4.
13 The matter is discussed in K. Swanwick, *A Basis for Music Education*, Windsor, NFER, 1979, pp. 104ff.
14 'Model curriculum for the secondary general school', *Soviet Education Study Bulletin*, 1985, vol. 3, no. 2, pp. 66–7, quoting *Byulleten' normativnykh aktov Ministerstva prosveshcheniya SSSR*, 1985, no. 6, p. 24.
15 'Ob utverzhdenii . . . ', op. cit., especially p. 21.
16 D.B. Kabalevski [sic], *Music and Education*, London, Kingsley/UNESCO, 1988.
17 For a substantial account of the Kabalevsky system, see J. Muckle, 'Dmitriy Kabalevsky and the three whales', *British Journal of Music Education*, 1987, no. 4, pp. 53–70. The Soviet music syllabus is: *Programma po muzyke 1–3 klassy* and *4–7 klassy*, Moscow, Prosveshchenie, 1985; a translation exists of the syllabus for year 1: 'The music curriculum for grade one of the four–year elementary school', *Soviet Education*, 1988, vol. 30, no. 1, pp. 94–101. Summaries of the music, art and literature syllabuses are to be found in J. Muckle, *A Guide to the Soviet Curriculum*, London, Croom Helm, 1988, pp. 105–28.
18 I am grateful to Professor Nemensky for sending me duplicated copies of the projected syllabuses which would otherwise have been hard to find: *Izobrazitel'noe iskusstvo i khudozhestvennyi trud. Proekt programmy dlya 1–10 klassov obshcheobrazovatel'noi srednei shkoly SSSR*, Moscow, 1976–9; *Programma: 'Izobrazitel'noe iskusstvo, pervyi klass' dlya obshcheobrazovatel'noi shkoly (eksperimental'naya)*. Moscow, 1981; *Programma: Izobrazitel'noe iskusstvo i khudozhestvennyi trud. 3 klass*, Moscow, 1983; and *Programma: Izobrazitel'noe iskusstvo i khudozhestvennyi trud. 5 i 6 klassy obshcheobrazovatel'noi shkoly*, Moscow, 1985. Publisher in each case: Union of Artists of the USSR (Soyuz khudozhnikov SSSR).
19 *Programma 'Izobrazitel'noe iskusstvo' 4–6 klassy*, Moscow, Prosveshchenie, 1988.
20 Actual examination questions from *Bilety dlya vypusknykh ekzamenov za kurs srednei shkoly na 1986/87 god*, Moscow, Prosveshchenie, 1987, p. 5.
21 I.D. Morozova, 'Obrazovatel'nye i vospitatel'nye zadachi urokov razvitiya rechi', *Russkii yazyk v shkole*, 1990, no. 4, pp. 3–6.
22 L. Zueva, 'Poeziya nashikh dnei (k ekzamenam po literature)', *Literatura v shkole*, 1989, no. 2, pp. 111–19.
23 M. Dronov, 'O Biblii i bibleiskom uchenii', *Literatura v shkole*, 1990, no. 2, pp. 57–69.
24 G. Mitin, 'Za chto otvechaet marksizm? Retrospektivnye zametki o "sotsialisticheskom realizme"', *Literatura v shkole*, 1990, no. 1, pp. 39–55.
25 D.N. Murin, 'Partiinaya literatura ili partiinost' literatury?', *Literatura v shkole*, 1990, no. 3, pp. 50–4.

26 See, for example, S.S. Martynova, 'Formy i priemy gruppovoi raboty', *Russkii yazyk v shkole*, 1990, no. 3, pp. 39–42, and Z.T. Veselova, 'Literaturnaya kompositsiya na urokakh literatury', *Literatura v shkole*, 1989, no. 1, pp. 58–63.
27 Veselova, op. cit.
28 A. Kosenkova, 'Esli ne my, to kto zhe?', *Literatura v shkole*, 1990, no. 1, pp. 140–4.
29 'Vozvrashchayus' k ekzamenatsionnym biletam', *Literatura v shkole*, 1989, no. 3, pp. 105–7.
30 'Guidelines for the Reform of General and Vocational Schools', *USSR: New Frontiers of Social Progress*, Moscow, Novosti, 1984.
31 ibid., pp. 61–3.
32 *The Intelligence of Feeling* is the title of Robert W. Witkin's book published in London by Heinemann, 1974.
33 G.P. Shevchenko, 'Dukhovnoe razvitie uchashchikhsya', *Sovetskaya pedagogika*, 1989, no. 10, pp. 26–30. The references to Vygotsky and Yevtushenko appear on p. 27.
34 *Muzyka v shkole*, 1990, no. 1, p. 68.
35 The lesson referred to is transcribed in J. Muckle, *Portrait of a Soviet School under Glasnost*, London, Macmillan, 1990, pp. 134–42.
36 The syllabus is published as *Programma 'Mirovaya khudozhestvennaya kul'tura' VIII–X klassy*, Moscow, Prosveshchenie, 1988.
37 For the renewal of the orders, see *Muzyka v shkole*, 1989, no. 3, p. 71; also *Muzyka v shkole*, 1986, no. 4, p. 6.
38 'Nachalo dialoga', *Muzyka v shkole*, 1989, no. 4, pp. 69–70.
39 N. Paltyshev, 'Muzyka na urokakh fiziki', *Muzyka v shkole*, 1989, no. 1, pp. 23–5.
40 A. Kolpakova, 'Obshirnyi vzglyad na mir', *Muzyka v shkole*, 1986, no. 1, pp. 31–2.
41 'O rabote po programmam "Muzyka" i "Izobrazitel'noe iskusstvo" v obshcheobrazovatel'nykh shkolakh RSFSR', *Muzyka v shkole*, 1989, no. 2, p. 73.
42 L. Predtechenskaya and colleagues, 'Kakim byt' uchebniku po mirovoi khudozhestvennoi kul'ture?', *Muzyka v shkole*, 1990, no. 1, pp. 7–18.
43 L. Predtechenskaya, 'Metod khudozhestvennoi-pedagogicheskoi dramaturgii v prepodavanii kursa M.Kh.K.', *Muzyka v shkole*, 1984, no. 4, pp. 10ff.
44 See note 36 above. In the absence of the syllabus referred to, the articles cited in notes 42 and 43 have provided good evidence as to the nature and content of the course.
45 'O vypuske posobii k programmam "Muzyka" i "Mirovaya khudozhestvennaya kul'tura" dlya shkol RFSFR na 1990 god', *Muzyka v shkole*, 1990, no. 1, p. 69.
46 Predtechenskaya, 1984, op. cit.
47 ibid., p. 13.

5

SOVIET UPBRINGING UNDER PERESTROIKA: FROM ATHEISM TO RELIGIOUS EDUCATION?

John Dunstan

INTRODUCTION

Viewing Soviet schooling from the standpoint of, say, January 1988, in the light of thirty years' study of it, one might have said this: whereas, with the pendulum swing between the general and the vocational, curriculum reforms come and go, upbringing (*vospitanie*) goes on for ever; its goals and objectives are immutable, and only its methods may change. Such a conclusion would have seemed to be confirmed a month later, when the CPSU Central Committee plenum had education at the top of its agenda and perestroika was officially extended to the schools. The plenum in effect rejected the central underlying concept of the 1984 school reform. This had amounted to the vocationalization of secondary general education, with the aim initially of doubling the proportion of 15-year-olds entering vocational schools and ultimately of merging the two sectors. Now, however, secondary general schooling was to form the main *basis* for training, though whether it should be for nine or eleven years was not specified and became controversial. The plenum approved various other measures to democratize school management and to diversify the curriculum, and innovatory teachers received M.S. Gorbachev's personal benediction. In the new democratic spirit, the detailed blueprint about how to make teaching and learning more efficient was left to the professionals and the public.[1]

Some of these decisions, if successfully carried through, would clearly affect upbringing. The 'pedagogy of cooperation' would bring a degree of democracy right into the classroom, improve teacher–pupil relationships, make children feel appreciated as individuals, create a more happy and active collective, and give greater scope for personal initiative and creativity within it. This would eliminate formalism and promote restructuring. It must be stressed, however, that in February 1988 there was no *official* suggestion of a change of aims or objectives. Similar ideas had been expressed thirty years earlier, for example, in the context of the scientific and technical revolution and the space race. What was demanded now was a change to a new methodology or methodologies – or partly new, since they were often reminiscent of the 1920s – and, more important still, a change in attitudes towards them. Anyone who might have been tempted to see this as a new philosophy implying radical transformations in ultimate societal goals was brought up short by some very familiar language later in the plenum resolution, with its call

> to step up the communist education of student youth and mould their consciousness in the spirit of restructuring . . . It is necessary considerably to intensify the patriotic and internationalist education of young people . . . Greater attention must be given to the moulding of communist morality and the atheistic education of the rising generation.[2]

Even 'in the spirit of restructuring', or of perestroika, the sky was not to be the limit.

Yet only three years later, much had changed. There were complaints that schools were not so very different; teachers are in general a conservative breed. But 'deideologization' had entered the language. The youth organizations that had been a principal tool for the fashioning of the New Soviet Person were in disarray and in some republics had been disbanded. The disintegrating mosaic of the USSR raised fundamental questions for patriotic education, as did the end of the New Cold War for internationalist upbringing. Revelations about Soviet history, its past distortions and some of its former heroes impugned for many the notion of communist morality. Some parents were even suggesting that upbringing should be taken out of the hands of the schools altogether.[3]

Within this process of deideologization, the case of atheistic education presents some particularly interesting features. At the time of writing it had been deposed from its pedestal but not ousted, and in this it was not unique. But to a certain extent, though limited so far, it had been replaced by its opposite, religious education; and the way to this had been paved by a rapprochement with the church in the name of that same communist morality to which it was frequently linked. This chapter will successively consider the traditional line on atheistic education – very briefly, because supplementary studies are available[4] – review the watershed year of 1988, scrutinize the various sectors of religious instruction and religious studies as they developed up to the enactment of the Law on Freedom of Conscience and Religious Organizations of October 1990, and discuss the new and continuing problems in this area.

SEVENTY YEARS OF ATHEISTIC EDUCATION

The Soviet state was atheistic from the start. For Marx and Engels, religion was a delusion, a perverted consciousness of the world; only matter was real, and societal development was determined by production relations; in this scheme of things there was no place for a divine being. For Lenin, religion was also a dangerous counter-attraction.[5] A decree of 20 January 1918 separated the church from the state and the school from the church, and prohibited religious instruction in schools, confining it to the private sphere. Many teachers actively or passively resisted this. During the late 1920s, school policy moved from non-religious education to anti-religious education. A law of 8 April 1929 reinforced the 1918 decree and forbade religious associations to conduct work among children and young people. On 5 September 1931 the Central Committee called for full 'communist upbringing in the Soviet school'.[6]

As the Second World War became the USSR's Great Patriotic War, church–state relations changed as Orthodoxy in particular harnessed itself enthusiastically to the national cause. The atheistic content of school syllabuses sank to a minimum, and their anti-religious component vanished altogether.[7] But this pragmatic and one-sided truce did not long survive the German defeat. As early as 1947 the educational press was again stressing that teachers must be active atheists, and 1954 saw the start of a new anti-religious campaign in the schools. This was reinforced and extended to higher education in 1959 and indeed continued after the ousting of its chief sponsor, Khrushchev, in 1964. For a few years in the early 1960s under-18s were even formally banned from church services, though legislation of 1975 was to restore such rights and also permit over-10s to assist in the ritual and to sing in choirs.[8] It is generally agreed that these regulations might be diversely honoured, in the breach or – especially – in the observance, depending on the attitude and energy of local secular officials. In consequence of providing a religious upbringing, in a few extreme cases, believers were actually 'deprived of parental rights' and thus of the care of their children.[9] This rarely happened in Orthodox families, partly because they might be ill-equipped to perform that function, and partly since they were more likely to keep a low profile.

The era of Brezhnev and his two immediate successors, Andropov and Chernenko, was not marked by the harshness that had preceded it under Khrushchev, but a fairly strict line on atheistic education was nevertheless maintained. Let us summarize its principles, practice and problems. It was part of communist upbringing. It had to serve the cause of communism by inculcating a materialist world view and by developing resistance to alternative ideological and moral positions. Religion was the only alternative belief-system that was grudgingly permitted to exist, so people, particularly young ones, had to be steeled against it. Atheistic education was to be effected through subject knowledge and through its application in individual and social activity. It operated through both the formal curriculum and extracurricular activities, and was indeed meant to be part of lifelong learning.

In the formal curriculum, atheism – pure but not simple – comprised only one small segment of one final-year subject, social studies, taken by senior students in all three sectors of secondary general, vocational and technical education. Most of it was taught through other subjects, natural sciences appealing to the intellect, literature and the arts to the emotions, and history to both.[10] Apart from formal teaching, there was overt propagation of secular values in slogans and displays bedecking the school walls and in preparation of students for such rituals as the internal passport conferment at age 16 in the RSFSR. The youth organizations for successive age-groups were intended to lead the children from discussion of silly superstitions and 'reactionary' religious ceremonies through talks, concerts and magazine-writing to atheistic propaganda among their own families and neighbours.

Experts on atheistic education agreed that approaches to the task should be varied according to the extent of pupils' psychological maturation and the nature of their atheistic or religious experience, if any. This meant progression from the concrete and the known to the abstract and the unknown, as with any kind of teaching, and from emotional appeal to intellectual. But it also meant attention to children as individuals, which had not always been conspicuous in collective-dominated Soviet upbringing. Thus it was not necessarily sufficient, given a class of youngsters of about the same age, to be content with such progression. Vague atheists, for example, had to be treated differently from vague believers, the teacher encouraging conviction in the former and doubt in the latter. Vague believers should not be approached in the same way as firm believers, and the same techniques would not always do with convinced Orthodox, inspired by ritual and tradition, as with convinced Reform Baptists, affected by and skilled in the spoken word. And gentleness encouraged trust; the frequently confrontational stance of the Khrushchev period was in disrepute by the late 1970s.

Since parents played such a crucial role in this whole matter, a similarly careful and differentiated approach was required towards them. There was a clear tendency for teachers to direct their efforts at believing parents, where they were most required; but non-believers who did not give their children proper atheistic enlightenment, the vast majority according to surveys, also came to be seen to need help. This was an important reason why the inculcation of atheism was regarded as part of continuing adult education. As with other aspects of *vospitanie*, however, the grand design was to target and activate the whole community.

In the mid-1980s atheistic education was faced with a number of problems. Some were pedagogical, others more generally philosophical. The pedagogical problems were rooted in teachers' perceptions and behaviour. Atheism was widely regarded as an arcane subject, inherently difficult to teach, and calls for a highly differentiated approach or set of approaches only made matters worse. The easy way to 'teach' a subject when one feels insecure is to drum in the basics, ensure that they can be reproduced, and discourage discussion. But this is no way to ensure assimilation of essentially debatable material. And many teachers did not even rise to these low heights:

since atheism was meant as a rule to be taught indirectly and did not form a specific section of any syllabus except social studies, it was easier still to disregard it altogether. One could always rationalize this attitude by claiming that religion was dead or dying anyway, and that in any case there was no point in drawing attention to it by criticizing it. Adolescent Eves and Adams often want not just to see but to taste and see.

Young people's quest for autonomy brings us to a series of wider philosophical issues. It seems to be intrinsic to the human spirit sooner or later to rebel against a monistic ideology of whatsoever kind. In the USSR, religion was not merely the single tolerated alternative, it had features which made it more attractive than the official secular creed. Faith and hope were not confined, for the individual, to his or her present life and a golden future for mankind; they promised a personal victory over death. Communism had a lot to say about friendship between comrades and nations, and hatred of its enemies, but the concept of love occurred infrequently in its lexis. People found religion more humane. In the crises of life it offered personal comfort which atheism was unable to supply. If religion had been truly internalized, it was impervious to the argumentation on which the atheist case depended. Atheistic education could scarcely operate within the terms in which religion presented itself. Even where it was able to overcome its pedagogical problems, its efficacy remained positively correlated with the extent to which religion was shackled and silenced. So when in the 1970s some Orthodox churchmen began to urge the Party to make common cause with the church in order to halt moral decline and achieve social and economic ideals,[11] the prevailing ethos ruled a positive response out of court. When the churches were hostile, atheists at least knew where they were.

1988: THE WATERSHED YEAR

And so we come back to the future and the year 1988. Even as the February CPSU plenum called for the stepping-up of atheistic education and the formation of communist morality, the straws of change in religious policy were floating in the wind. Dimitry Pospielovsky dates this back to 1985–6, with the publication of literary works and speeches at the VIII Writers' Congress which were supportive of Christianity and the church.[12] A criticism of such writing led in December 1986 to the young people's newspaper *Komsomol'skaya pravda* publishing a reply by the poet Yevgeny Yevtushenko on the value of religion in cultural life, together with an atheistic rejoinder on the all-sufficiency of Marxism-Leninism.[13] This launched a debate which, as we shall see, eventually reached the educational literature. During 1987 the press was characterized by a dwindling of anti-Islamic articles and the appearance of calls to reopen Orthodox churches.

The Orthodox millennium was due to be celebrated in June 1988. On 29 April M.S. Gorbachev received Patriarch Pimen and members of the Synod in the Kremlin to discuss the celebrations. This was exactly a week after the director Tengiz Abuladze had been awarded a Lenin Prize for his film trilogy ending with the enormously influential anti-Stalinist allegory *Repentance*.[14] This film has the demolition of a historic church as a leitmotiv and poses its final question as to the good of a street that does not lead to a church. Gorbachev spoke to Pimen of past 'mistakes' in church–state relations, promised a new law on freedom of conscience, and referred to perestroika, especially in the realm of ethics and morality, as 'our common cause'[15] – the cause of believers and non-believers alike. This speech is considered to have been the turning-point in Soviet religious policy. It gave no joy, however, to conservatively minded members of the leadership, and it might take some time to percolate to lower levels, away from the centre. In outlying republics with their own strong religious traditions, on the other hand, it was quick to take effect.

Some reformist educators gradually began to link the new methodologies and attitudes approved by the February plenum to the new approach to religion and religious morality heralded by the April speech. It became obvious that if they were to be harmoniously conjoined, there could be no peaceful coexistence with atheistic education of the traditional militant stamp. That component of the upbringing process, even though re-endorsed by the same plenum, was now thrown into question. Churchmen also started to consider the implications of Gorbachev's remarks for that long-standing desideratum, the religious education of children and young people. Controversial enough, and indeed illegal, as an out-of-school activity, it caused real consternation among many atheist teachers when proposed directly or indirectly for the school curriculum. Others saw it as a challenge to be encountered rather than a foe to be fought. These reactions will be reviewed below, after tracing the development of the various emergent forms of religious studies and the formulation of legal provisions.

THE RISE OF SUNDAY SCHOOLS

Well before 1988 there were attempts to circumvent the law restricting religious instruction to the family circle. The Baptists, for example, split over this issue in Khrushchev's time, and unregistered Reform Baptists operated illegally. Following the 1975 law which permitted children aged over 10 to sing in church choirs, some churches went further and formed youth choirs. The practices provided an opportunity for slipping in Christian teaching.[16] Seventh Day Adventists conducted similar activities. The religious instruction of children was one of the points raised by the Latvian Lutheran reformist group known as Rebirth and Renewal in June 1987 for discussion with the church's leadership. That quietist body reacted with sackings and suspensions, though within a year the climate had changed sufficiently for a 'pastor of the youth movement' to be appointed.[17] Protestants did not monopolize such initiatives, since Roman Catholic priests in Lithuania had a long and honourable history of preparing children for confirmation despite official interference and repression.[18] In Islamic areas there was a network of 'underground' schools, where members of the unofficial Sufi brotherhoods taught Arabic and elementary religious knowledge to both children and adults.[19] In contrast, Orthodoxy seems to have found it much more difficult to act in contravention of the law, although there were exceptions.[20]

This being so, it is noteworthy that the earliest Sunday school, whose establishment in the new atmosphere after April 1988 has been traced in the press, was an Orthodox one. At a round-table discussion convened by the newspaper *Moskovskii tserkovnyi vestnik*, Boris Kozushin, a Moscow psalm-reader, reported that a Sunday school had been organized at the children's place of residence in September 1988. They were taught Bible history, the lives of the Saints, Church Slavonic, liturgical singing, and drawing with Biblical subjects. He added, 'And we talk about life.' This was a lay endeavour; because of the law, they had not been able to find a priest willing to participate.[21] Perhaps it was for this reason that there was no mention of basic instruction in doctrine, which was to become a central feature of clergy-run schools a year later. Other initiatives were under way. In November 1988 it was announced that the Lithuanian representative on the USSR Council for Religious Affairs had proposed, with the backing of the Lithuanian authorities, that the draft law on freedom of conscience should permit priests to give children religious instruction, with their parents' consent.[22] Then in December some Orthodox laity set up an action group to promote catechetical instruction, Sunday schools and youth activities.[23]

The year 1989 brought its encouragements for religious people. In February a preliminary draft law on freedom of conscience was published with a commentary in the principal Soviet legal journal. Although this did not exactly suggest opening the floodgates to change, it did at last propose a definition of 'private' religious instruction (permitted but not elaborated in the 1918 law). In the past, religious instruction had at best been left to the family circle. In practice, as the commentator himself pointed out, any kind of religious instruction of minors had been banned, and parents had been prosecuted for failing to 'bring up their children in the spirit of high communist morality'. Now the draft made it specific: such instruction was permitted 'privately, at home or in a religious association'.[24] Some three other drafts were issued during 1989, but not published in the same way. Further positive developments during the year were the election of several churchmen to the USSR Congress of People's Deputies and the beginning of church involvement – strictly speaking, still illegal then – in charitable work.

Publication of a steady trickle of reports about Sunday schools, mostly but not exclusively Orthodox, in the official press from October 1989 makes one speculate on whether the ecclesiastical authorities had taken a decision to be more venturesome; as we shall see below, church involvement in state education was receiving similar exposure. One writer attributes this directly to the USSR's signing the documents of the Vienna Conference on Security and Cooperation in Europe.[25] The rest of this section is based on fifteen press items: eleven Orthodox (Moscow five, other RSFSR two, Belorussia two, Lithuania and Latvia one each), one Catholic (Lithuanian), two Lutheran (Latvia one, RSFSR one) and one Baptist (Uzbekistan). While it is true that Moscow took a clear lead for consistency in the spread of Sunday schools, the sample may well be biased in favour of the north-western USSR.[26] Let us now look briefly at the aims, structure, activities and reception of this newly developing sphere of Soviet schooling. Its problems will be best considered later, jointly with those of related areas.

Orthodox clergy seem to have disagreed as to whether Sunday schools had the purpose of making converts. While Father Grigorii, parish priest in Segezha, a district centre in the Karelian Autonomous Republic of the RSFSR, denied this,[27] Father Georgii of the Cathedral of the Holy Spirit in Minsk, Belorussia said: 'Our goal is to educate people who take part in the church's life with understanding, and to unite them with what is good and with the faith.'[28] Both these men were pioneers; this was the first Orthodox Sunday school in all Belorussia, and there was none in the Karelian capital, Petrozavodsk, over 250 km from Segezha, until the Lutherans stepped in, with Finnish assistance, in March 1990.[29] It is a well-attested fact that official attitudes to the church may lag behind in remoter places. Perhaps such constraints help to explain the unevangelistic stance, surprising to us, of a priest operating within his own domain. The two men would have agreed, however, on another aim. For Father Grigorii it was to make a contribution to the spiritual rebirth of society.[30] In saying this, he aligned himself directly with the position of President Gorbachev and others who made common cause with the church in moral renewal. Father Matvei of the Cathedral of the Epiphany, Moscow, put this in more down-to-earth terms: 'to make a contribution to the education of children, to bring them up to be spiritually healthy'. And he added: 'to instil love for the motherland'.[31] This was a traditional function of the Orthodox Church; but what motherland did he mean?

What was the scope and the structure of the earliest Sunday schools? At the big Moscow churches and in Minsk they were for children of school age, to either 14 or 16, usually divided into two groups. The roll was about 130 in Minsk and 200 at the Church of the Resurrection Moscow.[32] At the little church in Segezha, on the other hand, the unspecified number of children and adults present at the school's opening had dwindled over four months to about twenty people aged from 6 to 50. The priest planned to start a separate children's group in the autumn.[33] All of these schools appear to have been available to all who wanted to come, whether believers or not. At Minsk, pressure of numbers made it necessary to function on Saturdays too.[34] In Catholic Lithuania, things went much further: G. Zabulis, the Minister of

Education, and Cardinal Sladkevicius signed an agreement whereby, among other things, the state allowed the church to use school premises for voluntary religious instruction.[35]

We have descriptions of the curricula of five Orthodox Sunday schools. While all taught the principles of the faith, four of them provided Bible study, and some offered catechism, church history, Church Slavonic and/or liturgical singing.[36] The fullest of these brief accounts refers to the Church of the Resurrection of Slovushchii in Moscow. The day started with confession, then at 8 a.m. the children began their studies: the Bible, lives of the Saints, principles of doctrine, liturgical singing, Church Slavonic and Latin! To this already impressive programme it was planned to add painting, to develop skills in iconography.[37] At Easter 1990 this trail-blazing Sunday school organized a one-evening festival for children and adults, opening with a bazaar selling 'spiritual literature', Easter eggs and cakes, and proceeding to a performance by children's choirs with competitions and games in the Novorossiisk Cinema. This was advertised in the Moscow youth press.[38] The new Sunday school of the Church of St Andrew the First-Called at the Vagan'kov Cemetery, Moscow, planned a series of excursions to churches, monasteries, exhibitions and concerts, financed by the parish.[39]

When the secular press reported parents' reactions to the Sunday schools, they were usually favourable, which is no surprise since the parents themselves were directly or indirectly involved. Here are two such comments. Marina, a young mother attending the Segezha school with her husband and daughter, said: 'We don't come out of idle curiosity, we want to know more about what was persistently denied for years on end. Religion contains a lot of simple human values which we've lost.'[40] And a Minsk parent explained:

> I've been an atheist all my life, but now I've realised that people have to believe in something – in goodness and beauty. Sadly, our schools bring up people who are indifferent. I want to see my son [grow up to be] a sympathetic person, incapable of cruelty, so I've brought him here.[41]

But a history teacher from Voronezh Region, drawing a Tolstoyan distinction between the Bible and the church, was horrified by a television programme showing a Moscow Sunday school:

> When I saw the submissive, praying children and imagined my own grandchildren among them, I felt sick at heart. Those poor children had been deprived of the joy of childhood and an undistorted perception of nature and the human life around them.[42]

This was juxtaposed to a letter from another teacher bemoaning the lack of spirituality in the Soviet school. This is the more controversial area to which we now turn.

THE BEGINNINGS OF RELIGIOUS STUDIES IN STATE SCHOOLS

The prohibition of religious teaching in educational institutions under the laws of 1918 and 1929 was repeated in 1975; the sole exception was religious seminaries.[43] The principle of the separation of church and school and the firm secular control of state establishments ruled out infractions of the law such as we have seen with religious associations. A report which appeared in the government newspaper *Izvestiya* in the millennial year of 1988 was consequently all the more sensational.

This report described a visit to School No. 67, Moscow, by Father Aleksandr Men', biologist, theologian and philosopher, and parish priest of Novaya Derevnya. Aged 53, he was a distinguished pastor, writer and advocate of reform in the Orthodox Church. The school provided special classes for talented youngsters in the humanities and physical sciences. Father Aleksandr talked to the pupils about culture, moral values and the history of Christianity, and then answered questions ranging from 'Which team do you support?' to 'What is the ultimate goal of human existence?' E. Topaler, the head teacher who in arranging the visit had played an equally trail-blazing role, told the journalist:

> The prescribed form 'think like this and not like that, believe in this and not in that' is no method of educating the younger generation. The children must themselves learn to choose between what is good and what is bad, and to determine their own stance for living and their own world view.

The report was remarkable not only for what it said but also for the objective and even friendly way in which it said it.[44]

As with Sunday schools, there was rather a long delay before this straw in the wind was followed by others. The draft law and exegesis published experimentally in February 1989 reiterated the separation of church and state and of church and school; religious associations were not to set up educational institutions also teaching general subjects.[45] This meant, more broadly, that religious education and general education must be kept strictly apart. It was nothing new, but it served to reaffirm the illegality of events such as those at School No. 67, and conservative opposition to them was only to be expected. About the same time, however, TASS reported the introduction of an experimental course on the 'History of Religion' for seniors in several schools in Tbilisi, Georgia. They had been issued with a textbook of excerpts from the Bible, including a commentary. This provides a particularly interesting link with the educational innovation movement inasmuch as the course was devised at the Georgian Institute of Pedagogical Sciences, directed by Professor Shalva Amonashvili. He stated that the texts had been selected for their reflection of historical facts, folk wisdom and the development of moral principles. The new subject was also to embrace 'other great faiths'.[46]

In autumn 1989, reports and discussion of religious studies in state schools began to appear more frequently. While some schools allegedly brought in the priests so as to be in the forefront of fashion,[47] worthier goals were usually put forward. They can be summarized under two potentially connected headings: appreciation of the cultural heritage, and moral education. As teachers and parents knew from practically any visit to a public gallery, it was difficult or even impossible to understand many masterpieces of art – or literature – without a knowledge of the scriptures concerned. 'We can't fully explain the natural system of a tree if we go by its trunk and crown and ignore its roots.'[48] A knowledge of religious teachings would also help educators to deal properly with believing parents and children and to understand the local nationality.[49]

Religious morality had also a contribution to make to the spiritual regeneration of society. The communist world view was difficult to form and to sustain when words had lost the meaning they once had and people no longer had confidence in them. A vacuum had been created. Religious morality, it was said, was the only practical positive means of filling the gap. If not, then there was the danger of drifting into a world of illusions.[50] The flourishing of occultism among school pupils was an ominous example of this.[51] Educators who favoured religious studies and the clergy whom they co-opted denied any intention to proselytize.[52] As we shall see, however, with increasing openness of discourse the attempt to separate religious morality from personal faith came more and more into question.

Religious studies in schools were of two kinds: one-off talks by invited priests, and optional courses which might be given by visiting clergy, other guest teachers, the school staff, or a combination of these. In Moscow one of the functions of the Centre of the Mother of God (*Bogorodichnyi tsentr*), an independent educational organization, was to supply priests as guest lecturers on Christian history.[53] The example of Father Aleksandr Men' was followed by Father Aleksandr Borisov with a talk on 'The Gospel Today' at School No. 36, Moscow, and by two priests in Kazakhstan who had a two-hour session with senior pupils and teachers at School No. 56, Alma-Ata. When they affirmed that man could achieve moral perfection only through religion, they provoked a lively reaction from their attentive audience.[54] In Latvia, many headteachers called in Lutheran clergy to inaugurate the 1989/90 school year.[55]

There was a variety of elective courses.[56] The titles of some of them, in the outlying republics, might be best translated 'religious instruction' (*zakon Bozhii, veroispovedanie*). Catholic Lithuania apparently introduced this into its general schools in January 1990, and by February 16,000 pupils had opted for it in the city of Kaunas alone.[57] Teachers in the Ararat District of Armenia were reported to be preparing to teach a course in general theology, Armenian church history and ritual.[58] Occasionally calls were published to go the whole hog in Russia too,[59] but the well-known independently minded

Father Dmitrii Dudko was opposed to this on the grounds that religious education would then become just another unimportant subject.[60]

More often the idea of religious instruction was deliberately avoided. The most frequently mentioned course-title in 1990 was 'History of Religion', either as a component of the course on 'World Artistic Culture' (see Chapter 4) or in its own right. Thus, under the former arrangement, teachers at a school in Khabarovsk in the Far East called in a priest to give a talk on iconography.[61] Under the latter, School No. 470 in the Kalinin District of Leningrad invited Father Vasilii Lisnyak to give an entire course. Originally intended for senior students only, it was made available also to younger ones, teachers and parents. Each meeting had three parts: a talk, a 'moral sermon' (*nravstvennaya propoved'*, as on television) and a half-hour session of questions and answers. I.N. Safonova, the headteacher, later remarked with approval that a lot of the children had managed to obtain Bibles and Testaments and to bring them to the lessons. It was important to go back to primary sources. She also commented that, since this course had been the first of its kind in Leningrad, there had been hassle from the local authorities, especially the party, on the grounds that priests were not allowed into schools by law. Because of the non-neutrality of the visitor, they subsequently proposed that an atheist took part as well, so that both sides could be heard. The head resisted this, fearing – from experience, no doubt – that the two speakers would monopolize the discussion. She wanted the youngsters themselves to have the chance of disagreeing.[62]

Other courses were said to have been tried out or to be in preparation. At School No. 284, Leningrad, the head, L.V. Kuznetsova, found it very difficult, when teaching her first-year seniors, to deal with Ostrovsky's heroine Katerina Kabanova aside from her religious consciousness. Then there were Tolstoy and Dostoevsky. S.I. Makov, paediatrician and theologian, helped her to devise and teach a Saturday option on 'Ancient Culture and the Present Day', including a study of the Book of Genesis (the Creation and man's place in it, ecological problems, the Fall) and the Ten Commandments.[63] At the Academy of Pedagogical Sciences, however, I.A. Galitskaya, an authority in the field of atheistic education, continued to bear the torch that she herself saw as a 'very unpopular notion'. Her institute was preparing courses entitled 'Introduction to Religious Studies' and 'Stories and Legends of the Peoples of the World'.[64] E. Korol'kova had written a two-year elective for 13 to 14-year olds on 'Young People, Atheism and Religion'.[65]

It is difficult to judge how widely religion had spread in the school curriculum by the end of 1990. We know that, fuelled by nationalistic aspirations and cultural traditions, it had become popular in the Baltic republics, especially Lithuania, and to a less clear extent in the Transcaucasus. The Centre of the Mother of God claimed that its priests were 'constant guests in dozens of Moscow schools', whereas an APN survey in 1989/90, claiming a representative sample of over 150 Moscow schools, found that no more than twenty paid any attention to religion or atheism; under 2 per cent of the total were engaged in old-style atheistic upbringing, about 5 per cent had options or clubs studying atheism and religion in the context of world culture, and 7 per cent were teaching religion.[66] Outside Moscow and Leningrad, the paucity of references and the tone of the existing ones suggest that religious education and instruction were little in evidence elsewhere in Russia. A Belorussian priest gives the impression that they were virtually non-existent in his republic.[67] The position in Islamic areas awaits elucidation.

There are probably three main reasons why religious education was slow to develop in Russian schools. The first was its exceedingly dubious legal basis. The second was the conservatism of teachers and education officials, let alone party people, tending to intensify with age and the remoter they were from the metropolis. A third has been suggested: teachers' self-esteem and difficulty in coming to terms with gaps in their professional competence.[68] They could not be blamed for this; they had had no training in the history of religion and were unfamiliar with arguments against atheism. Nor were they often much more familiar with arguments for it. If they balked at the teaching of atheism, as we saw earlier in this chapter, how much more would they fight shy of religious subjects! Yet to call in a priest would be tantamount to admitting their impotence. Parental objections seem to have been an insignificant factor. Most parents were ready to accept or even welcome religious education as a facilitator of the upbringing task in an increasingly complicated and topsy-turvy environment. The lengths to which some of them would go are graphically shown in the next item on our agenda.

RELIGIOUS INSTRUCTION IN PRIVATE SCHOOLS

The reader is forgiven for gulping at the need to swallow two of the great banes of Soviet education in one mouthful. It is nevertheless a fact that at the end of 1990 there were two independent day schools in Moscow, one Jewish and one Orthodox. The first was essentially illegal and the legal basis of the second was cleverly contrived.

The Jewish School or *kheder* was set up at the Moscow Choral Synagogue in autumn 1989, and by May 1990 had over ninety boys and girls on its roll. Its premises were unsuitable, lacking laboratories and a sports hall, and it could not award school-leaving certificates. It was, however, the only school where for five days a week Jewish children could study their history, language and scriptures along with general subjects. The teaching was in small groups, and there were daily 90-minute tutorials on Jewish tradition, with an interval for breakfast. The director said that the pupils often went well beyond the ordinary school syllabus. Interestingly, there were some Gentile children on the books too, Soviet Germans and others whose parents were delayed in Moscow while trying to emigrate, and who would otherwise have been in an educational limbo.[69]

The Orthodox Classical Gymnasium opened a year later on the initiative of the Radonezh Christian Education Society.[70] The Moscow education authorities seem to have accepted the argument that since the Society was a voluntary public organization and not an ecclesiastical one the law was not infringed. From about 1,000 applicants, 180 children were chosen for the first seven school-years on the basis of interviews and tests and their parents' attitude to Christianity; they had to be believers or sympathizers, with priority being given to pupils of the Radonezh Society Sunday School. The Gymnasium occupied part of the premises of School No. 1106, sharing its director, L.I. Slezeneva, and six selected teachers and having the services of several visiting specialists. The salaries for general-subject teaching were met by the state but topped up by Radonezh Society funds. Parents paid for additional subjects and extracurricular activities, but only for the first child.

The day of the visit by the journalist from the teachers' newspaper began with a service in the first period, conducted by Father Artemii, and parents were invited to stay. The five-day week was more intensively taught than in other schools overall. There was less science and technical subjects and a modified history course, stressing church history, and in the first year slightly less maths but twice as much physical education. The foreign language began in the second year, along with 'Principles of Spiritual Culture' (in effect, religious education), liturgical singing and religious art. At the middle stage, ancient culture and classical Greek were studied, and Latin, Church Slavonic and rhetoric were planned for the future eighth-year pupils. According to the head, the school's aim was 'to train . . . people with a conscience, able to make decisions for themselves';[71] children should be able to choose their world view. Father Artemii couched this in more particular terms: 'to give the child a knowledge of himself, to immerse his mind in his conscience, and to build a temple of the soul, not on the sands of ideology but on the rock of faith.'[72] The Patriarch and Synod are reported to have accorded their blessing to this experiment, and, given success, intended to spread it throughout Russia.

RELIGIOUS STUDIES IN HIGHER AND ADULT EDUCATION

The tertiary sector of Soviet education also saw important changes in 1989 and 1990. Vilnius University in Lithuania actually founded a chaplaincy.[73] Elsewhere there was a re-naming of departments, a switching of courses and a grafting-on of religious components. Moscow State University's Department of Scientific Atheism became the Department of Social Sciences. One of the most striking statements about all of this was made by Yu.N. Solonin, Dean of the Faculty of Philosophy at Leningrad State University, on the occasion of an international seminar, hosted jointly with Metropolitan

Aleksii, the future Patriarch, to commemorate the seventy-fifth anniversary of the Russian Bible Commission. S.P. Merkur'ev, Rector of the University, had described the Bible as part of world culture, and Solonin referred to it as the basis of 'our morality'. Asked whether the history of religion would gradually replace scientific communism, atheism and Marxism, he replied:

> The idea of socialism is also a general cultural idea, and there is an incredible number of variants . . . The one called scientific socialism or communism and connected with the world-view of Marx, Engels and Lenin is one of the possible ones. In the Faculty of Philosophy, the Department of Scientific Atheism has already been transformed into the Department of Philosophy and History of Religion. This is not just a change of name; the syllabuses are being changed, and there will obviously be a re-orientation of the lectures and of research. Not only shall we provide options in Bible history, but also we do not rule out the introduction of a course for the whole Faculty on the basis of the Biblical text.[74]

The re-orientation was not achieved by the wave of a wand. An anonymous writer to the Moscow evening paper complained that mostly the same lecturers (at an unnamed institute) were teaching 'History of Religion' as had taught 'Scientific Atheism', and the content had changed very little. The editors replied that the Moscow Institute of Physics and Technology, with ministerial approval, had engaged clergy from the Zagorsk Academy for this purpose.[75] At Erevan Pedagogical Institute the Scientific Atheism course was replaced by one entitled 'History and Theory of Religion and Atheism'. One 20-hour component of this, intended for third-year students but open to all, was 'The Bible as a Monument of World Culture'; Echmiadzin Seminary helped to set it up, and the Catholicos Vazgen I gave the first lecture at his own request.[76] No doubt the organization of this course was facilitated by Armenian pride in the national culture. In general, pedagogical *vuzy* (*vysshie uchebnye zavedeniya*, higher education establishments) are extremely conservative places, but their response to the new thinking in the area of atheism and religion is clearly quite crucial.[77] In 1989/90 the problem had scarcely begun to be addressed.

There were various reports of elements of religious studies becoming available to *vuz* students as open lectures or as components of their main courses. At the Far East Polytechnical Institute, Vladivostok, the Philosophy Department arranged a series by Father Anatolii on 'Problems of Religion and Atheism'. Open to all, the programme was said to be justified by the growing interest in religious matters and by the common upbringing role of church and party. The latter's efforts had failed and morality had collapsed because of the double standards of the bearers of the ideology.[78] There were also plans for a course on the 'History of the Christian Church' (on what basis was unclear) at Kishinev State University and other Moldavian *vuzy*, with the understandable but rather opaque aim of promoting peace among the nationalities.[79] In 1989/90 journalism students at the University of Moscow were studying the Old Testament in their course on classical literature and the New during that on literature in the Middle Ages, taught by regular staff. Journalists could greatly benefit from Biblical knowledge, the dean said, above all because of cultural references to Bible stories.[80] Local priests gave thirty lectures to language and literature students at Krasnoyarsk University, to help them to understand 'Christian mythology' and Church Slavonic texts.[81]

Atheistic work had long had a place in the sphere of adult education. In 1990 it became clear that religion was making an entry there too. One example comes from the extreme north-west of Russia, where Orthodoxy is expanding rapidly. Bishop Panteleimon was asked by the director of the Dobrolyubov Library in Arkhangel'sk to organize a series of lectures, of which he gave two himself. It was obvious from the questions that the spiritually hungry audience knew nothing about religion. They needed an idea of the Bible, the mysteries (Eucharist) and certain aspects of Christian doctrine.[82] In Moscow, a 'Sunday Orthodox University' was initiated. Voluntary public societies were formed to engage in these and other educational and charitable activities. The Radonezh Society and the Centre of the Mother of God have been mentioned already. Another was the St Ignatii Bryanchaninov Society for Russian Orthodox Culture, Leningrad.[83] The Russian Christian Democratic Movement, a party with monarchist sympathies founded in April 1990 in Moscow, has also launched educational initiatives.[84]

THE LAW OF 1 OCTOBER 1990

Earlier in this chapter we surveyed the laws affecting religious education to 1975 and the changes proposed in February 1989. The official draft or bill 'On Freedom of Conscience and Religious Organizations' was issued in June 1990. Towards the end of our period under review, on 1 October, the law was finally enacted by the USSR Supreme Soviet.[85] Let us trace the fate of the provisions that related to education. The Orthodox Church was very concerned that religious organizations' rights here should be clearly laid down.[86]

When the official draft appeared on 5 June, it showed some significant differences from the discussion document of February 1989. Citizens still had the right to profess any religion or none, and to bring up their children accordingly, though without coercion (art. 3), but there was no longer any mention of the right to atheistic education. In fact the words 'atheistic' and 'atheism' appeared nowhere. The principle of the separation of school and church was reasserted (art. 6); a sentence guaranteeing access to the various forms and levels of education irrespective of citizens' attitudes to religion was added; and the 1989 point about religious instruction being permitted privately, at home or in a religious association, was put more positively: 'Citizens may teach religious doctrine and receive religious education in the language of their choice individually or together with others, at home, in a religious organization, etc.'[87] So far, believers must have thought, so good.

Then, however, the draft added a possible insertion: 'The teaching of religious doctrines in educational establishments in which general school subjects are taught is not permitted.'[88] This replaced sweepingly the circumlocutory ban on church schools in the 1989 document. It also ruled out the use of state school premises by religious bodies for their own educational purposes. The fact that it was the only 'variant' in the whole draft suggests that it was controversial. The new Patriarch, Aleksii, expressed dissatisfaction with the draft almost entirely in terms of education: the religious education of children, young people and adults must become one of the church's responsibilities, and schools should offer basic extracurricular religious and Biblical teaching.[89]

The bill underwent a fairly lengthy debate before it became law on 1 October. Religious people did not gain all that they wanted, but further progress was nevertheless made. Article 3 followed the draft. Atheism returned to the text, but in a way which could have brought its proponents little joy: 'The state does not fund religious organizations or activity associated with the propaganda of atheism' (art. 5). This could be taken to imply also that atheistic teaching no longer had a place in the school curriculum. (Some school staffs were already deciding this for themselves.)[90] Article 6 again attested to the separation of state education from the church and to access to education regardless of religious stance. Citizens might be taught religious doctrine and receive religious education in their chosen language individually or with others. But the vaguely-worded phrase about the location of such teaching was replaced by a separate paragraph: registered religious organizations had the right 'to set up educational establishments and groups for the religious education of children and adults, and also to engage in teaching in other forms, making use of premises that they own or that are placed at their disposal for this'.[91]

The legitimization of religious education was clearly a giant stride forward. Nevertheless, the final text of article 6 seems to have increased the studied ambiguity. 'In other forms'? 'Premises . . . placed at their disposal'? Day-to-day reports revealed that following publication of the draft law a final paragraph had been added to article 6 whereby state educational institutions could offer their premises to religious organizations outside teaching hours for the purpose of religious instruction of pupils. Despite strong advocacy by the Patriarch, Amonashvili and others, this controversial provision was finally deleted on a vote of 303 to 46. It is fair to add that the 'variant' banning religious teaching from state schools had also disappeared along the way, and that, in the words of a commentator, 'anything that is not prohibited is permitted, as deputies agreed!'[92] It subsequently transpired that the churches had been at loggerheads on the question of religion in the school curriculum.[93] Presumably all churchmen, however, would have preferred a more specifically positive statement addressing the key problem of accommodation for Sunday schools.

ATHEISTS AND BELIEVERS: ADVERSARIES OR ALLIES?

The debates in the Supreme Soviet over believers' rights epitomized a dichotomy of feeling in the country as a whole. How far was it possible, after the Gorbachev–Pimen meeting, for atheists and churchmen to make common cause in the upbringing of children? Believers – unless living in places where the light was slow to penetrate – could only rejoice at their new-found freedoms. Atheists had a harder time. One should distinguish between the leadership and the rank-and-file. While the general staff and officers were calling for reconciliation, the frontline troops felt increasingly beleaguered if not betrayed.

During the winter of 1989–90 the party announced plans to expand the dialogue between atheists and believers. Atheism, said a *Pravda* editor, needed to drop its dogmatism and intolerance. This was difficult for the dedicated pioneers of antireligious propaganda. But it did not mean capitulation. Rather, the search now must be for common ground.[94] At about the same time people were being reminded that communism had borrowed the doctrine of the New Person from Christianity, and that both church and party had the role of 'fishers of souls'.[95] (Earlier, that had been a term of abuse used by atheists of clergy.) An educationist called upon atheistic propaganda to modify its approach; by refusing to acknowledge the church's historical role in the development of spiritual culture it brought discredit upon itself.[96] And when the conservatively inclined *Sovetskaya pedagogika* opened its pages to the debate in September 1990, reporting a round-table discussion on 'Mass Culture and Morality' convened by the Patriarchate, V.V. Amosov from the Moscow City Committee on Public Education, said that cooperation with the Church was indispensable.[97]

The extent to which leading atheists had modified their ideas was brought home with remarkable force in a survey of experts conducted by the USSR Academy of Sciences Institute of Sociology and the journal *Nauka i religiya*. The private religious instruction of children was favoured by 73 per cent of the atheists, while 68 per cent thought that religious organizations should have their own mass media; 56 per cent considered that the principle of social justice was being infringed in respect of believers (one in six cited higher educational opportunity). The only proposition to be rejected was that the state should stop financing atheistic propaganda (49 per cent), but here the majority was a mere 1 per cent.[98] One doubts very much that these views were replicated by atheists at the chalkface. Although the voices of Christian teachers were occasionally heard in the press,[99] they were

98

outnumbered by those who deplored the replacement of Marxism-Leninism by religion and its invasion of the schools.[100]

Believers' opinions were more muted; they had nothing to gain by aggressiveness, or at least they were still chary of committing themselves to print. Enthusiasm for cooperation with atheists was also slow to find expression by ordinary people. In Dzerzhinsk, however, Archbishop Nikolai of Gorky and Arzamas took part in a meeting of propagandists and university of Marxism-Leninism students. Speaking of social morality and the family, and the need to 'emancipate woman from direct presence at the workplace', he said: 'It's our common cause, and we must work with you hand in hand.'[101] It is also interesting that in the sociological survey mentioned above only 20 per cent of the experts from traditional confessions (Christians and Jews) favoured the cessation of atheistic funding by the state – fewer than the atheists themselves![102] This is hard to explain other than by the wish to avoid unnecessary contention at a time of improving relations. All the same, controversies and problems were not far to seek, and we shall end with a review and discussion of them.

PROBLEMS AND CONTROVERSIES

In the early 1990s religious education in the USSR was faced with a number of practical problems and philosophical issues, usually interrelated. The practical questions might be categorized as essentially objective on the one hand and subjective or attitudinal on the other. The former were about supply and demand. There was a shortage of accommodation for Sunday schools, and their financial basis was sometimes unsatisfactory. There was a lack of suitable teachers. Clergy and others needed to be not only willing but also able to teach in Sunday schools and respond to invitations from day schools; the pioneers celebrated in the mass media and their kindred spirits were a finite pool of special talent. Among professional teachers there were some Christians, but if the options in 'History of Religion' were taken on by the atheists responsible for the most ideologically oriented subjects, history and social studies, as sometimes happened, one might well wonder about the outcome. The expunging of the atheistic content of syllabuses and textbooks in general subjects, as in 1942, would be an earnest of authority's intentions. Training was needed all round. There was an extreme shortage of Scriptures, textbooks and teaching aids that particularly affected, but was not restricted to, the private sector. Effective Sunday school books required expert authorship by educators.

We must pause here to comment that by the end of 1990 the literature problem was beginning to be addressed. By mid-1989 the Baptists had started a publication which was also relevant to young people and Latvian Lutherans had a children's magazine.[103] The comic *Veselye kartinki* began to issue a selected cut-out 'Children's Bible' for pre-schoolers.[104] From 1990 a bi-monthly Islamic newspaper appeared in Tashkent; one of its purposes was to assist families with religious upbringing.[105] *Sem'ya i shkola* started a regular series, headed 'Sunday School', to help parents, and the three main central educational periodicals began to devote space to questions of religious education.[106] The history teachers' journal *Prepodavanie istorii v shkole* promised to publish materials from 'World Religions', a course for seniors in preparation by Academy of Sciences historians.[107]

A practical problem of a more subjective nature was resistance by atheist teachers and entrenched attitudes on the part of some officials, especially in the Slavic republics away from the centres of power. Take the case of Elena, schoolgirl Komsomol member and a Christian, writing from Pyatigorsk in the North Caucasus to the teachers' newspaper about being reprimanded by her teacher for her 'religious delusion' and about being advised by her friends to believe what she liked but to keep her mouth shut lest her references were spoiled; this was in April 1990, with the new policy well under way in Moscow.[108] The vagueness of the October 1990 law as to the use of state school premises – quite possibly the only ones available – for Sunday schools left matters very much to the discretion of local authorities. Even on points where it was specific there could be no firm guarantee that it would be observed.[109]

The two great philosophical problem areas may be linked directly to the two main spheres of influence of religious education that have dominated Soviet policy and practice: the cultural heritage, and public and private morality. Although the new law was scrupulous not to distinguish between faiths, there is nevertheless a close connection between church and state in Russian history. There was sometimes the half-uttered suspicion that the state was exploiting the church by limiting its message and its activities to those which the state deemed most serviceable;[110] more of that presently. That the new approach was more of a strategic truce than a permanent reconciliation is supported by an interesting fact. Just a few weeks before Gorbachev had his famous meeting with Patriarch Pimen, the Party's theoretical journal *Kommunist* called for a more sophisticated way with believers. This subtler line, though relatively recent, was nothing new in atheistic education. The whole tenor of the article was that 'atheistic activity too must undergo radical restructuring'.[111] There was no hint of abandonment of ultimate goals. For the moment, the church has a client relationship to the state, as in days of old.

And it always was, of course, the Orthodox Church. The activities of that Church in the Baltic Republics have received a relatively large amount of attention in the Soviet press. Orthodoxy is rightly concerned to serve the needs of the principal non-native minority there, but in so doing it may be seen willy-nilly as an agent of Soviet power unless there is a deliberate distancing. In Russia proper with its own nationalistic aspirations, the role of the Orthodox Church as a potential arm of secular authority is different, reinforcing aspects of the indigenous traditional culture. In these unsettled times, however, its role is also hard to predict, other than to expect support of the dominant temporal power. It is possible that this will lead to preferential treatment for it over other denominations, educational activities included, as was characteristic of the imperial past. The Baptists are certainly fearful of this.[112] It has been clear in these pages that the incipient religious teaching in Russian schools is very much of the Orthodox stamp. Those Orthodox who would wish it otherwise, such as Father Dmitrii Dudko, must be very few. And it was but a small step from 'no morality without faith' (see below) to 'no spirituality without Orthodoxy'. In Moslem areas, for Orthodoxy we should presumably read Islam, but educational developments there await exploration.

Turning to the question of morality, one cannot but agree with atheists and some impartial observers that both the secular authorities and churchmen as well as ordinary citizens have exaggerated the moral potential of religion. The Christian would add: at least within the limits that it has been officially encouraged to operate. Religious and non-religious people alike recognized the danger of the moral vacuum created by the collapse of communist ideals, long undermined but suddenly falling apart. Nature's abhorrence of a vacuum led to the spread of unhealthy introspective cults, pornography and criminality. So the call went forth to pursue the common cause of spiritual and moral regeneration. Since then, however, no palpable improvement has been detected; indeed, circumstances have caused the continued decline of national morale. Christians have countered the charge of ineffectiveness by stressing their conviction that morality has no operational basis apart from a living faith. Yet churchmen invited to appear on TV were apparently given strict warnings to talk only about morality and not to say a word about faith.[113] Some clerical preachers and educators denied that they sought converts. Others described the school 'History of Religion' course as a half-measure and claimed that to broadcast 'Sunday moral sermons' was putting the cart before the horse. Thus in 1990 people with these concerns were faced with what might be termed a dilemma of public purpose. At the same time, paradoxically enough, the still officially atheistic state appeared to be favouring very limited religious instruction rather than religious education in the 'stances for living' sense. Perhaps the latter looked too much like exploring the vacuum. And perhaps it seemed more comprehensible to deal in instruction, more manageable to replace a temporal didacticism by a restricted spiritual one.

With the Soviet Union's very brief and narrow experience of relatively free religious teaching, whether as instruction or education, it is clearly far too soon to talk about results. Prospects, however, are another matter. In December 1989 there was an all-Union survey on the 'Soviet person', with 2,696 respondents. Of these, 20 per cent said that they were atheists; 48 per cent professed a religion (significantly more than the 15 per cent in urban and 40 per cent in rural areas and the Ukraine presented in data from *circa*

1970).[114] Some of the other findings were debatable, but the most interesting one for our purposes was that 39 per cent 'wanted to teach their children to believe' in God,[115] which goes much further than to know about religions. This level of parental support suggests that in the Soviet Union religious teaching has a future not only in the private domain but also in the public sector.

NOTES AND REFERENCES

1 *Summary of World Broadcasts* (hereafter *SWB*), SU/0079 C/1–21, 19 February 1988; SU/0081 C/1–2, 22 February 1988; SU/0082 C/1–5, 23 February 1988.
2 *SWB*, SU/0082 C/4, 23 February 1988.
3 O. Mudrova, 'Massovaya kul'tura i nravstvennost'', *Sovetskaya pedagogika*, 1990, no. 9, p. 66.
4 For a general overview of the rationale, scope and efficiency of the atheistic component of Soviet education up to 1985, see J. Dunstan, 'Atheistic education in the USSR', in G. Avis (ed.), *The Making of the Soviet Citizen*, London, New York and Sydney, Croom Helm, 1987, pp. 50–79. For a more particular examination of the aims, content and methodology of atheistic education in the school curriculum and in extracurricular activities, including problems encountered and attempts to deal with them, see J. Dunstan, 'Soviet schools, atheism and religion', in S.P. Ramet (ed.), *Religious Policy in the Soviet Union*, Cambridge, Cambridge University Press, forthcoming.
5 These points are elaborated in Dunstan, 1987, op. cit., pp. 52–3.
6 ibid., pp. 50–1; P.B. Anderson, *People, Church and State in Modern Russia*, London, SCM Press, 1944, pp. 15–16; D.V. Pospielovsky, *A History of Marxist-Leninist Atheism and Soviet Anti-religious Policies*, Basingstoke and London, Macmillan, 1987, pp. 45–6, 57, 133–4, 141.
7 Biology syllabuses of 1939 and 1943 are briefly discussed in J. Dunstan, 'Soviet schools in the Great Patriotic War' in R. Lowe (ed.), *Education and the Second World War*, Brighton, Falmer Press, forthcoming.
8 Pospielovsky, op. cit., pp. 70, 74–5, 78–9, 84–7, 120.
9 J. Ellis, *The Russian Orthodox Church: A Contemporary History*, London and Sydney, Croom Helm, 1986, p. 195. On the legal basis see Pospielovsky, op. cit., pp. 86–7, 117.
10 For details and illustration see my forthcoming article mentioned in note 4 above.
11 Ellis, op. cit., pp. 310, 350–1. For a typical hardline CPSU response see Ligachev's remarks in *Pravda*, 2 October 1986.
12 D.V. Pospielovsky, 'Religious themes in the Soviet press in 1989', *Religion in Communist Lands*, 1990, vol. 18, no. 4, p. 319.
13 Cited in M. Bourdeaux, *Gorbachev, Glasnost and the Gospel*, London, Sydney, Auckland and Toronto, Hodder & Stoughton, 1990, pp. 17–18.
14 R.W. Davies, *Soviet History in the Gorbachev Revolution*, Basingstoke and London, Macmillan, 1989, p. 150. Davies, p. 8, calls the release of the film (in January 1987) 'perhaps the most important single event' in the upheaval in Soviet historical consciousness.
15 Bourdeaux, op. cit., p. 44.
16 ibid., p. 119.
17 M. Sapiets, '"Rebirth and Renewal" in the Latvian Lutheran Church', *Religion in Communist Lands*, 1988, vol. 16, no. 3, pp. 242, 244, 249.
18 Documented in M. Bourdeaux, *Land of Crosses*, Chulmleigh, Augustine

Publishing Company, 1979, *passim.*
19 A. Bennigsen, 'Modernization and conservatism in Soviet Islam', in D.J. Dunn (ed.), *Religion and Modernization in the Soviet Union*, Boulder, CO, Westview Press, 1977, pp. 264–5.
20 Ellis, op. cit., pp. 194–5.
21 'Voskresnaya shkola? Da!', *Moskovskii tserkovnyi vestnik*, 1989, no. 10, p. 7.
22 P. Anilenis, 'Believers' legitimate requests are being satisfied', *Current Digest of the Soviet Press*, 1988, vol. 50, no. 47, p. 11 (from *Sovetskaya Litva*, 11 November 1988).
23 Bourdeaux, 1990, op. cit., p. 106.
24 Yu.A. Rozenbaum, 'K razrabotke proekta Zakona SSSR o svobode sovesti', *Sovetskoe gosudarstvo i pravo*, 1989, no. 2, pp. 91–8, especially pp. 94–5.
25 I. Aref'eva, 'Party v tserkovnom pridele', *Sovetskaya Litva*, 25 November 1989.
26 Probably because most of it was supplied by a press agency in Leningrad (which raises the interesting question why that city was not represented). I should like at this point to acknowledge the assistance of Keston College (Mr Malcolm Walker, Librarian).
27 T. Chervova, 'Voskresnaya shkola dlya vzroslykh i detei', *Komsomolets* [Petrozavodsk], 11 January 1990; T. Chervova, 'Vozlyubi blizhnego tvoego', *Komsomolets*, 22 May 1990.
28 L. Isaenya, ' . . . I rai narisovat'', *Znamya yunosti* [Minsk], 12 March 1990. Father Nikodim of the Danilov Monastery, Moscow, saw the goal as to give children the ideal of Christ (S. Latsis, 'Verim – ne verim . . . ', *Komsomolets* [Petrozavodsk], 15 March 1990).
29 V. Kiiski, 'Voskresnaya shkola v kirke', *Leninskaya pravda* [Petrozavodsk], 21 March 1990.
30 Chervova, 1990 (January), op. cit.
31 G. Digtyarenko, 'Urok v voskresnoi shkole', *Moskovskaya pravda*, 24 January 1990.
32 ibid.; Z. Eroshok, 'Voskresnaya shkola', *Komsomol'skaya pravda*, 20 December 1989; Isaenya, op. cit.; Latsis, op. cit.
33 Chervova, 1990 (May), op. cit.
34 Isaenya, op. cit.
35 'Zakon Bozhii v shkole', *Trud*, 20 January 1990.
36 Chervova, 1990 (January), op. cit.; Digtyarenko, op. cit.; Eroshok, op. cit.; Isaenya, op. cit.; N. Orlova, 'Genka, ponomar' i drugie . . . ', *Moskovskii komsomolets*, 25 February 1990.
37 Eroshok, op. cit.
38 'Paskha v "Novorossiiske"', *Moskovskii komsomolets*, 18 April 1990.
39 E. Strel'chik, 'Shkola rabotaet po voskresen'yam', *Vechernyaya Moskva*, 5 February 1990.
40 Chervova, 1990 (May), op. cit.
41 Isaenya, op. cit.
42 A. Emel'yanov, 'Vnov' Zakon Bozhii', *Uchitel'skaya gazeta* (hereafter *UG*), 1990, no. 40, p. 4.
43 Pospielovsky, op. cit., p. 141.
44 E. Isakova, 'Svyashchennik Men' beseduet so shkol'nikami', *Izvestiya*, 22 October 1988. See also M. Bourdeaux, 'Fr Alexander Men', *The Independent*, 14 September 1990, p. 28 (this is an obituary of the priest, who was murdered by an unknown hand).
45 Rozenbaum, op. cit., pp. 93–5.
46 'News roundup', *Keston News Service*, 16 February 1989, p. 19.
47 E. Mikhailova, 'Svyashchennik v shkole', *UG*, 12 December 1989, p. 3.

48 ibid.; N. Sokolova, T. Petrova, L. Soldatkina, L. Mikhailynk, N. Dovbilo, D. Poperechnyi and others, 'Urok kul'tury', *Tikhookeanskaya zvezda* [Khabarovsk], 20 May 1990.
49 E. Mikhailova, 'Proshla pora emotsii', *UG*, 1990, no. 28, p.10.
50 ibid.; Mikhailova, 1989, op. cit.
51 'Voskresnaya shkola? Da!', op. cit.
52 S. Krayukhin, 'Svyashchennik v shkol'nom klasse', *Izvestiya*, 29 October 1989.
53 A. Pavlov, 'Shkola po abonementu', *Trud*, 30 April 1990.
54 Mikhailova, 1989, op. cit.; S. Stepanov, 'Svyatye ottsy v shkole', *Kazakhstanskaya pravda*, 26 November 1989.
55 Bourdeaux, 1990, op. cit., p. 157.
56 Religious subjects aside, the principle of electives was nothing new. Their early development is surveyed in J. Dunstan, *Paths to Excellence and the Soviet School*, Windsor, NFER, 1978, pp. 177–96.
57 '"Pyat"' po Bozh'emu zakonu?', *Komsomol'skaya pravda*, 3 December 1989; 'V raspisanii – novyi urok', *Sovetskaya Litva*, 28 February 1990.
58 'Pervyi urok v tserkvi', *Komsomolets* [Erevan], 7 April 1990.
59 O. Nikolaeva, 'Re-thinking religion', *Moscow News*, 1990, no. 6, p. 14; N. Sakidon, 'Urok religii – v shkol'noe raspisanie', *Izvestiya*, 17 July 1990. For a frustrated attempt, see N. Savel'eva, 'O prikaze, kotorogo ne bylo', *UG*, 1990, no. 43, p. 3.
60 O. Murova, 'Massovaya kul'tura i nravstvennost'', *Sovetskaya pedagogika*, 1990, no. 9, p. 65.
61 Sokolova *et al.*, op. cit.
62 Krayukhin, op. cit.; '"Kruglyi stol" . . . ', *Prepodavanie istorii v shkole*, 1990, no. 5, pp. 12–13.
63 ibid., p. l5.
64 ibid., pp. 18–19.
65 Mikhailova, 1990, op. cit.
66 Pavlov, op. cit.; I.V. Metlik, 'Religiya v shkole: opyt izucheniya problemy', *Sovetskaya pedagogika*, 1990, no. 12, p. 37 (percentages derived).
67 L. Lomsadze, 'Vozvysit' cheloveka', *Sovetskaya Belorussiya*, 17 April 1990. He mentions just one lesson!
68 Mikhailova, 1990, op. cit.
69 E. Fattakhov, 'Kaplya meda', *UG*, 1990, no. 20, p. 4.
70 This account is based on A. Trushin, ' . . . I "Zakon Bozhii"', *UG*, 1990, no. 43, p. 3, supplemented by R. Osorio, 'On a wing and a prayer in Moscow', *Guardian*, 27 November 1990, p. 27.
71 Osorio, op. cit.
72 Trushin, op. cit.
73 Bourdeaux, 1990, op. cit., p. 147.
74 D. Mishin and Ya. Grigor'ev, '"Voskreshenie" Biblii?', *Sovetskaya Rossiya*, 24 February 1990.
75 *Vechernyaya Moskva*, 29 December 1989.
76 D. Saakyan, 'Lektsiya Katolikosa Vazgena I', *Kommunist* [Erevan], 1 March 1990.
77 See comments in Mikhailova, 1990, op. cit. In 1989, however, atheist students at the Herzen Pedagogical Institute, Leningrad, were holding friendly discussions with young Baptists and their pastor (Bourdeaux, 1990, op. cit., p. 113).
78 T. Shkarban, 'Religiya, ateizm, dukhovnost'', *Krasnoe znamya* [Vladivostok], 31 January 1990.
79 'Pastyr' chitaet lektsii', *Lesnaya promyshlennost'*, 2 December 1989.
80 N. Davydova, 'Journalism students need Bibles', *Moscow News*, 1989, no. 48, p. 14.
81 V. Pyrkh, 'Za kafedroi – svyashchennik', *Sotsialisticheskaya industriya*, 13 December 1989.

82 A. Mozgovoi, 'Priglashaite – otzovemsya', *Pravda severa* [Arkhangel'sk], 18 February 1990.
83 'Odnim abzatsem', *Vechernii Leningrad*, 4 April 1990.
84 'There are such parties!', *Moscow News*, 1990, no. 28, pp. 8–9.
85 'O svobode sovesti i religioznykh organizatsiyakh', *Izvestiya*, 5 June 1990 and *Pravda*, 9 October 1990; *SWB*, SU/0902 C1/1, 23 October 1990.
86 'The Holy Synod on freedom of conscience', *Moscow News*, 1990, no. 17, p. 1.
87 'O svobode sovesti . . . ' (June), op. cit. In the original, the last part of this sentence reads awkwardly, which may indicate problems of formulation.
88 ibid.
89 G. Alimov and G. Charodeev, 'Vera bez del mertva', *Izvestiya*, 16 June 1990.
90 'Razgovor stoit prodolzhit'', *UG*, 1990, no. 40, p. 4.
91 'O svobode sovesti i religioznykh organizatsiyakh', *Pravda*, 9 October 1990; *SWB*, SU/0902 C1/1–2, 23 October 1990. For a full account, see O. Antic, 'The new law on religion', *Report on the USSR*, 1990, vol. 2, no. 47, pp. 9–10.
92 *SWB*, SU/0886 C1/1, 4 October 1990.
93 I. Kozyrev, 'Teper' vse zavisit ot nas samikh' (interview with E.V. Chernetsov), *Protestant*, 1990, no. 11, p. 2.
94 O. Boguslavskaya, 'Whom Raphael depicted', *Current Digest of the Soviet Press*, 1990, vol. 42, no. 8, p. 27 (from *Pravda*, 24 February 1990).
95 Shkarban, op. cit.
96 Mikhailova, 1990, op. cit.
97 Mudrova, op. cit., p. 62.
98 S. Yakovlev, I. Polulyakh, V. Lokosov, V. Medvedeva and P. Olovyannikov, 'Kakoi byt' Tserkvi', *Argumenty i fakty*, 1990, no. 6, p. 5.
99 For example, Z.F. Svetova, '"Nichego net nuzhnee very"', *Sem'ya i shkola*, 1990, no. 9, pp. 24–5; N. Avdeeva, 'Kogda, zabludshie, ochnemsya?', *UG*, 1990, no. 40, p. 4.
100 For example, letter, *Sem'ya i shkola*, 1989, no. 6, p. 14; Mikhailova, 1990, op. cit. (various references); F. Gorelik, 'Poteryali pokolenie?', *UG*, 1990, no. 43, p. 3.
101 N. Kalkun, 'Arkhiepiskop na zanyatii . . . po ateizmu', *Gor'kovskaya pravda*, 10 February 1990. This view of women's emancipation reflects a recent line in official discourse.
102 Yakovlev *et al.*, op. cit.
103 Bourdeaux, 1990, op. cit., pp. 115, 155.
104 A. Mosesov, 'Bibliya dlya . . . doshkolyat', *Sovetskaya kul'tura*, 28 October 1989.
105 V. Mizhiritsky, 'First newspaper for Moslems', *Current Digest of the Soviet Press*, 1990, vol. 42, no. 22, p. 28 (from *Pravda vostoka*, 24 May 1990).
106 Svetova, op.cit.; Metropolitan Yuvenalii, 'Poluchit' obrazovanie ili byt' obrazovannym?', *Narodnoe obrazovanie*, 1990, no. 6, pp. 28–33; Mudrova, op. cit.; *UG* from December 1989, *passim*, but note especially 'Kak chitat' Bibliyu', *UG*, 1990, no. 43, p. 3.
107 '"Kruglyi stol" . . . ', op. cit., p. 10.
108 'Kogda rushatsya idealy', *UG*, 1990, no. 16, p. 11.
109 Kozyrev, op. cit.
110 An unusually explicit instance is Eroshok, op. cit.
111 'Sotsializm i religiya', *Kommunist*, 1988, no. 4, p. 120; reference owed to J.B. Dunlop, 'The Russian Orthodox Church and nationalism after 1988', *Religion in Communist Lands*, 1990, vol. 18, no. 4, pp. 292–306.
112 Kozyrev, op. cit., p. 3.
113 Eroshok, op. cit.
114 C. Lane, *Christian Religion in the Soviet Union*, London, Boston and Sydney, Allen & Unwin, 1978, p. 223. She had no data on Central Asia.
115 'Homo sovieticus: a rough sketch', *Moscow News*, 1990, no. 11, p. 11.

6

REFORM OF THE SOVIET GENERAL SCHOOL AND THE LIKELY EFFECT ON CHILDREN WITH LEARNING DIFFICULTIES

Avril Suddaby

INTRODUCTION

In many education systems slow-learning pupils are a visible and clearly identifiable group. They might, for example, be differentiated from other pupils by being educated in separate classes for the less able, with perhaps an easier, more appropriate curriculum. They might differ from other pupils by their lower success rate in school-leaving examinations, or by the fact that they drop out of education at an earlier age than most of their coevals. In the Soviet education system such considerations do not pertain to slow learners, because there has been, at least until very recently, the same curriculum for virtually all pupils, with no streaming. The same school-leaving examination was taken by everyone, and it was claimed that all except an insignificant percentage were successful in this exam. It was therefore difficult to discern Soviet slow learners as they were lost from view in the mass of children in the general (comprehensive) schools.

Nevertheless there were, of course, indications that the Soviet education system had not found solutions to the intractable problem of non-able, non-academic pupils. Some failed in their end-of-year exams and were forced to repeat the year; and where the problem of repeating appeared to have been solved, there were suspicions of what Soviet educationists call 'percentomania' (passing pupils who should fail, in order to achieve the recommended pass-rate). There was evidence that some teachers tried to use special schools for the mentally handicapped as places to dump troublesome, ill-disciplined pupils who would not, or could not, learn. Educational problems were a feature of the further education system (the vocational-technical schools or *proftekhuchilishcha*), where most of the less able completed their secondary general education whilst acquiring a certain amount of vocational training.

The Soviet education system has undergone changes as it tries to correct its deficiencies and make improvements, and the focus of this chapter is the changes affecting slow learners which have taken place in the last decade. The first of these changes was at the start of the 1980s, when the major educational reforms of 1984 were under consideration; then a new type of differentiated education appeared for a tiny proportion of less able pupils. Since M.S. Gorbachev started the processes of perestroika, most of the 1984 educational reforms appear to have been abandoned, but a differentiated provision for the less able has continued and increased, making them a more visible and identifiable group. Therefore following the fate of the less able in the Soviet education system over the past decade involves consideration of differentiated educational provision for non-academic children.

The children with learning difficulties who are the subject of this chapter are those in the Soviet system of general education rather than those in special education. This means children in the ordinary or 'mass' schools rather than those in special schools. In order to define the group under consideration, we must first define those who are *not* included, because they come under the umbrella of special education. We therefore begin with a brief account of the history and recent development of that educational sector.

DIAGNOSIS FOR SPECIAL EDUCATION

The fundamental distinction between children in Soviet special education and those in ordinary schools is to be found in the difference between the concept of oligophrenia (*oligofreniya*) and other forms of backwardness. The classifications of mental handicap and the terminology used sound to Western ears archaic. The term oligophrenia, or mental deficiency, includes three grades or levels: idiots, imbeciles and debiles. Idiots, the lowest grade, rarely master speech; imbeciles attain limited speech; debiles, the least severely handicapped, are educable, within limitations, and usually employable. Debiles, and also occasionally imbeciles, are educated in the so-called auxiliary or special schools.

Luriya describes the concept of oligophrenia:

Mentally retarded children, or oligophrenic as the doctors call them (from the Greek words *oligo*, small, *phrenos*, mind), have suffered from a severe brain disease while in the uterus or in early childhood and this has disturbed the normal development of early childhood and produced serious anomalies in mental development.[1]

The concept of oligophrenia is therefore physiologically based. An oligophrenic child has incurred damage to the central nervous system (CNS); only when the damage to the CNS has led to impaired mental functions (such as memory, attention, verbal thinking) can mental deficiency correctly be seen to exist. Selection of children for special education is undertaken by medical-pedagogical commissions, multidisciplinary panels consisting of doctors, speech therapists, psychologists, defectologists and teachers. Important among the arsenal of methods for diagnosis are tests based on Vygotsky's theory of the 'zone of next development', used to investigate whether the impairment of mental functions is so great as to make satisfactory development of such functions impossible.[2]

Thus Soviet methods of diagnosis for special education contrast with other models which are more based on the child's educational performance. Sutton cites from Soviet sources case-studies of two children, outwardly very similar as both children performed equally badly in schoolwork. One boy, when tested to ascertain his zone of next development, was found to have such limited capacity for development that he was sent to a special auxiliary school. The other boy, outwardly very similar, showed greater potential and was returned to normal education.[3]

INNOVATION IN SPECIAL EDUCATION: ZPR SCHOOLS

At the end of the 1970s (and indeed still today in 1991) classes in ordinary Soviet schools were large, usually exceeding thirty and sometimes even forty pupils. There was no streaming, and a common curriculum was used in all schools. In order to progress to the next class, children had to pass end-of-year exams with a mark of at least '3' (satisfactory) in all subjects, as there was no dropping of difficult or unpopular subjects. The teacher was held responsible for the success or failure of her pupils. If any were doing poorly, she was supposed to arrange extra tuition for them. If, despite this extra help, they still failed the end-of-year exams, there was a possibility of resitting in September, and extra tuition would be arranged during the summer vacation. The onus was firmly on the teacher; if fewer than 97–98 per cent passed the end-of-year exams, the teacher was seen as incompetent.

Inevitably the pressure was great on teachers, on weaker pupils, and on their parents. Eventually, however, in 1981 Soviet educators dealing with 'difficult' pupils obtained some relief in the form of a new category of children recognized as being in need of special education. This referred to youngsters with a 'temporary delay in mental development' (*vremennaya zaderzhka psikhicheskogo razvitiya* or ZPR). These were children who had formerly been borderline cases, not quite serious enough to be included in the special education system but beyond doubt presenting considerable difficulties to the teacher in the ordinary school. Regulations issued in 1981 set up new forms of special education for such children, as boarding or extended-day schools.[4]

The 1981 regulations specify which categories of children should and should not be admitted to the new type of special school. Children who should not be admitted are those suffering from oligophrenia, defective vision, hearing and/or speech, and physically handicapped children, who should be educated in the auxiliary (special) schools. While the regulations are not so specific about those who should be educated in the new type of school, they all have the following in common:

Specific defects occur in the development of the cognitive and emotional-volitional spheres.

Deviations in the cognitive sphere are manifested in inadequately developed mental activity, a limited fund of the knowledge and concepts which are essential for mastery of school subjects, and a low level of intellectual activity.

The emotional-volitional sphere is characterized by inadequately developed school interests, pronounced play motivation, and inadequate goal-orientation of activity.[5]

The delay in mental development is usually the result of infection or injury which has affected the nervous system, although it can more rarely be the result of genetically conditioned handicap. Thus the basis of diagnosis is CNS damage, although not as serious as in the case of oligophrenia. The difference between ZPR children and oligophrenes is shown by the possibilities for intellectual development which remain, as children with ZPR 'make good use of help, and achieve the transfer of acquired knowledge and skills to new material'.[6] The medical-pedagogical commission is responsible for the diagnosis and selection of children who are to attend the new ZPR schools. Even though there is a distinction made between the concepts of ZPR and oligophrenia, it must in practice be difficult to achieve accurate diagnosis and to ensure, sometimes doubtless in the face of parental opposition, that the child is correctly placed.

Special schools of the new (post-1981) type admit 6 to 9-year-olds who are not yet ready for school or who are having difficulty there. The regulations ensure that ideal conditions are provided in which the child's delay in mental development can be corrected. There must be no more than twenty pupils in a class, and one speech therapist (*logoped*) is provided for every twenty-five to thirty children with speech problems. Teachers and upbringers must be trained defectologists, as in auxiliary schools, and they receive the 20 per cent supplement to normal salary for staff in special schools. Facilities are provided so that all children can have a daytime nap. Lessons are shorter and there is more time given to physical exercise than in normal schools.

The standard timetable of the ordinary schools is used, including labour training and the full range of academic subjects, such as science subjects, foreign language. The principle of the timetable is to allow extra time to cover the standard eight-year (now nine-year) programme of the ordinary school, by providing an extra year for completion of the formerly three-year and now increasingly four-year primary stage.

The reason for using the curriculum of the ordinary school is that the aim of the ZPR school is to correct the delay in mental development and to return the child to mainstream education. After completion of the primary stage all children are assessed by the commission responsible for placement to see if they are capable of continuing their education in the ordinary school. Only the more severe cases of ZPR stay in the special school for the duration of their education. According to reports, the success rate for returning children to mainstream education is 40–50 per cent; also, when children stay in the ZPR school for the duration of their compulsory education, most continue their education in some way.[7]

CATCHING-UP CLASSES AND THE QUESTION OF INTEGRATION

Despite this very commendable success rate, ZPR schools did not become widespread. Two years after publication of the 1981 regulations there were just thirty-four in the whole of the USSR. By 1988/9 they numbered only eighty-one, with 17,844 children (some 3 per cent of the total of special schools for the handicapped and of special pupils).[8] Possibly the expense of such schools was a reason. Instead another development, which appeared first in the Baltic republics and later in Moscow, was that of 'catching-up classes' (*klassy vyravnivaniya*).[9] These too seem to be classes for children with ZPR, since they are governed by the same 1981 regulations as apply to the ZPR schools, and they are similarly staffed by defectologists receiving the 20 per cent salary increment. This, however, is an instance of anomalous children receiving their education on the premises of ordinary schools, an uncharacteristic development in an education system where segregation of such children is seen as the best method for their eventual integration into society.

Professor V.I. Lubovsky, director of the Institute of Defectology, claims that about 4.5–5 per cent of all primary pupils suffer from ZPR but, in his opinion, by no means all of these should receive special education in special schools. In an article on the deficiencies in Soviet care of the handicapped, Lubovsky approves the American system of providing remedial lessons for backward children rather than segregating them in special schools. He writes of the Soviet provision:

> Unfortunately the only way to help such children is to send them to special schools, but there are far from enough of these schools, or to send them to special catching-up classes for children with delay in mental development, of which there still exist rather few.[10]

Lubovsky's comments indicate that Soviet educationists felt that there remained a need for more help for backward children, and also that such help should not come in the form of special segregated education. The Soviet education system differs markedly from the British model in that, as mentioned above, it has traditionally been opposed to the idea of integration.[11] Perhaps the advent of perestroika and the resultant receptiveness to alternative educational theories was necessary for the development of yet another type of educational provision for slow learners, this one within ordinary schools. Towards the end of the 1980s there appeared the first reports of classes for remedial education in general schools.

INNOVATION IN GENERAL EDUCATION: CORRECTIONAL CLASSES

Correctional or corrective classes (*korrektsionnye klassy*) are also referred to as adaptation or health classes (*klassy adaptatsii, klassy zdorov'ya*). They seem to have the official approval of the Soviet Academy of Pedagogical Sciences (APN) as it was in the former Institute of General Pedagogy of the APN that the Laboratory of Correctional Pedagogy (director: G.F. Kumarina) was established. The approach of these classes is described in a booklet by Kumarina.[12]

The preamble to the booklet begins by stating that the former approach, which saw children as either healthy or sick, as normal or pathological, is too crude and that finer distinctions should now be taken into account. There are conditions when one is neither 100 per cent fit nor can correctly be described as ill; this in-between state, however, can prevent the individual from functioning effectively. Over 20 per cent of all young (primary and pre-primary) children fall into the group with which the Laboratory of Correctional Pedagogy is concerned (*gruppa riska*). The approach of correctional classes, tried out in the Baltic republics, the Ukraine and several cities of the RSFSR, has been found to be the most effective method of dealing with this group.

Correctional classes apply to years 1–3 of the general school. They consist of a maximum of twenty pupils (as in ZPR classes) and the overwhelming majority of pupils (about 80 per cent) are boys. Classes, which can be set up in any type of general school (day or boarding), are likely to draw children from a number of pre-school and primary classes in the region. The classes comprise, first, children who are not yet ready for school and, second, children who are having problems in adapting to school. The first category has been identified at the pre-school stage, whilst the second will have been transferred from ordinary classes. The complement of correctional classes is not static, as transfer of children to and from these classes into normal classes occurs.

The causes of the learning difficulties which result in children falling into the 'at risk group' are asthenia, infantilism and pedagogical neglect. Asthenia (a state of general debility resulting from a childhood illness) is the most common cause. Infantilism has three identified types: first, poor personality development while the intellect is normal; second, poor cognitive development; and third, inadequate speech development. Pedagogical neglect is generally caused by poor social conditions which have prevented satisfactory development during the pre-school period.

How does this compare with the causes of ZPR identified in the 1981 regulations? The latter, which are phrased in typically ponderous official jargon, state that the main cause of delay in intellectual development is CNS damage, which could be genetically caused but is more likely to be the result of injury in the very early or prenatal stages of development. Nevertheless, three types of exceptional cases are also permitted: first, children may be backward because they suffer from infantilism, or simply develop more slowly than their peers; second, they may be asthenic so that poor health makes them backward; third, they may suffer from a severe form of neurosis which prevents their personality from developing as it should. In the words of the 1981 regulations:

> the chief medical indication . . . is a delay in intellectual development of a cerebral-organic origin (usually of a residual nature as a result of infection, trauma or intoxication of the nervous system, more rarely as a result of genetically conditioned handicaps to development); the following clinical variations of ZPR may be allowed in exceptional cases:
> (a) constitutional, mental and psychophysical infantilism
> (b) ZPR of somatogenic origin accompanied by forms of persistent somatic asthenia and somatically conditioned infantilism
> (c) ZPR of psychogenic origin following pathological personality development of a neurotic type, accompanied by signs of mental inertia and psychogenic infantilism.[13]

Thus the causes of delay in development are, it would seem, similar both for children in correctional classes and for those exceptional cases in the catching-up (ZPR) classes. A different predominance in causes is shown in the differing order in which the causes are placed, with asthenia being most common in the case of correctional classes and infantilism in that of ZPR classes. In the case of ZPR classes, however, infantilism, asthenia and pedagogical neglect are supposed to be the exception rather than the rule, as mild CNS damage is the most usual cause of the child's backwardness. Therefore the establishment of correctional classes indicates a widening of the band of children for whom some sort of differentiated education is provided in the Soviet system.

Selection of children for correctional classes is undertaken by the school pedagogical commission, consisting of the head of primary education in the school, the school doctor, the speech therapist and the school psychologist (if there is one). It is therefore a simpler and more school-based version of the more professional medical-pedagogical commission which diagnoses ZPR and oligophrenic children for special education. An important function of correctional classes is diagnosis, taking some pressure off the overworked medical-pedagogical commissions.[14] Doubtful cases will come under observation for some time in the correctional class until a decision can be reached on the child's suitability for special education. In making their decisions, members of the commission rely on the judgement of the teacher of the correctional class. In the assessment of children, guidance is provided for teachers by a manual published by the Laboratory of Correctional Pedagogy.[15] There are two basic components in this assessment: first, the teacher must familiarize herself with the child's home and developmental conditions and his or her state of health and medical history; second, the process of the child's learning must be studied. Tests of the Vygotskian teaching experiment type[16] are provided for the teacher to use in analysing the pupil's learning activity: for example, the pupil is given the task of arranging beads of different colours and shapes according to a pattern which has been demonstrated. If the pupil has difficulty, help can be given by the teacher; such help may take the form of words of encouragement, a suggestion as to how to continue with the task, or even in the last resort showing the child the start of the next step. This diagnostic teaching experiment should take place and be recorded regularly, approximately once every month.

In the case of children who have not yet started school, the tasks of the commission are to organize the collection of data on those who will shortly do so, to analyse the data, and to identify the group of children who are 'at risk'. It is important that strong links are established with feeder pre-school institutions from which the children will come, and that efforts are made to acquaint staff and parents with the purpose of correctional classes.

The timetable (*uchebnyi plan*) is that of ordinary classes, and correctional classes operate on an extended-day basis with special classes and logopaedic exercises in the later part of the day for helping the children with their particular problems. It is recommended that correctional classes are set up in those schools where a speech therapist already has a consulting room. Children in these classes must also have a medical examination twice every year.

While teachers of ZPR classes are trained defectologists who receive the additional salary increment, teachers of correctional classes are merely described as the best qualified, best trained teachers, who know how to establish contact with children. Although there are no financial inducements for this demanding work, practical help is provided by the Laboratory for Correctional Pedagogy in the form of pedagogical literature. Two such guides for teachers are a manual giving recommendations on the evaluation of students[17] and the already mentioned teacher's manual on diagnostic methods to be used in the correctional classes.

What, then, are the principal differences between ZPR classes and correctional classes? ZPR classes are of a more permanent nature. Children attend these classes for a minimum of three years. About 50 per cent remain for the duration of their schooling and cover the primary and middle stages of compulsory education. The population of correctional classes, however, is transitory, and the impression is that such classes are established (and disbanded) according to local needs; they are of a far more *ad hoc* nature than ZPR classes. Correctional classes apply to only the first three years of primary education. The timetables used differ in so far as ZPR children are allowed extra time to complete the standard programme, whilst children in correctional classes have exactly the same amount of time as those in ordinary ones. There is, at least in theory, a distinction between children suffering from ZPR and those in the correctional classes, who have fallen behind in their education for various reasons. The former have a mild and often remediable form of CNS damage, and research into their educational problems is conducted by the Institute of Defectology, the APN institute concerned with research into special education. Research into the educational problems of children in correctional classes is conducted by the Institute of Theory and History of Pedagogy (until 1990 General Pedagogy).

SLOW LEARNERS AND THE IMPACT OF PERESTROIKA

Since the advent of perestroika the educational establishment in the form of the APN has been subjected to fierce criticism. This attack was spearheaded by the teacher-innovators, who were later joined by progressives in the APN.[18] The APN was criticized for its remoteness from the actual problems of contemporary education and for its failure to give any practical help to teachers. The criticism became so vociferous that eventually a commission was set up to report on the work of the APN and to make recommendations for its reform. Teachers were meanwhile setting up their own groups to devise their own solutions to educational problems. Such groups were organized in the Eureka clubs of creative pedagogy or in schools participating in the *avtorskaya shkola* movement, coordinated by the teachers' newspaper *Uchitel'skaya gazeta* (see Chapters 1 and 2).[19]

The approach of correctional classes which has been described can be taken as the officially approved APN approach. It was developed in an APN research institute and the APN has published teachers' manuals written by staff in the Laboratory for Correctional Pedagogy. Before considering alternative approaches recommended by the innovators and other progressives, the drawbacks and the advantages of correctional classes should be considered.

Correctional classes can be criticized as an attempt to supply education for the less able in a cheaper form than is possible in ZPR classes, since teachers are not trained defectologists and the provision of facilities would certainly cost less than in the ZPR schools, if not the ZPR classes. Doubts immediately arise, however, as to the possibilities of correctional classes being successful in dealing with educational problems. Remedial work is difficult and often seen as unrewarding, and Soviet teachers of remedial classes are not to receive the salary increment accruing to their colleagues in special education. One suspects that heads of schools will be reluctant to have correctional classes opened on their school premises, as such classes will inevitably be seen as a gathering of all of the difficult pupils from the schools in the area. There is also the problem of accurate diagnosis; how to differentiate between ZPR pupils and pupils for correctional classes is a problem which the Soviets admit that they have not yet solved.[20] The correctional classes can be seen as a way of shifting some of the burden of diagnosis on to teachers and away from the specialists who comprise the medical-pedagogical commissions. Of course, involving teachers increases the danger that the classes could become dumping grounds for the use of teachers wishing to dispose of their problem pupils. The official intention, however, is definitely not one of using correctional classes as a convenient way of tidying all problem pupils out of the way, since such classes apply to only the first three years of schooling, and it is generally accepted that the worst discipline problems arise with older adolescent pupils.

On the positive side there are clear goals to aim for, as the purpose of the correctional classes is to return pupils to ordinary classes, and the success of the classes can be measured by how well pupils subsequently progress with their education. There is the research conducted by the Laboratory of Correctional Pedagogy, and the manuals produced to assist teachers with the difficult work with such classes. Many a British remedial educationist would welcome the materials provided in these manuals. There is, for example, a format for the appraisal of children and a format for the resultant profile (*pedagogicheskaya karta*); also a recommended standard letter to parents is provided for the commission to use, so that parents learn of the value of correctional classes and do not view them with distrust.

What approach is recommended by the progressive camp, the teacher-innovators who led the attack on the APN? In the innovators' manifesto of 19 March 1988 separate classes for less able students were roundly condemned. Catching-up classes are seen by them as dangerous; pedagogical lessons should be learned from the 'tracking' which is standard in American schools and which has produced so many illiterates, because children give up when they are relegated to the bottom streams. According to the innovators: 'Children should be differentiated according to their interests and their special talents and not according to their abilities'.[21]

A comment made to me on a visit to VNIK 'Shkola' (see Chapter 1) in 1989 was that, as long as the educational conditions were right, correctional classes were unnecessary. All children, it was stated, should be provided with the ideal educational conditions which such classes offered. Of course, the commentator was right; every child should ideally receive an education which matches his or her individual needs and interests. But what country has ever managed to provide such a level of educational funding that ideal conditions can be given, never mind a country like the Soviet Union which has yet to solve so many basic economic problems? In this light the statement of the VNIK educationist seems as Utopian as that of Lunacharsky, the first Soviet Education Minister, who said in an early speech: 'In the proper sense of the word, defectiveness depends not so much on bad inheritance as on the

115

milieu. Change conditions, and there will not remain a trace of defectiveness in these children.'[22] Such was the boundless optimism of the early years. A similar Utopianism can be discerned in the views of some of today's progressive Soviet educationists.

CONCLUDING REFLECTIONS

In the new freedom which Soviet education is experiencing there will undoubtedly be some educationists with an interest in and talent for developing education for the less able, and creative educational experiments are likely to appear, as happened in the 1920s and early 1930s. At the start of the 1990s, many educationists look back nostalgically to this early Soviet period and authors quote from educational psychologists such as Blonsky to support their points of view. Many of the progressives turn to Western models of education in the hope of finding there the solutions to numerous problems besetting Soviet education. Again, this interest in Western theories is a repetition of what happened in the 1920s and 1930s. There is an interest in the theories of Karl Rogers, and *avtorskaya shkola* projects have been developed which are based on his ideas. Some of these projects will probably result in successful schemes for educating children with learning difficulties.

Nevertheless some Western observers of Soviet special education will feel unease. A specifically Soviet model of special education had developed with its roots in the psychological theories of Vygotsky and his followers. It was a model of special education very different from those in the West, but it had much to commend it. For example, it had a sound theoretical basis in Vygotskian psychology; it claimed to have the same egalitarian ideals as the rest of Soviet education; and Western visitors reported favourably on the staffing ratios and standard of care in special schools.[23] It must be conceded that Western observers also had various doubts. How even was provision throughout the country? How effective were the diagnostic methods in selecting children for the appropriate type of school? But now the inevitable question is raised as to how the cold winds of market forces will affect this marginal type of educational provision. There will be disquiet on the part of Western observers that the Soviet model, which offered many instructive lessons, is in danger of disappearing in the hotch-potch of experimentation which has appeared with glasnost and perestroika. The danger is especially great when new models present themselves as more economical alternatives.

NOTES AND REFERENCES

1 A.R. Luriya, *The Mentally Retarded Child*, Oxford, Pergamon, 1963, p. 3.
2 T.A. Vlasova, K.S. Lebedinskaya and V.F. Machikhina, *Otbor detei vo vspomogatel'nuyu shkolu*, Moscow, Prosveshchenie, 1983.

3 A. Sutton, 'Backward children in the USSR: an unfamiliar approach to a familiar problem', in J. Brine, M. Perrie and A. Sutton (eds), *Home, School and Leisure in the Soviet Union*, London, Boston and Sydney, Allen & Unwin, 1980, pp. 181–4. See this source, pp. 171–2, 180, for explanation of the concept 'zone of next development'.

4 'Tipovoe polozhenie o spetsial'noi obshcheobrazovatel'noi shkole-internate (shkole s prodlennym dnem) dlya detei s zaderzhkoi psikhicheskogo razvitiya', *Byulleten' normativnykh aktov Ministerstva prosveshcheniya SSSR*, 1982, no. 3, pp. 29–38.

5 ibid., p. 27.

6 ibid.

7 'O predvaritel'nykh rezul'tatakh obucheniya i vospitaniya detei s zaderzhkoi psikhicheskogo razvitiya v spetsial'nykh shkolakh i klassakh', *Byulleten' normativnykh aktov Ministerstva prosveshcheniya SSSR*, 1983, no. 6, pp. 23–4.

8 *Narodnoe obrazovanie i kul'tura v SSSR*, Moscow, Finansy i statistika, 1989, p. 129 and derived.

9 G.F. Kumarina, 'Individualizatsiya obucheniya slabouspevayushchikh shkol'nikov', *Sovetskaya pedagogika*, 1987, no. 2, pp. 40–5.

10 V.I. Lubovsky, 'Zavtra budet pozdno', *Narodnoe obrazovanie*, 1989, no. 9, pp. 54–61.

11 For the traditional view see, for example, V. Lubovskii [sic], 'Against integration', *Special Children*, 1988, no. 23, pp. 6–7.

12 G.F. Kumarina, *Korrektsionnye klassy v strukture srednei obshcheobrazovatel'noi shkoly*, Moscow, NII obshchei pedagogiki APN, 1988.

13 'Tipovoe polozhenie . . . ', op. cit., p. 28.

14 A. Izmaganbetova and V. Lubovsky, 'Problemy raboty mediko-pedagogicheskikh komissii', *Defektologiya*, 1989, no. 4, pp. 3–8.

15 G.F. Kumarina, *Pedagogicheskaya diagnostika razvitiya i obucheniya shkol'nikov v sisteme korrektsionnogo obucheniya*, Moscow, NII obshchei pedagogiki APN, 1989.

16 For an account of the teaching experiment see Sutton, op. cit., p. 184.

17 G.F. Kumarina, *Individualizatsiya otsenochnoi deyatel'nosti pedagoga v sisteme korrektsionnogo obucheniya*, Moscow, NII obshchei pedagogiki APN, 1989.

18 A. Suddaby, 'An evaluation of the contribution of the teacher-innovators to Soviet educational reform', *Comparative Education*, 1989, vol. 25, no. 2, pp. 245–56.

19 A. Suddaby, 'Perestroika in Soviet education', *Soviet Education Study Bulletin*, 1989, vol. 7, no. 1, pp. 14–21; J. Sutherland, 'Soviet education since 1984: the school reform, the innovators and the APN', *Soviet Education Study Bulletin*, 1989, vol. 7, no. 1, pp. 21–33.

20 Izmaganbetova and Lubovsky, op. cit.

21 'Metodika obnovleniya', *Uchitel'skaya gazeta*, 19 March 1988, pp. 2–3; translated as Sh. Amonashvili, I. Volkov, I. Ivanov, E. Il'in, E. Kurkin, S. Lysenkova, L. Nikitina, B. Nikitin, V. Shatalov and M. Shchetinin, 'The methodology of reform', *Soviet Education*, 1989, vol. 31, no. 7, pp. 44–77, at p. 72.

22 A.V. Lunacharsky, speech at the First Congress of Workers in the Struggle against Defectiveness, 1920, quoted in A.I. D'yachkov, 'Teaching handicapped children', *Soviet Education*, 1967/68, vol. 10, no. 5, p. 45.

23 A. Suddaby and A. Sutton, 'Special education for handicapped pupils in the Armenian SSR', *Soviet Education Study Bulletin*, 1988, vol. 6, no. 2, pp. 33–9.

7

THE V.I. LENIN SOVIET CHILDREN'S FUND: COMMUNITY SUPPORT FOR THE SPECIAL CHILD IN THE SOVIET UNION?

Landon Pearson

INTRODUCTION

This contribution examines the origins of the V.I. Lenin Soviet Children's Fund, describes its purpose and structure, and looks at the role that the Fund has undertaken with respect to the exceptional child in the Soviet Union, especially the child who is at a disadvantage for learning in a regular school for socio-economic, physical, or psychoneurological reasons. It advances the proposition that the Fund is more likely to achieve its objectives by raising public awareness and putting pressure on decision-makers, or by making use of the other means employed by children's advocates in the Western world, than by direct intervention in the school system. The use of these techniques requires considerable practice, however, and to be effective, organizations that use them must remain in close contact with their own grass-roots. Concern has been expressed that the Soviet Children's Fund has become bureaucratized and over-centralized as it has grown. Yet its commitment to respond to the plight of disadvantaged children in the Soviet Union remains genuine. With all of the work that needs to be done on their behalf, it is to be hoped that the organization will be able to retain some of the freshness and imagination with which it began.

THE ORIGINS OF THE V.I. LENIN SOVIET CHILDREN'S FUND

'The only privileged class': all through the Brezhnev years this was the phrase that Soviet authorities used to describe the situation of children in the Soviet Union not only to foreigners but also to Soviet citizens as well. At that time the Soviet state certainly did appear to value children, if only for ideological and patriotic reasons, as potential 'builders of communism'. Soviet society valued them partly because there was little else of promise for people to value. In spite of this, children were not really a privileged class; many, particularly those who were in the sole custody of the state, were spending

118

their childhoods in miserable circumstances. It was the unhappy plight of this last category of children, the thousands of inmates of infants' and children's homes, that inspired the creation of the V.I. Lenin Soviet Children's Fund.

There have been children's homes in the Soviet Union since the time of the Revolution. Their continued existence has mirrored the tragic history of the country: the misfortunes and deprivations of the Civil War, the human wastage created by collectivization, the purges, the Second World War, and the difficult post-war years. By the early 1980s, material conditions had eased but new social trends ensured that many children continued to require residential care. The children who were now living in Soviet children's homes were seldom orphans, as had formerly been the case. They were children whose parents, unable to cope, had been deprived of parental rights; children, that is, who had been neglected, abandoned, abused, or humiliated. Yet the residential homes to which they were sent for care and protection were often intolerable, badly built and improperly staffed. Amonashvili, the well-respected educator and a member of the Soviet Children's Fund, characterized the prevailing mood in the homes as *zapugat', potom vospitat'* (intimidate, then educate).

Albert Likhanov, a journalist and writer with a passionate concern for children, was then the editor-in-chief of *Smena*, a monthly magazine for young people which was published under the auspices of the Komsomol. He organized round-table discussions on the subject and published a number of articles urging the public to pay attention. In the mid-1980s two excellent films, whose titles may be translated as *The Mistress of the Orphanage* – this was also shown on television – and *Games for Adolescents*, broadened public awareness of the issue; both vividly depicted how children and adolescents were actually living in these homes. Likhanov continued to make statements and his message obviously touched a sensitive public nerve. What he wrote in *Pravda* on 13 August 1987 is typical:

> Let us begin from the beginning. Let us carry out all our other transfor-mations – in the spheres of the economy, social restructuring, ecology, culture and art – asking ourselves not at the end, but at the very beginning: how is this going to affect our children, their souls and minds?
>
> Spontaneous undertakings, grass-roots initiative, the energy of kind and selfless actions – this is what we can only dream of and what we have been willingly or unwillingly killing in ourselves, in our con-sciousness and in our people by endlessly repeating 'you must not' (*nel'zya*) where one should hear 'you may' (*mozhno*).

In spite of *nel'zya*, Likhanov and others persisted in trying to turn their concern for unfortunate children into real action. Organized charity was not always so frowned upon in the Soviet Union as it came to be later, when the state claimed that it was no longer necessary. An aid fund for children's homes named after Lenin had existed in the USSR from 1924 to 1938. Likhanov proposed that this be revived and given a broader mandate. The CPSU undoubtedly approved, although it is not listed with the other founding organizations. These included the Soviet Women's Committee, the USSR Writers' Union, the USSR Film Workers' Union, the USSR Union of Journalists, the Red Cross and Red Crescent Societies, the All-Union Central Council of Trade Unions, the Komsomol, the USSR Cultural Foundation, *Komsomol'skaya pravda*, *Smena*, the Children's Musical Theatre, the USSR Peace Fund, the Soviet Peace Committee and the All-Union Society of Book Lovers.[1]

On 14 October 1987, the founding conference of the V.I. Lenin Soviet Children's Fund took place in Moscow. M.S. Gorbachev sent a message of support. There were several speeches pledging commitment to improving the conditions of Soviet childhood, notably by Likhanov, who was elected as the first chairman of the Fund. The statute adopted by the founding conference confirmed the Fund's structure as a self-governing organization, enjoying tax-free status and capable of receiving funds from the public at large and disbursing them on behalf of children without government interference. It listed as one of the Fund's main purposes the task of uniting citizens 'in order to carry out concrete social undertakings aimed at protecting the health and interests of children and at bettering all aspects of their upbringing and development',[2] with a particular emphasis on children lacking parental care, disabled or invalid children, and gifted children.

THE STRUCTURE OF THE CHILDREN'S FUND

As a resident of Moscow in the early 1980s, and a frequent visitor since, I have been observing the evolution of the Children's Fund with considerable interest. The need for such an organization is transparent, given the burden of suffering carried by so many Soviet children and the obvious incapacity of the system to respond to their needs. Most Western countries have long recognized that governments are ill-suited to the direct solution of children's problems. As a result, thousands of non-governmental organizations have come into existence to deal with the variety of specific challenges related to children and their welfare. Most of them flourish with small staffs and many volunteers. The formality of the proceedings and the scope of the issues addressed by the founding conference of the Soviet Children's Fund were in striking contrast to the way in which most national and international non-governmental organizations concerned with children operate.

Nevertheless, Gennady Savinov, the first deputy chairman (executive director) of the Fund, assured me when I met him in a tiny temporary office in the Yunost Hotel in March 1988 that the Fund would resist bureaucratization. Although a year later I found him in an imposing office in the Fund's new quarters, surrounded by papers and supported by a growing staff,[3] he continued to assure me that the responsive structure that he had described to me at our first meeting was evolving according to plan. An interview with Albert Likhanov in Moscow in November 1990 confirmed the structure which Savinov described to me and is set out below, although Likhanov admitted that some aspects of the Fund's activities were proving to be more effective than others.

The Soviet Children's Fund is a membership organization managed by a board of directors and supported by a paid staff. The entire membership meets every five years to set policy directions. The board of directors meets at least once a year and the executive considerably more often. The board has the capacity to set up committees (councils) to focus on specific issues, such as the family, children in institutional care, and gifted children. Members of these councils serve on them as volunteers. The staff administer the Fund and manage the projects recommended by the councils. Because the Fund is a juridical person capable of lodging a complaint on behalf of a child, it also has a legal section enabling it to act as an ombudsman for children.

Membership in the Fund is open to both individuals and organizations whose interests and activities conform to the objectives listed in the Fund's statute. Members must be prepared to 'render material, organizational or any other necessary assistance to the Fund' and to coordinate their activities with the board or with local branches of the Fund. Foreigners and foreign organizations may also become full or associated members.

The Fund receives the money that it disburses for charitable purposes from public donations, either individual or collective. In 1988, its first full year of operation, it received 43m roubles in donations. It also raises money through telethons (a 24-hour telethon in January 1990 raised 61m roubles)[4] and galas. Both types of event allow the Fund to engage in consciousness-raising with the general public. Operational money comes from the profits earned by a number of cooperatives with which the Fund is associated, toy manufacturing for example. The most important source of funds appears to be the revenues from the Fund's popular weekly newspaper, *Sem'ya* (Family). The editorial board of the newspaper is made up of young and imaginative journalists, and circulation is limited only by the shortage of newsprint. For disaster-related activities, such as medical assistance for children injured during the Armenian earthquake or help for children who are refugees from areas of ethnic conflict, the Fund seeks support from its many local and regional branches.

The Children's Fund also has a political role to play and the structure of the Congress of People's Deputies, elected in 1988, provides it with the means. The Fund is one of the so-called public organizations that has been guaranteed representation in the Congress: five places are reserved for it. Other members of the Fund also became people's deputies; altogether thirty prominent members of the Children's Fund were elected to (or selected for) the Congress. These people have tried to maintain the place of children on the public agenda. They helped to ensure that the USSR was among the first group of nations to sign the UN Convention on the Rights of the Child in January 1990, and they pushed successfully for ratification of the Convention by the Congress in August 1990. When I first met Likhanov at a meeting convened by Unicef in New York in April 1989, he was still hoping that the Supreme Soviet would establish a permanent commission for children's issues. This has not happened and children's issues are (in 1991) still subsumed under the Standing Commission on Women's Affairs, Protection of Family, Motherhood and Childhood (formerly Commission for Work and Welfare of Women, Protection of Motherhood and Childhood, a standing commission of the Supreme Soviet created in 1976). Likhanov, however, is himself a member of the Supreme Soviet, and is sufficiently influential to have been included on the USSR delegation to the World Summit on Children held at the United Nations in September 1990.

DAY-TO-DAY ACTIVITIES

As the founding conference intended, many branches of the Fund have sprung up in various parts of the Soviet Union to deal directly with local issues. A brief look at what was happening in Irkutsk should give some idea of the Fund's day-to-day activities in 1990.[5]

The population of Irkutsk and its surrounding region was 2.82m among whom were 3,700 orphans in twenty-three residential and four family-type children's homes. Children in foster care or under the guardianship of other family members totalled 4,419. There were also a certain number of children in labour colonies for offences against the law. An inventory taken by the Children's Fund determined that there were 3,158 severely disabled children in the region, many of whose parents were unaware of the availability of allowances and other forms of state assistance. Of all of the families in the Irkutsk region, 34,467 were headed by single mothers and 12,214 had more than three children. All of these people comprised the field of action for the Irkutsk branch of the V.I. Lenin Soviet Children's Fund.

The branch had a board of directors made up of twenty-five volunteers, an executive committee of six, and five staff employees comprising an executive director, an administrator, and three 'inspectors' (project officers) who did the bulk of the field work. There were several volunteer councils. The council on large families acted as their advocate with schools, pre-school institutions, shops, and polyclinics. The special council made up of former inmates of children's homes offered counselling to senior students still living in these homes and helped them to adjust to the outside world. The council on disabled children was responsible for the inventory mentioned above, and the council on family-type children's homes pressed for the creation of more of these. Transforming the old residential children's homes into children's villages on the Austrian model, where small groups of children live with houseparents in separate homes clustered around a central facility, is one of the major thrusts of the Soviet Children's Fund everywhere in the Soviet Union.

The Irkutsk branch earned its core money by publishing calendars, selling plastic bags, and holding special events. Money for its charitable activities came from personal donations, and donations from churches, cooperatives and small organizations, notably women's collectives. In 1988, 200,000 roubles was received in donations, of which 40 per cent was channelled to the central 'piggy-bank' for all-Union projects. The rest was spent on hiring more personnel for local infants' homes, upgrading the local reception centre where children go when taken into care and where they wait to be placed, and equipping a computer room in one of the residential children's homes.

A typical week of one of the project officers consisted of the following activities, undertaken during a trip to Bratsk. The officer visited a children's home to observe whether it had been successful in dividing its children into 'family' groups made up of children of various ages, instead of grouping them by age as had previously been done. Then she went to the city council to put the case on the children's behalf for a summer cottage and a minibus. Some of the children's relatives were employed at a local factory, so she went there to talk about the work of the Fund. Initially she was received with suspicion because the workers were weary of contributing to compulsory funds such as the Peace Fund, but she persuaded them that the Children's Fund was entirely voluntary and they need not contribute if they did not want to do so. The important thing was to understand what the Fund was all about and to help children in whatever way they could. Finally she visited a family whose three daughters had been badly burned in the gas explosion near Ufa in 1988. The Fund was monitoring the progress of their long course of treatment and trying to obtain help for them as needed. The project officer enjoyed her work because it was practical and she felt the weight of a community board behind her.

THE FUND AND SPECIAL EDUCATION

While the V.I. Lenin Soviet Children's Fund is much preoccupied with the plight of handicapped children, it does not intervene directly in the development of the school curriculum. It sees this as the responsibility of the State Committee for Education. What the Fund is interested in are the conditions in which handicapped children live. Ilya Lebedev, the staff member responsible for handicapped children at the Fund's central office in Moscow, said when interviewed in 1990 that more alternatives should be created to the residential schools for the handicapped that are considered the norm. At issue is not the educational experience offered by these schools but the degree to which students emerge from them ill-equipped to deal with the challenges of ordinary living. This is a result, according to Lebedev, of the fact that these children are almost totally isolated from the outside world and are given insufficient instruction in life skills. Besides, the fact that a child in a special residential school for the handicapped is separated from his or her parents for long periods often contributes to the disintegration of that child's family. The Children's Fund has urged the government to incorporate facilities for the physically disabled into the design of new schools. The Fund also wants ramps placed in old schools. The response has been favourable.

Another issue being tackled by the Children's Fund is the inadequate amount of time allotted by existing placement teams, known as medical-pedagogical commissions (see Chapter 6), to the assessment of children who are having difficulty in school. The Fund is concerned that a major decision may be made without adequate consideration on the future of a child with a minor problem. As a result, the Fund is pressing for the creation of permanent consultation centres in every town and region, where parents and others may seek advice on children with learning difficulties and which will be responsible for monitoring the progress of children placed in auxiliary schools. Such centres would be of particular importance for children who have been in institutional care since birth.

Another project of the Fund is the creation of family-based children's homes for mentally-handicapped children, which are focused on nurturing their capacity for social adaptation. The model being used is a Finnish one, and Finnish experts have already conducted a number of workshops in Moscow to explain their approach.

With the Fund's participation, a centre for the creative rehabilitation of disabled children has been formed in Moscow to search out gifted children among the handicapped, to develop their creative powers, and to ease their way into society. The Children's Fund will grant a certain number of scholarships to these children, to augment those that they have already granted to gifted children in the general population (14 in 1989 and 145 in 1990), in order for them to study at premier artistic institutions such as the Moscow Conservatoire of Music.

Judging by our interview with Lebedev[6] and other available materials, the bias of the Fund is towards integration of the handicapped child into the regular school system. This is not the position of the Institute of Defectology in Moscow, which has long been responsible for setting standards for educating children who suffer from mental or physical disabilities. The Institute supports differentiated education for a number of carefully considered reasons, based on L.S. Vygotsky's observations of how physiologically based disabilities distort the social interaction that is so important for the development of children's higher mental functions. The concern of the Institute is that ordinary classroom teachers have neither the training nor the opportunity to make use of the highly differentiated teaching methodologies that it has designed after years of experimental work with children suffering from a variety of mental and physical disabilities. Therefore the Institute would prefer to improve the general conditions for children who are placed in the special schools that it monitors in order to help them to reach their full intellectual and vocational potential, rather than see more disabled children integrated into ordinary schools that are not structured to receive them. To finance this objective, as well as to support more research, a separate Fund for Disabled Children was set up in the spring of 1990 under the chairmanship of V.I. Lubovsky, director of the Institute for Defectology, and named after Vygotsky.

THE FUTURE OF THE V.I. LENIN SOVIET CHILDREN'S FUND

The V.I. Lenin Soviet Children's Fund emerged from a recognition that the Soviet system as it existed before the period of perestroika was quite incapable of responding to the needs of its most vulnerable children. Since its formation in 1987, it has been able to elicit widespread public support for its philanthropic mission. That support is especially available for children who are seen to be deprived of a normal family life. In the case of a country as materially disorganized as the Soviet Union is today, money and other material assistance will make a real difference. The Fund is to be commended for its support for children suffering from the after-effects of Chernobyl, for example, and for its attempt to establish a rehabilitation centre for physically disabled youngsters which is based on Variety Village, a long-established centre in Toronto, Canada that has had some notable successes. This latter project is being funded by a joint Soviet-Canadian group sponsored by George Cohon, the Canadian entrepreneur who opened the first McDonald's restaurant in Moscow in January 1990. If the Fund concentrated on these activities alone it would be performing an invaluable service. The Fund, however, has assumed a wider mandate for itself; it would like to better the lives of *all* Soviet children. This is where it is encountering criticism, from the public as well as from specialists in child development. If the Soviet Children's Fund is to be effective in this wider mandate then it must resolve three fundamental problems.[7]

The first of these is the relationship of the V.I. Lenin Soviet Children's Fund to the CPSU as well as to the government. A non-governmental organization does not have to be against the government to be credible, but it must be seen as autonomous in its policy-setting function. The establishment of the Children's Fund was one of several similar moves taken in the Soviet Union in the late 1980s, signalling the belated emergence of a civil society in which communities take charge of their own issues. But excessive involvement with the government, and particularly with the CPSU, will be detrimental to the authenticity of the Children's Fund. There have been some complaints in the media that the Fund is serving as a dumping ground for old communists who have little or no knowledge of children's issues. What is worse, according to a TV programme from Leningrad in March 1990, these people have been allowed to retain the special benefits, the black cars, the dachas, and suchlike, that are so loathed by the general public. The chairman of the Latvian branch of the Soviet Children's Fund, A. Berzinsh, was even asked outright: 'Is the Children's Fund a shelter for apparatchiks?' He denied it, of course, and went on to relate all of the good things that the Fund was doing, but the question remains.

A second issue, which was brought to my attention in November 1990 by Dr Igor Kon, Dr V. Lubovsky and Dr V.V. Davydov, all members of the Academy of Pedagogical Sciences (Davydov is vice-president) and distinguished intellectuals, is the credibility of the Fund's research activities among members of the academic community. The Fund has been responsible for the creation of a new research institute, under the auspices of the Academy, called the Institute of Childhood. Established research institutes are entering the 1990s under constraints imposed by the chaotic economic conditions. Salaries are inadequate; good researchers have left to work in joint ventures, new ones are hard to attract. The social and political climate does not promote sustained research. In consequence, a new institute, no matter how well-intentioned, is bound to have difficulty in establishing its legitimacy. The first task of the Institute of Childhood was the production of a 'State of Soviet Children' report modelled on UNICEF's annual 'State of the World's Children'. Likhanov told me that he had seen the galleys and that the report would be released early in 1991. While this carefully researched report may be a useful advocacy tool for change, it does not represent the same level of academic research as the other institutes have been pursuing. The tension that I detected may be only a function of role clarification but it does represent a challenge to the Fund's credibility.

A third issue which the Fund must resolve is related to attitudes about the family. Dr Kon, who is the Soviet Union's leading expert on sexuality, told me in November 1990 that the Council on the Family, of which he is a member, had not been able to achieve very much because of a lack of agreement. The definition of family roles has been a major problem in the Soviet Union for decades and there is some indication that the Fund's leaders are stereotypical in their views about women and about family dynamics. According to a report in *Pravda* of 4 June 1989, Likhanov and V. Matvienko, the head of the Supreme Soviet's renamed Standing Commission on Women's Affairs, Protection of Family, Motherhood and Childhood, could not even agree on who should raise the children – women, men, or both of them together. In my view, the Soviet Children's Fund will have to be flexible and realistic in its approach to the family if children are to be helped. The solution is to put the child first and to support any model of family living that is able to respond to a child's need for love, safety, nurture and respect.

The Soviet Children's Fund is a firmly established entity and will be a significant feature of the Soviet social landscape for many years to come. The direction that it takes will depend to some degree on how it responds to the issues that I have just raised. As a writer, Likhanov is an excellent publicist, and his deep commitment to the well-being of Soviet children is clear. So far the strength of the Fund has been shown in its philanthropic projects and, to a certain extent, its political activities on behalf of children. Creating a cultural climate that will make children a truly 'privileged' class is a much more complicated task, for which neither the Fund nor any other single organization may be suited.

NOTES AND REFERENCES

1 Listed in Albert Likhanov, *We are All Responsible for Our Children*, Moscow, Novosti Press, 1987.
2 From the statute of the Lenin Soviet Children's Fund, Moscow, Novosti Press, 1987.
3 Full address of V.I. Lenin Soviet Children's Fund: 11, Armyansky per., Moscow 101000, USSR.
4 Telethon reported in *Pravda*, 9 January 1990.
5 Account of Irkutsk branch published in *Sem'ya*, no. 13, 1990.
6 Lebedev interviewed on my behalf by Nina Ryan in March 1990.
7 The present manuscript was completed in January 1991.

8

REFORMS IN SOVIET VOCATIONAL EDUCATION: THE INTERFACE OF ECONOMIC, LABOUR AND EDUCATIONAL POLICIES

Friedrich Kuebart

INTRODUCTION

In the course of a few years since 1984 the reform process within Soviet education has been marked by various stages and turning points. The reform preceded the general social and political happenings in 1985. The socio-economic process of change ushered in by perestroika and glasnost swiftly revealed the failure of the 1984 concept of educational reform, leading to an awareness of the depth of the crisis in the educational system as a whole.

The changes in the economic and political framework have been accompanied by a change in the reasoning behind the educational reforms. With its focus on vocational education and training, the 1984 reform concept was based on the constellation of problems confronting the labour market. It envisaged solutions characterized by a perception of the education system as a mere 'component of the economy'.[1] The new reform ideas, which have been taking shape particularly since the turn in educational policy-making marked by the plenary session of the CPSU Central Committee in February 1988, no longer insist on linking the education system so closely to the system of employment. The introduction of a relationship similar to that in a market economy, with enterprises acting as customers for qualifications and educational institutions as their 'producers', provides a bridge to a new type of allocation process. This is still 'tailor-made', but less rigid and more achievement-orientated than traditional planning mechanisms.

With its goals of achieving a comprehensive improvement in the efficiency of the educational system, the reform is in line with Gorbachev's aims of 'radical economic reform'. In addition, educational reform is situated in the context of a comprehensive social reform which has not only been set in motion 'from above' but is also supported by a widespread grass-roots movement in favour of educational renewal. The core values of this movement, such as the decentralization of decision-making powers, differentiation of educational structures, emphasis on a more humanistic content of

128

education and individualization of instruction, have also been adopted by official educational policy-making. It is on these ideas that the new conceptions for the various sectors of the education system are based, which themselves are likewise supposed to find their functional position within the framework of a future system of 'permanent education'.

Like Soviet society as a whole, the education system faces a difficult and contradictory situation of radical change. This applies in particular to vocational training, which is in its turn closely dependent on the fate of economic reform. This paper is limited to analysing what can be viewed as central problems of vocational education.[2] The starting point for this must needs be the reform of 1984, which has already been intensively investigated both as a whole and as regards vocational training.[3] We shall focus, therefore, on the new developments in the reform of vocational education in the context of perestroika policies. Since 1988, when the radical turn in the course of reform spelt the end of the 1984 approach, a structural change in vocational training has moved to the centre of attention. Second, the curricular shaping of training has been affected by the new concepts and thinking. A third important issue is the financial organization of vocational training and the relationship between vocational training institutions and enterprises.

THE 1984 EDUCATIONAL REFORM: THE UPGRADING OF VOCATIONAL TRAINING

As far as vocational training was concerned, the 1984 reform of the general and vocational school incorporated two basic decisions. In the first place, the senior classes of the secondary general school were assigned the task of providing a vocational skill in addition to the secondary education certificate entitling its holders to apply for admission to higher education. Approximately one day a week was set aside for training for comparatively simple jobs.[4] Thus, in practice, the general school was incorporated in the 'system' of vocational training. The second decision concerned the PTU (*professional'no-tekhnicheskoe uchilishche*, vocational-technical school), the Soviet full-time vocational school, whose status was substantially raised by the reform in two respects. First, the SPTU (*srednee professional'no-tekhnicheskoe uchilische*, secondary vocational-technical school), which had been constantly extended since the end of the 1960s and which provides both the secondary leaving certificate (usually after a 3-year course) and a vocational qualification, was made the standard type of vocational school. The ordinary PTUs, with one to two-year courses not leading up to the certificate of secondary education, had to reorganize their courses to meet these requirements within an extremely short space of time, often without the facilities necessary for providing higher level vocational skills. Second, the reform envisaged a doubling of the number of SPTU students, a decision geared to a profound reorganization of the senior level of secondary education.

129

This massive reallocation of pupils was to be carried out at the expense of the last two classes of the general school by redirecting up to 50 per cent of pupils to the SPTU when they had finished the 'incomplete' secondary general school at age 15. Both this and the orientation of general school leavers towards the labour market at age 17 by vocationalizing the senior stage were a reaction to complex problems and contradictions within the education system that had accumulated during the Brezhnev era. Aspired to since the mid-1960s, the main goal of introducing compulsory secondary education for all had been pursued primarily by expanding the system of secondary general education. The orientation of general school leavers towards higher education and their rejection of low-skilled manual jobs conflicted increasingly with the demands of the labour market.

Satisfying the economy's need for skilled labour, particularly for qualified workers in a number of blue-collar jobs or in branches with a high proportion of physical labour, became increasingly problematic. School leavers encountered difficulties in settling into work on the shop floor, and there was a high rate of turnover among young workers. These were dysfunctional developments for which previous educational policies and the inadequate socialization achievements of the schools were made largely responsible.[5]

One of the extremely complex causes of this development was to be found within the employment system. Its chronic shortage of workers resulted from the 'extensive' type of economy typical of the Soviet Union, a state of affairs which had been aggravated by demographic developments since the end of the 1970s. The annual increase in the number of workers, which had slowed down during the last five-year plan periods, virtually came to a standstill during the mid-1980s,[6] although there were considerable regional imbalances owing to demographic factors. Areas with a considerable dearth of workers contrast with a surplus elsewhere, particularly in the Central Asian republics.[7] Other sectors of the labour market also show a heterogeneous situation. But, generally speaking, the employment situation has been characterized for a long time by a shortage of blue-collar workers and an excess supply of graduates from higher education, particularly engineers. At the same time the enterprises are overmanned as it is economically to their advantage to hoard workers. This enables them to cope with bottlenecks in production, changes of plan, supplementary assignments and the consequences of the high rate of fluctuation, the more so since wage expenditure has so far not been a decisive factor.[8] Ageing and technically out-dated equipment along with a too narrowly specialized workforce are also amongst the factors influencing the great demand for workers.

The new goal of educational policy, 'vocational training for all young people', proclaimed by the 1984 reform was intended, in the long run at least, to guarantee that young people already had some vocational qualifications before they entered the labour market. To safeguard standards, this qualification was preferably to be gained in some form of schooling within the vocational-technical system. The expansion of the PTU on a nationwide scale, which was envisaged by representatives of vocational education as early as the 1970s, proved impracticable, not least for financial reasons, and so the senior classes of the secondary school were once again assigned the task of providing vocational training, even though a similar reform model had run aground under Khrushchev. It was alleged that early physical and 'socially useful' work together with the acquirement of a trade skill would result in the increased orientation of young people towards blue-collar jobs.

PERESTROIKA AND THE REFORM OF THE REFORM

Looking back over developments since the launching of the reform of the general and vocational school in 1984, one can say – not without a touch of irony – that one of its basic mistakes was its premature conception and introduction. It was a far-reaching attempt to tackle the growing problems of an important area of Soviet society, which made it a trail-blazer in the 'clearing up' of the legacy of the Brezhnev era; but its aims and methods were not yet aligned to the basic restructuring of the economy and society. This was to take shape as the new leadership's political programme after Gorbachev had come to power. It was endorsed by the XXVII Party Congress in 1986.

The implementation of the 1984 reform had started with the endeavours of the educational bureaucracies to turn the reform documents and their provisions into directives and regulations for reforming the general and vocational school system 'from above'. Less than two years after its announcement, however, it became clear that the reform was increasingly meeting with resistance and contradictions. The bureaucratic style of implementation was showing few signs of success, and increasing criticism of the reform became apparent in public discussion.

At the XXVII CPSU Congress, when the perestroika programme was approved, it was already becoming clear that the 1984 education reform plan was not capable of matching the whole range of requirements connected with the reform of the economy. Economic authorities and the enterprises in particular had so far failed to cooperate adequately in providing the necessary millions of pupil work-places. Critical questions concerning the cost-efficiency relation of the general-school training scheme were provoked by the realization that only about 11–14 per cent of graduates took up jobs for which they were trained at school.[9] Experts also criticized the fact that this type of training did not result in adequately qualified young people, as pupils could only be given instruction in narrowly specialized jobs which would soon become obsolete in an economy involved in rapid technological modernization.

At the other end of the scale, similar doubts were growing as to the ability of the vocational-technical schools to provide the pupils allotted to them with a proper general education at the same level as the secondary general school. As recent research has again confirmed, school achievement decisively influences the choice of further courses of education at the upper secondary level. Whilst more successful pupils tend to go on to the senior classes of the general school, the vocational school is left to recruit its pupils from the pool of the less able and the less well motivated. This 'negative selection' is reflected in the low social prestige of the PTU, which again does little to attract high achievers.[10] Thus, it soon became apparent, and had to be admitted by those responsible, that the reform was expecting too much of the vocational schools by requiring the attainment of complete secondary education along with a vocational skill by all pupils. The result was the manipulation of marks and 'dishonest' leaving certificates.[11]

The expectation that the attempts to allocate the projected number of students to the SPTU would soon meet with success was in no way confirmed by actual developments. While in the first three years of the reform between 1985 and 1987 the proportion of pupils entering the senior stage of the general school indeed dropped slightly from 62.2 to 59.8 per cent, the number of pupils transferring to the SPTU during this period remained at 24.5 per cent. At 12.5 per cent in 1987, the proportion of transfers to the third type of upper secondary school provision, the specialized secondary school (or technicum, training 'medium specialists'), likewise showed little alteration. At the same time, the proportion of those leaving school for good after class 9 and entering employment without a secondary leaving certificate proved to be on the increase again. This is in contradiction to the legal regulations on compulsory education, but in view of many young people's lack of interest in school this is tolerated by a more liberal-minded educational administration.[12]

It was in the context of the public debate on the principles of economic reform that fundamentally new aspects, which were not apparent in the 1984 reform concept, entered the discussion on vocational training. Some of the features of the economic reform affecting the reform of vocational training in various ways and directing it along new paths can be summed up only very briefly: technological modernization of the production sphere, decentralization of economic organization and administration, along with profitability and self-financing of enterprises (khozraschet) and income structures more aligned to achievement. The new law on state enterprises adopted on 30 June 1987, which came into force on 1 January 1988,[13] widened the enterprise's scope for independence. It has thus been able to act more flexibly, placing the profit-making aspect at the centre of its activities. As the rate of pay, alongside investment, depends on profits made, this principle is expected to provide both an achievement-oriented stimulus and a more economical approach to labour and material resources.

These innovations are linked to far-reaching employment policy problems and consequences, the solution of which will itself be decisive for the success of the programme of economic and social reform. Perestroika is, for two separate reasons, going to lead to a massive reduction in the number of workplaces. It is expected that the projected technological refurbishing of the production sphere is to reduce drastically the amount of manual work, involving an equivalent loss of jobs. The enterprise law has likewise emphasized that in future millions of jobs will be axed. In line with the principle of self-financing, it will be to the advantage of the enterprise to shed unproductive and superfluous jobs. For the workers concerned this will involve transfer to other jobs within the enterprise or dismissal.

The reduction in the number of jobs resulting from the change in employment policy also affects school leavers, who have to compete with those affected by loss of employment for any jobs available. The tools provided by the 1984 general and vocational school reform for carrying out the strategy of 'vocational training for all young people' no longer fit the new situation. It is no longer a question of introducing to the labour market as many school leavers as possible, with qualifications for which there will perhaps soon be no demand and which have little competitive value. As it is becoming increasingly difficult for leavers from vocational-technical schools (as well as for those from specialized secondary schools and graduates from higher education) to find a job related to their training or even a job at all,[14] the quantitatively oriented re-allocation of pupils to the SPTU no longer makes sense.

The point which marked a decisive change of direction in the development of the school and vocational training reform was, just four years after its launching, the plenary session of the Central Committee of the CPSU on 17 and 18 February 1988. This had been specially called to discuss the state of the education system and to readjust the reform to the new perestroika conditions. The change of course embarked on by the February plenum concerned the organizational structure of vocational training, a rearrangement of the relationship between the various forms of training, the structures governing the planning and financing of training courses, and lastly a reorganization of the links between the systems of general and vocational education within the framework of the education system as a whole.

Both the general school and the vocational-technical school systems were affected by the revision of the regulations directing the 1984 reform. Vocational training at the general school has virtually been dropped as a compulsory subject area, although it may be offered 'at the wish of the parents and children and if the necessary arrangements are available'.[15] Thus the differentiated senior stage of secondary general education that is planned for the future is to offer a vocational course with a skill qualification as an option, along with academic instruction, under the assumption that there will still be a demand for such a course at the upper secondary level. But on the whole the general school is once again to be limited to offering polytechnical pre-vocational education which is intended primarily to provide vocational orientation. In line with the decentralization of curriculum strategies, the individual republics and even the individual school will be permitted a greater conceptual scope and improved organizational openings for determining its length and its concrete goals and contents. As local requirements are increasingly to be taken into account, future solutions will probably vary considerably and a rigid system with obligatory provisions will no longer prevail. The central task of the school is to provide 'basic secondary education', which is regarded as the foundation of all further educational processes in a future system of permanent education.

In this sense the February 1988 plenum also opted for a solution for vocational training which was based 'predominantly' on complete secondary general education. In this consecutive model, which had been favoured by a number of vocational education experts a few years earlier, the main route to acquiring a vocational qualification at the level of blue-collar jobs was to take pupils through the post-secondary TU (*tekhnicheskoe uchilische*, technical school) which had been amalgamated with the reformed SPTU after 1984. Although the SPTU with its combination of general and trade qualifications was to be retained as a parallel path, the goal of forcing its expansion, as described above, without regard to existing conditions was in fact revoked by the plenum. This decision virtually marked the withdrawal from an educational strategy which was aimed at achieving general education for all combined with a vocational skill. This combination, which was originally intended to be the common feature for all types of upper secondary courses, including the specialized secondary school, and thus affected all students whatever their prospective course of further training, has not proved successful as a general, suitable and applicable solution. Wherever it was enforced without regard to individual and material limitations, it tended to be educationally counter-productive. The plenum, in its attempt to replace the uniform approaches of the 1984 reform with more flexible strategies offering more choice and variation, also explicitly recognized initial vocational training on the job as an alternative to in-school vocational training at the PTU, whereas the 1984 reform was partially designed to squeeze on-the-job training for school leavers out of existence.

Resulting from the reassessment of educational policies at the February plenum, the system of vocational education in the Soviet Union is in a state of transition, characterized both by the search for a new, lasting conceptual and organizational framework and by the continuation of long-term reform work on the content of training geared to the new requirements. Not all of the orientation points introduced by the plenum for the 'reform of the reform' within vocational training were paid equal attention in the ensuing efforts to develop new and alternative concepts of reform. In contrast to previous political practice the plenum merely laid down a minimum number of basic provisions and guidelines without stipulating ready-made, detailed regulations. These formed the basis for creating a comprehensive reform conception for a system of 'permanent education', as well as for the individual sectors of the education system ranging from pre-school to higher education. The most controversial of these remains the reform conception for the system of general education, as it raised the question of dismantling a number of basic ideological and educational tenets which have moulded the shape of the school for decades. 'Temporary model statutes' passed in the summer of 1989 for the various sectors of education represented a first attempt at a codification of the new reform ideas. These seem, however, to have limited chances of being put into practice as long as the Education Act has not been adjusted accordingly.

STRUCTURAL CONSEQUENCES OF THE NEW REFORMS

Any attempt to outline the structural problems of Soviet vocational training in the reform process must proceed from the existing situation whilst one bears in mind the new focus set in and after February 1988. One feature of Soviet vocational training that has survived various periods of development is the parallel, in many instances even dualist, existence of forms of training at vocational schools, which include phases of practical instruction on the shop floor, and on-the-job training courses which are organized in the enterprises and which are generally shorter and more specialized. Government vocational educational policy has given priority to in-school training for some time now because of its alleged higher quality and the increasing demand for qualifications geared to technological change. Owing to the present developmental stage of employment structures and the weaknesses of the vocational-technical school system, however, training on the shop floor has largely retained its position.

Another basic feature of Soviet vocational training is its administrative diversity. Up to 1988, the various institutions of upper secondary education were in the hands of three different administrative bodies. It was not until the USSR State Committee for Education was founded in March 1988 that a common education administration was created. As far as on-the-job training within the enterprises is concerned, however, its powers are still limited, and for vocational training within the vocational schools responsibility is divided between the educational administration and economic branch administration agencies.

The vocational training system – which so far lacks the coherence of a 'system' not only in the administrative and organizational sphere but also as far as its content and final qualifications are concerned – is comprised of the following separate components: the vocational-technical school system; the institutions providing qualifications within the enterprises; the specialized secondary schools; and the upper level of the general school. The last of these, as already mentioned, is to retain to some extent its function of providing vocational qualifications in the future, particularly where the necessary infrastructure will remain in the form of efficient 'inter-school training and production combines'.

The efforts at 'reforming the reform' in the vocational education sector are aimed at integrating existing institutions with new structures which are both better coordinated and more diversified. Approved in December 1988 by the All-Union Education Congress, the 'Conception for Permanent Education' represented an educational framework programme for the restructuring of the education system as a whole.[16] This statement of policy is to provide the general guideline for interlocking the reform processes in the various sectors of the education system – particularly the school and vocational education reform and the reform of higher and specialized secondary education. It is also intended to allocate a concrete position, within the structure of the education system as a whole, to each sector along with its differentiated internal structures. For individuals it is to guarantee the continuity of the educational ladder from pre-school education to adult and continuing education, so that they are able to satisfy their own educational aspirations in an optimal manner.

Parallel to this comprehensive approach, a 'Conception for Vocational-Technical Education' was also elaborated under the auspices of the 1988 Education Congress.[17] It was the result of the cooperation of an interdisciplinary team of experts working at the Leningrad All-Union Research Institute for Vocational-Technical Education and headed by its director, V.V. Shapkin. This document outlines a new organizational structure for vocational education, proceeding from the existing institutional situation whilst attempting to supplement it in line with present-day and future qualification requirements. The vocational education institutions are to be divided into three structural levels, thus distinguishing their functions more clearly than is frequently the case at present. These structural levels are geared to the various qualification requirements of the Soviet economy and expressly take into account the considerable variations in the stage of technical development reached in its various branches.[18]

The planning of developments in vocational education is faced with somewhat contradictory trends in this area. Despite the continuous growth of higher skill grades since the 1960s, the average level of qualifications among the industrial labour force has not kept up with the demands of production, particularly in jobs and branches with a highly dynamic rate of technological development. In fact, Soviet research has shown a constant widening of the 'skill gap' since the 1960s.[19] On the other hand, the mainly manual jobs with low skill requirements are only gradually disappearing,[20] and if training were to take place at the SPTU it would result in over-qualification. This also explains the reserved attitude of some firms and branches to training at the vocational-technical schools. The new 'Conception for Vocational-Technical Education' has reacted to this situation by

136

offering a programme with more differentiated courses at various levels, which is also to cater for differences in both ability and motivation among young people.

At a basic level the first stage of vocational training aims at narrowly specialized mass jobs with fewer theoretical demands. This type of qualification is to be acquired both in vocational classes at the general school, in affiliation to an inter-school training and production combine, and in the appropriate departments of the vocational-technical school. At this level, on-the-job training within enterprises is also to be continued; it normally takes only six months and is popular with industry for two reasons. First, the vocational-technical schools can provide training for only about a quarter of the specializations in the production sphere and about two-thirds of new entrants to the workforce.[21] Second, it can be adjusted more flexibly to the specific and immediate demands of the individual enterprise. It retains its popularity despite the fact that numerous investigations have shown PTU training courses to be qualitatively superior.[22]

According to the reform conception, the second stage is to be reserved for the vocational-technical school as an intermediate level of vocational training. As is already the case, it is to be linked to the acquisition of the certificate of secondary general education after transfer from the incomplete secondary school. As an alternative – there is no longer any mention of the 'main path' as in the CC plenum resolution of February 1988 – a qualification at this level can also be acquired in a shorter course at a TU after completion of the senior classes of the general school. Thus the SPTU is evidently to remain the backbone of training courses for jobs with a broader qualification profile and higher theoretical requirements, which will form the largest section of the industrial vocational structure in the context of the technological modernization of production.

In the course of the post-1984 reform, only a few of the rapidly reorganized SPTUs have been able to comply with the ideal of a progressive institution providing a high standard of training for jobs in modern technology within industry and in non-industrial spheres alike. The above-mentioned low prestige of this type of school used to make it difficult for it to recruit achievement-oriented pupils. Moreover, the reduction of state pressure in controlling the transfer to the upper secondary stage along with the increasing difficulties for SPTU graduates in finding jobs in certain branches and areas has led to a drastic drop in applicants for this type of school. In 1988 only 87 per cent of the existing course places as allotted by the plan could be filled, and there was no change in 1989 either.[23] Thus, in the wake of the recent upheavals, the SPTU is confronted from both a quantitative and a qualitative point of view with increasingly urgent problems.

The innovative steps taken at the new, third level of vocational training aim particularly at consolidating its situation and modernizing its structure. Previously this level had been represented solely by the post-secondary form of the specialized secondary school (technicum). The reform 'Conception' introduced a new type of school, the 'higher vocational school' (*vysshee professional'noe uchilishche*), for training workers at the higher skill levels for jobs making heavy demands both theoretically and practically. This level is intended primarily to produce top-grade workers for modern occupations in innovative spheres of production. Initially two forms are being tried out, a 'technical college' (*tekhnicheskii kolledzh*) in the sphere of secondary specialized education, and a 'technical lycée' (*tekhnicheskoe litseum*), which is to provide an additional stage of vocational-technical schooling. This new term has been adopted from the example of a Russian elite school of the nineteenth century and is also reminiscent of the French upper secondary school. The few existing examples of either form have mostly been created since the autumn of 1989 on an experimental basis by the redesignation of either a SPTU or a specialized school. The lycée follows on from the incomplete secondary school and is to take at least four years, with pupils completing both the lower and the intermediate skill levels. It is possible to transfer to an appropriate occupation at any stage, whilst a continuation of the course is to depend on a rigorous selection procedure. The final certificate will be a new 'worker's diploma'. The curriculum of the final year is to be dovetailed to higher education so that graduates will also be enabled to continue their training in a shorter course of higher education. This opportunity to go on to higher education is particularly intended to enhance the attractiveness of the vocational alternative on the education ladder. If they chose this path to their degree, future engineers will have simultaneously completed their training as skilled workers.

So far there has been a considerable degree of uncertainty as regards the functional dividing line between the lycée and the college. It is not even clear whether their parallel existence is due to specific skill profiles or rather to vested interests of the responsible bodies involved in their setting up (despite the amalgamation of the various education administration machineries in 1988). The somewhat controversial position of the specialized secondary schools or technicums between higher education and vocational education cannot be discussed in detail here. It is obvious, however, that the dividing line between the training of technicians and qualified workers and thus between the vocational school and the technicum has become blurred as an increasing number of technicum graduates take on positions as skilled workers. This has resulted from a lack of suitable jobs for technicians or from better pay or from the demand for higher qualifications in modern occupations.[24] Figures given for 1986 indicate that over 20 per cent of those trained as technicians were working in blue-collar jobs in industry.[25] What the quantitative development of the two types of higher training will be like cannot yet be surmised. Variability of educational provision and variety of organizational forms are, however, among the new catchwords of state educational policy-making in the Soviet Union. The intention is gradually to eliminate rigid centralized manpower planning, with individual demand for education and the regional labour market as the regulating factors.

CURRICULAR CHANGES

The envisaged structural changes place new demands on curriculum development, making new approaches necessary. Amongst the curricular problems confronting the planners in 1984 was the tension between centrally oriented, state-guided curriculum development, with its concern for uniformity of form and content, and the varying requirements of individual regions or branches of the economy. The post-1984 curriculum reform retained the traditional bureaucratic principle of uniformity. The new curricula for individual occupations were devised centrally and adhered largely to uniform structural features. Especially in the case of general education as part of the SPTU curriculum, the principle of uniformity was taken to extreme lengths: common standards of general education were expected to demonstrate the equality of the various types of school at the upper secondary level. Both the range of subjects and the content of the general secondary school were to apply to the vocational schools as well. Within the SPTU, the range and structure of general education subjects was likewise identical for all occupations. Thus the SPTU was, to a large degree, marked by the mere joining together of the general school and the PTU curricula.

In contrast, from the point of view of the theory of vocational education, a closer linkage of general and vocational curriculum elements was demanded, as the various occupational fields place different demands on general education according to the dominant type of work and the technological processes involved. Batyshev, for example, deduced from this the necessity to differentiate according to specific occupations and specializations in both technological and general academic SPTU courses. Among other things, he suggested extra mathematics and physics for occupations in the metalwork industry and additional chemistry and biology for agricultural ones.[26] Such ideas were seen to contradict not only the dominant educational goal of the basic equality of all secondary school certificates but also the vocational school's official function of promoting the all-round development of its pupils rather than merely 'training workers as the bearers of certain occupations'.[27]

This lack of flexibility in the curriculum concept undoubtedly contributed to the SPTU's inability to fulfil the role allotted to it by the 1984 reform and to the reform's failure in this sector. It also jeopardized the socially and politically motivated goal of 'secondary schooling for all'. The original enthusiasm was soon followed by the realization that a considerable number of SPTU students were unable to meet the rigorous performance targets of the general education curriculum alongside those of the vocational training subjects. In the wake of glasnost it was finally officially acknowledged that 'a large number of graduates' acquired the secondary education certificate without meeting the required standard.[28]

The new conception of vocational training has adopted the demand for greater integration of general and vocational curriculum elements which are specific to individual occupations or groups of occupations.[29] In the context of the general principles of flexibility and diversity of approaches to curriculum construction, attention is also being paid to various ethnic and national cultural traditions and to special conditions of local industry. Thus the new generation of curricula is to break with the tenet of uniformity and the 'strict regulation of educational content'[30] and is to adopt a curriculum structure founded on official specification of basic requirements and guidelines only. Within this framework there will be a considerable decentralization of decision-making powers, enhancing the responsibilities of the republics on the one hand and of the individual vocational school on the other. Thus various components of the curriculum will be determined by the central and republic authorities and others by local bodies. The basic parameters as laid down in the new conception form the starting point for working out experimental model curricula at the central level or by the republic authorities.[31] The curricula are to combine a number of basic common features with a variety of structural approaches. SPTUs are actively encouraged and given the scope to develop their own 'tailor-made' curricula and syllabuses, taking into account the specific requirements of the 'customers' within local industry. The SPTU's flexibility in constructing curricula is to be increased both by enabling it to introduce its own optional courses and by allowing it to alter and vary the vocational contents to fit specific requirements. The problems ensuing from increased flexibility obviously lie in the fact that it becomes even more difficult to guarantee generally binding standards for the qualifications offered.

Within the minimum requirements determined by the central authorities, more emphasis is to be laid on the humanities. Instruction in mathematics and the natural sciences is to pay greater attention to practical application, thus bringing these subjects closer to those involving technological knowledge. This marks a new approach to the integration of vocational and general education in the curriculum, indicating that the SPTU is still regarded as the mainstay of the vocational education system. On the whole, a shift of emphasis in favour of theoretical components can be observed whilst practical training on the shop floor seems to be allotted a more peripheral role. The reason for this is that the authors of the reform 'Conception' are particularly mindful of those innovative occupations of modern industry whose content places growing demands on theoretical knowledge. Whether an appropriate and well-balanced relationship between theoretical and practical training can be found remains to be seen. It will probably have to be worked out at the interface of the individual PTU and the enterprise. Likewise, it is still necessary to find a clearly defined mechanism for dividing responsibilities among the various decision-making levels.

Another central problem, particularly relevant in view of the above-mentioned issues, has as yet not been satisfactorily solved and can be only briefly mentioned here.[32] It is the question of how to define those trades and specialisms for which training courses are to be given at the various levels of the vocational-technical school and within the other forms of training. The list of such occupations, containing job descriptions, skill requirements and entrance requirements, is a government document, which is used as the basis for constructing curricula for the individual specialisms. There is a total of 7,000 different trades and specialisms within the Soviet economy. In the mid-1980s, however, the SPTU was providing training for some 1,600 occupations – a qualification for the others can only be acquired on the shop floor. In either case, these are generally narrowly specialized jobs as required in the various branches of industry. The mass of pupils in the SPTU are concentrated in no more than about 200 occupations comprising 87 per cent of all graduates.[33]

In the 1970s vocational education research and, subsequently, the vocational school itself started to integrate narrowly specialized but related occupations into new, so-called 'broad-profile' occupations. Training for such occupations is to make the worker more independent and mobile within his or her occupational sphere. In the process of formulating these occupations special attention has been paid to finding definitions not limited just to one branch of industry. In 1987 the list of occupations already contained some 600 such combined specialisms.[34] Since the introduction of modern technological equipment and the reorganization of work in the enterprises has been a slow process so far, opportunities for integration will be limited for some time to come.

PTU–ENTERPRISE LINKS

Under the 1984 reform the enterprises or their supervisory industrial agencies have retained their powers to decide on the allocation of investments for setting up vocational-technical schools. Thus the decision to establish new vocational schools or to expand existing ones may be governed by the specific needs of the enterprise or agency, although planning must be carried out jointly with vocational training administrative bodies. Each school continues to be attached to a so-called 'base enterprise' which functions as a sponsor whilst the school retains its organizational independence. This mainly entails the enterprise providing the facilities for pupils' practical training and making contributions in the social sphere, e.g. subsidizing a student hostel or students' meals. In turn, the PTU provides training in line with the qualification requirements of the base enterprise, on which its specialist profile and course specialisms thus primarily depend.

Needless to say, the relationship between PTU and enterprise is not always harmonious and the close links to the base enterprise can even present an obstacle to efficient training. The main complaint directed at the enterprises is that they fail to provide the facilities necessary for an up-to-date technological standard of training. This applies particularly to the technologically innovative spheres where rising costs reduce the enterprises' willingness to provide the schools with modern equipment for training purposes.[35] The consequences are an obsolescent collection of machines in the schools as well as neglected school buildings. The legal regulations concerning the enterprises' obligations have evidently proved to be too weak and are frequently interpreted as not binding. Thus the provision of proper facilities seems to depend largely on the subjective attitude of enterprise managers towards vocational training.

The new economic mechanism embedded in the recent enterprise law also offered an opportunity to reorganize the relationship between school and enterprise by making the school less dependent on the enterprise. The educational reform concepts and new legislation point in the same direction. Vocational education administrators used the logic of the enterprise law to argue that not only should the technological equipment and other resources be funded by the enterprise, but also the cost of producing qualified workers should be subject to the principle of profitability and self-funding.[36] The financing of training would thus be shifted from the state budget to the enterprises employing the workers (only some of the eligible enterprises actually function as base enterprises). This would force the enterprises to plan their qualification requirements more carefully and to employ graduates more rationally and in accordance with their qualifications.

In this mode, which was at first received with great enthusiasm by vocational education decision-makers, the connection between school and enterprise is to be based on a formal contract between both parties. This is to stipulate on the one hand the skills to be provided by the vocational school, and on the other the funds to be provided by the enterprise to cover the cost of the facilities required by the school. Such an arrangement alters not only the form of funding but also the financial opportunities of the vocational school. The schools will generally sign contracts with a number of enterprises which they have to find themselves, thus acquiring an income of their own which is no longer dependent on the goodwill of a single base enterprise. Even though the contract may not entail the abandoning of the principle of the base enterprise, it promises to release the vocational schools from their dependence on enterprises and economic branch administration agencies.

Some of the vocational-technical sector's visions of being able to form a kind of independent economic unit in the future are, however, way ahead of economic and educational reality. The introduction of a comprehensive system of direct contracts presupposes a sufficient number of enterprises functioning according to the self-financing system, and it will take time to achieve. Central issues, such as tax incentives for enterprises providing training, which are anchored in the enterprise law, have scarcely been touched on. For this reason state funding of vocational training is for the time being indispensable if a qualitatively and quantitatively satisfactory provision of training is to be made at all. Budget deficits and the general financial crisis, however, cast serious doubt on the government's ability to fulfil this task.

CONCLUDING REMARKS

The problems of vocational training for which the reform is to find a solution are rooted partly in long-term historical developments still affecting the present. They have also, however, been partly triggered off by perestroika and the dynamics of socio-economic change that it set in motion. Since 1984 one of the main issues has been the restructuring of the upper secondary stage and the defining of the function of general and vocational schools. The notion of integrating vocational and general education as envisaged by the 1984 reform has proved too rigid in the way it was conceived, and the regulating of the flow of students through bureaucratic planning mechanisms has not proved feasible either.

The reform ran aground on other factors, too, which continue to affect the new reform conception. With regard to perestroika these are possibly even more serious, particularly where it is a question of modernizing training and improving its quality. One of these factors is, for example, the lack of material resources for training and its underfunding, which likewise affects the quality of the teaching staff. Another problem area is the attitudes of large parts of industry and the employment system to vocational training, as these have often proved to be either ambivalent or even downright uncooperative. Under changing economic circumstances, as envisaged by the aims of perestroika, managers seem to be guided even more in their attitudes to training policies and programmes by short-term interests and economic considerations.

Besides the differences in the various branches of the economy, one must take account of the considerable regional differences in the stage reached in the expansion of the vocational education system. Thus the general impression of vocational education being enmeshed in a crisis needs to be more carefully differentiated, and special regional investigations are essential for obtaining a realistic picture of the reform of Soviet vocational education and its chances of success.

The above-mentioned framework factors, to which others could be added and on some of which educational policy-makers have little or no influence, are a considerable burden for the implementation of the new reform strategies. The as yet unsolved relationship between the elements of a planned economy and those approaching the conditions of a market economy likewise presents additional pitfalls. With the more liberal policy of educational choice at the upper secondary stage and more achievement-oriented differentiation, the vocational-technical schools face difficulties in holding their position. Their popularity will depend largely on whether they succeed in achieving the competitiveness for their graduates on the labour market which the new reform conception for the first time proclaims as an aim of vocational education, and which gains in importance at a time of increasing unemployment among young people.

NOTES AND REFERENCES

1 E.M. Kozhevnikov, 'Razvitie srednego obrazovaniya v SSSR: problemy i perspektivy', *Sovetskaya pedagogika*, 1985, no. 3, p. 28.
2 This paper is largely based on the results of a research project carried out at the Comparative Education Research Unit, Ruhr University, Bochum. For a full report see F. Kuebart, 'Union der Sozialistischen Sowjetrepubliken', in W. Hörner, F. Kuebart and B. Himmel, *Technisch-ökonomischer Wandel und Reformen in der Berufs- und Allgemeinbildung sozialistischer Staaten – Deutsche Demokratische Republik, Sowjetunion, Polen, Tschechoslowakei*, Bochum, Arbeitsstelle für vergleichende Bildungsforschung, 1989, pp. 81–170.
3 See, for example, O. Anweiler, 'Die sowjetische Schul- und Berufsbildungsreform von 1984', *Osteuropa*, 1984, vol. 34, pp. 839–60; B.B. Szekely, 'The new Soviet educational reform', *Comparative Education Review*, 1986, vol. 30, pp. 321–43; J. Dunstan, 'Equalisation and differentiation in the Soviet school 1958–1985: a curriculum approach', in J. Dunstan (ed.), *Soviet Education under Scrutiny*, Glasgow, Jordanhill College Publications, 1987, pp. 32–69; O. Anweiler and F. Kuebart, 'Berufsausbildung in der Sowjetunion im Schnittpunkt pädagogischer Ziele und ökonomischer Interessen', *Osteuropa*, 1988, vol. 38, pp. 562–77.
4 See for the curriculum concept F. Kuebart, 'School reform, technological modernisation of the economy and vocational training in the Soviet Union', in Dunstan (ed.), op. cit., pp. 70–87.
5 See, for example, M.N. Rutkevich and L.Ya. Rubina, *Obshchestvennye potrebnosti, sistema obrazovaniya, molodezh'*, Moscow, Politizdat, 1988, p. 113.
6 F.R. Filippov, 'Sotsial'nye garantii effektivnoi zanyatosti', *Sotsiologicheskie issledovaniya*, 1988, no. 5, p. 27.
7 M.Kh. Titma (ed.), *Nachalo puti. Pokolenie so srednim obrazovaniem*, Moscow, Nauka, 1989, p. 6.
8 V. Kontorovich, 'Labor problems and the prospects for accelerated growth', in M. Friedberg and H. Isham (eds), *Soviet Society under Gorbachev: Current Trends and the Prospects for Reform*, Armonk, NY and London, M.E. Sharpe, 1987, pp. 30–51.
9 A. Novikov, 'Povtoryat' proidennoe ne nado', *Uchitel'skaya gazeta*, 6 August 1987, p.3.
10 Titma (ed.), op. cit., pp. 49, 78.
11 A. Dumachev, 'Lomat'-to legche . . . Chto zhdet proftekhshkolu', *Pravda*, 29 December 1987, p. 3.
12 *Vestnik statistiki*, 1988, no. 8, p. 66.
13 *Izvestiya*, 1 July 1987, pp. 1–4.
14 Filippov, op. cit., p. 27; Titma (ed.), op. cit., p. 90.
15 *Materialy plenuma Tsentral'nogo Komiteta KPSS, 17–18 fevralya 1988 goda*, Moscow, Politizdat, 1988, pp. 20, 64.

16 Vsesoyuznyi s"ezd rabotnikov narodnogo obrazovaniya, *Kontseptsiya nepreryvnogo obrazovaniya*, [Moscow], 1988; this document was finally approved by the State Committee for Public Education of the USSR and the All-Union Education Council on 18 March 1989.
17 Gosudarstvennyi Komitet SSSR po narodnomu obrazovaniyu, *Kontseptsiya professional'no-tekhnicheskogo obrazovaniya*, Leningrad, 1989.
18 ibid., p. 10.
19 A. Zvontsov, 'Kvalifikatsiya: firmennye garantii', *Professional'no-tekhnicheskoe obrazovanie* (hereafter *PTO*), 1989, no. 2, p. 83.
20 B.D. Breev, *Chelovek i proizvodstvo*, Moscow, Mysl', 1989, p. 218; M.A. Kovrigin, *Obnovlenie rabochikh kadrov*, Moscow, Mysl', 1989, p. 115 *et passim.*
21 Kovrigin, op. cit., p. 180.
22 L.A. Kostin (ed.), *Upravlenie trudovymi resursami. Spravochnoe posobie*, Moscow, Ekonomika, 1987, p. 141; N.I. Latysh, *Trud i professional'naya podgotovka molodezhi*, Minsk, Universitetskoe, 1987, p. 95.
23 *Izvestiya*, 21 January 1989 and 28 October 1989.
24 D.I. Chuprunov, *Spetsialisty srednego zvena. Planirovanie, podgotovka, ispol'zovanie*, Moscow, Ekonomika, 1984, p. 120.
25 S.Ya. Batyshev, *Reforma professional'noi shkoly. Opyt, poisk, zadachi, puti realizatsii*, Moscow, Vysshaya shkola, 1987, p. 11.
26 ibid., p. 102.
27 V.V. Shapkin, *Obshchetekhnicheskaya podgotovka kvalifitsirovannykh rabochikh v usloviyakh nauchno-tekhnicheskoi revolyutsii*, Moscow, Vysshaya shkola, 1985, p. 112.
28 'Dopusk v zavtrashnii den'', *PTO*, 1987, no. 9, p. 3.
29 For theoretical considerations underlying the integration approach see A.P. Beyaeva, 'Integratsiya soderzhaniya professional'no-tekhnicheskogo obrazovaniya', *Sovetskaya pedagogika*, 1989, no. 1, pp. 86–9.
30 Gosudarstvennyi Komitet SSSR, op. cit., p. 7.
31 For examples of model curricula for the SPTUs developed at the central level and by the education authorities of the Russian Republic (RSFSR) respectively see A. Leibovich, 'Model' uchebnogo plana: poiski i nakhodki', *PTO*, 1989, no. 4, pp. 14–18 and K. Kyazimov, 'Uchebnyi plan: model' Rossii', *PTO*, 1989, no. 7, pp. 23–8.
32 For more details, see Kuebart, 1989, op. cit., pp. 118–25.
33 'Dopusk k zavtrashnii den'', op. cit.
34 ibid., p. 2.
35 V.A. Kaznacheev, 'Put' iz zony zastoya', *Molodoi kommunist*, 1987, no. 12, pp. 49–55; Dumachev, op. cit.
36 A. Dumachev, 'PTO v zerkale NTR', *PTO*, 1986, no. 6, pp. 2–8; 'PTO: voprosy otkrytye i zakrytye', *PTO*, 1988, no. 4, pp. 2–9.

9

DEBATE AND CONTROVERSY IN SOVIET HIGHER EDUCATION REFORM: REINVENTING A SYSTEM

Stephen T. Kerr

INTRODUCTION

It has been four years since the promulgation of a wide-ranging reform programme for the Soviet system of higher education. During that time, much has changed in Soviet society in general, and there have been some changes in higher education. None the less, serious problems remain. At the moment, it seems clear that the reforms as originally proposed and adopted cannot be carried out in anything like the ways originally conceived. Indeed, given current conditions in Soviet society, it may be better that the original reforms not be put into practice exactly as foreseen. In fact, the entire reform of 1986–7 might well be seen as a kind of 'last gasp' of old-style Soviet educational decision-making, and the predecessor for changes now under way that may mould the educational system into new forms.

The review here starts with a look at educational reform in the Gorbachev era. The higher education reform of 1986–7 is then considered, and the attempts to put it into effect are chronicled. Next, some specific recent developments in higher education since 1987 are examined, with a highlight on the rise of a social agenda superseding the economic focus that was primary when the original reform proposals were made. Finally, the conclusion identifies two dilemmas with which reformers must cope. Solution of these is necessary for deeper reform efforts to take effect.

EDUCATIONAL REFORM AND PERESTROIKA

Reform of higher education is only one of the shifts in the Soviet education system that M.S. Gorbachev has pushed since coming to power in 1985. A general school reform that was crafted in 1984–5 was at least partly Gorbachev's own doing and showed at an early point his desire to go beyond tinkering with the balance between vocational and academic tracks that had characterized many reform efforts since the 1940s.[1] Among other elements, the school reform of 1984–5 proposed providing some support for

Soviet working mothers by reducing the school starting-age from seven to six, thus presumably opening up thousands of slots in the day care system that had been occupied by 6-year-olds. A strong shift in emphasis away from advanced and specialized secondary education and toward lower-level vocational education was intended to improve the mix of native-Russian-speaking workers in the industrial heartland of the USSR and thus hopefully revive moribund, labour-intensive Soviet factories. And a new nationwide course in computer literacy was established (see Chapter 3) to show parents and educators that there could indeed be new things done in schools. The last of these changes was reportedly Gorbachev's own idea.

Whatever else they were intended to do, this school reform and the reform proposals for higher education that followed it by two years were at their heart economic. More than anything else, they were tied to the inefficiencies that the Soviet system had developed in training, assigning and updating its millions of workers. Education was to be improved, but with an eye principally toward how it could better serve the economy, how it could alleviate regional labour shortages in key industries, and how new technologies could find their way more rapidly into the workplace through industry–education collaboration. In vision and intent, the reforms of both general and higher education were consummately traditional Soviet plans – centrally developed, conservative in form and substance, submitted for popular inspection through controlled discussion in the press, and designed ultimately to change little in the structure of the system of education itself.

THE HIGHER EDUCATION REFORM OF 1986–7

In early 1986 there was published a draft document describing a proposed thoroughgoing reform of the Soviet system of higher education. After discussion in the press, a final version appeared in April 1987.[2] Since this proposal defined the landscape with regard to change in higher education, it makes sense for us briefly to review here its main provisions. For the purposes of the review that follows, the ten sections contained in the original reform plan are collapsed into three main themes: higher education and the economy; the form, content, and processes of higher education; and improved organization and administration of higher education.

Higher education and the economy

The 1986–7 reform put improvement of the economy in first place and stressed that this was the primary reason for undertaking the reform. The relationship among institutions of higher education, planning agencies, and firms and factories in the country's industrial sector was to be significantly altered. Graduates (*spetsialisty*) were to be trained in a more carefully co-ordinated fashion so that their skills would be both up to date and relevant to current industrial needs. Institutes and universities were to be encouraged to enter into long-term collaborative research and development activities through establishment of joint 'scientific-instructional-production combines'. Some of the funding for these was to come from government, but some was also to come from the firms and factories themselves – a form of self-financing *khozraschet* applied to universities' work. More (and more frequent) opportunities were to be provided for workers to receive continuing education and skill updating on the job. Such retraining was to be made available for three months every five years, with higher education forced to assume responsibility for workers' productive capabilities throughout their entire careers. Academic staff at institutions of higher education were to gain new skills and to sharpen old ones by taking 'practical sabbaticals' involving work in industry.

The form, content and processes of higher education

The reform recognized that changes needed to be made also in the ways in which students were taught, in the resources and facilities that supported students' work, and in the ways in which students were evaluated. Students quite clearly had not been very pleased with the day-to-day experience of education in classrooms of universities and institutes, nor had the professorate been satisfied with student entry-level preparation or abilities. The 1986–7 reform proposed tighter standards for admission to higher educational institutions (*vuzy*), and more leeway for administrators to dismiss those students unable to make satisfactory progress. Instructional programmes in the various defined specialisms were to be restructured to include more independent study and fewer weekly hours of lectures, and generally were to shift from narrow specialized training to 'broad-profile' preparation. Accompanying this, however, was a demand that graduates also be more able to step right into productive responsibilities in the workplace, and so arrangements were to be made with individual factories to join in the 'goal-directed preparation of specialists' (*tselevaya podgotovka spetsialistov*). Some specific subjects were singled out as areas where virtually all graduates would need more support than they had been getting – foreign languages and computer science were noted. And, perhaps as a sop to the traditionalists, there was to be new emphasis on finding better and less dogmatic ways to teach ideology, including practical experience through enhanced and more truly responsible student government.

Improved organization and administration of higher education

The 1986–7 reform also foresaw the need to make rather substantial changes in the organization and administration of institutions of higher education. Paradoxically, one such shift was to a more centralized form of planning in the hope of eventually encouraging a less bureaucratic, less centrally directed system. Coordination and control of general policies was to be taken out of the hands of individual ministries and centrally determined by the Ministry of Higher and Specialized Secondary Education (absorbed since March 1988 into the State Committee on Public Education, along with the former Ministry of Education and former State Committee on Vocational Education). Regional methodological centres for instructional development were to be established at leading institutions so as to help weaker *vuzy* to make changes in their ways of teaching. Additionally, academic staff were to receive new powers of self-government, including the power to elect rectors; they also were to receive added support in the form of defined programmes of study leading to the doctorate and better research and instructional facilities (laboratories, computers, audio-visual equipment), and were to have the opportunity to define locally a portion of the curriculum in any given specialism. Improvements were to be made in evaluation of academic staff, administrators and institutions at all levels. This was to extend all the way to a rector's right to establish, where needed, annual 'qualification' competitions for all academic posts – the equivalent of abolishing tenure and requiring a kind of annual probationary trial.

THE HIGHER EDUCATION REFORM SINCE 1987: CHANGE AND STASIS

In the three years since the higher education reform was finalized, changes have taken place in Soviet institutions of higher education. A few of those changes have followed the programme laid out in the 1987 reform document, while during the same period other shifts have occurred that reflect the rapid evolution of Soviet society more generally. For higher education, the results have been disappointing. The changes anticipated in the 1987 reform have been slow to come, partly because of the innate conservatism of portions of the educational system, and partly because the reform was predicated on the creation of new kinds of administrative and economic structures that have proved immensely difficult to bring into being, again because of the basic conservatism of portions of the social and economic system. In reviewing what has happened, it will be useful to organize the first part of the discussion around the changes proposed in the 1987 programme and the three rubrics identified above.

Higher education and the economy since 1987

While the 1987 reform foresaw great changes in the ways that *vuzy* and industry would interact, it has become quite clear that the difficulties in fostering such interaction are much stronger than originally thought. It is true that a good many (500) branch *vuz* departments have been established in

149

workplaces, and that some fifty-five *vuzy* have established 100 joint 'scientific-instructional-production combines'.[3] But problems persist; a poignant article by S.K. Yakubovich, a frustrated instructor at Kuibyshev Polytechnic Institute who tried to set up such a unit, suggests the scope of difficulties. Although a combine was established and a special instructional centre created to link the institute with schools and industry, the author makes it clear that such activities are just not high enough on the priority list of industry to gain much attention: 'There were discussions in various organizations, and diametrically opposed positions appeared, but further talks didn't move things forward. There were no definitive decisions and no help in practical matters.'[4]

Those in higher education perhaps naturally lay the blame for such problems with their would-be colleagues in industry. In a 1989 interview with A.A. Logunov, Rector of Moscow State University, factory managers are excoriated as the principal barrier to economic development. Universities, notes Logunov, have by virtue of their scientific heritage and research focus a 'stake' in pushing back the frontiers of knowledge and practice. But factories are often still monopolies controlled centrally by a ministry, and hence have no incentive to change. Further independence for firms and factories may therefore be a precondition for further development of the kinds of relationships depicted in the reform document.[5]

The attempts to improve the quality and quantity of research done at universities and institutes have also met with mixed success. While billions of roubles have been invested for new research, some institutes actually do *less* research now than they did previously. The Karaganda Cooperative Institute, for example, saw its funded research drop from 90,000 to 50,000 roubles from 1986 to 1988, while academic staff published an average of only 1.2 article pages per year.[6] One government estimate suggested that only 5 per cent of *vuzy* are at a 'world level', and only 20 per cent are in a position to contribute actively to the country's further economic development. A full 60 per cent of all research is conducted at 60–70 of the leading institutions (out of more than 800 nationwide).[7] Academics also seem recalcitrant about the initiatives to engage them more directly in practical work. A staff member at the Novosibirsk Electrotechnical Institute noted that attempts there to restructure the curriculum, so as to involve students with local firms, required an initial 'scientific reorientation of the institute's researchers'.[8] Grekova and Myshkis (1988) decried the lack of thoughtfulness about either teaching or research on the part of many staff, casting them as 'school-type instructors'.[9]

Problems have also persisted in the attempt to train graduates more effectively to step directly into productive roles in the economy. If industry is to bear more of the costs of preparing specialisms, argue some, then a more precise accounting is needed of the educational costs for various specialisms; engineering education is a particularly problematic case, since it is both expensive and critical to economic development, yet even estimating demand for engineers under the new system of factory–*vuz* collaboration is very difficult.[10] The arguments suggest a continuing desire for precision and control in the old style, and less recognition than one might expect of the effectiveness of market mechanisms as a method for dealing with the uncertainties in calculating both costs and rewards of training.

Revision of the officially defined preparation plans for specialisms has also been difficult. Although the absolute number of specialisms has been reduced by 27 per cent (to 301, in thirty-one groups), ministries and *vuzy* have resisted radical changes in a system whose rewards and penalties are well understood by all.[11] Coming to an agreement on new specialism definitions also means agreeing on how the work to be done in firms is to be defined, and this kind of task analysis is exacting and time-consuming,[12] to say nothing of its being potentially threatening.

There have also been sharp disagreements about the role of the *vuz* in providing continuing education. It appears that there is a trend toward providing more continuing education opportunities through the so-called People's Universities (*narodnye universitety*), a network of continuing education sites which has been in existence since the 1920s but which has recently come to assume more of a role in updating the knowledge of teachers, medical and legal personnel, and other white-collar workers.[13] Figures based on the 1987 roster of those institutions (Table 9.1) suggest, first, that more such institutions have been created recently (of the total of almost 48,000, more than 22,000, or 46 per cent, have been founded since 1980) and, second, that more recently established *narodnye universitety* tend to favour one-year courses of study over two- or three-year courses. This trend is even more pronounced in urban locations, suggesting that these institutions are to cope with some of the demand for continuing education that the *vuzy* are unable or unwilling to meet.

Some would like to see a new system of continuing education arise with strong links to individual firms, providing the worker with flexible habits of thought so as to allow future problems to be dealt with easily 'as happens now in the USA'. But such a system cannot be expected to arise on its own; 'natural regulation' can only lead to disaster.[14] Indeed, one gets a strong sense that there persists among those making key decisions a set of tacit, somewhat wistful assumptions about the nature of the relationships between higher education and the economy: 'If only we could understand the links better,' they seem to be saying, 'we could really determine how best to plan and direct the preparation of students.' This assumption not only that there is 'one best system' but also that it is one amenable to rational calculation, correction and control is a powerful determinant of official behaviour on the part of *vuz* administrators, government functionaries, and industry representatives. Only a few officials appear willing to make a further leap in conceptualizing a continuing education system which would strengthen the connections among education, science, and society at the same time as it would encourage self-development and initiative.[15]

151

Table 9.1 Changes in People's Universities, USSR, 1970–87

Institution organized	1970 and earlier	1971– 1975	1976– 1980	1981– 1985	1986– 1987	Total
Number of institutions (thousands)						
Urban	4.9	5.1	9.8	10.2	6.2	36.2
Rural	0.9	1.4	3.5	3.7	2.0	11.5
Total	5.8	6.5	13.3	13.9	8.2	47.7
Length of programme of study (percentage of institutions offering)						
Urban						
One year	48	49	52	54	64	54
Two year	41	39	34	34	30	35
Three year	11	12	14	12	6	11
Rural						
One year	42	40	39	38	51	41
Two year	39	39	34	35	37	36
Three year	19	21	27	27	12	23
Total						
One year	47	47	49	50	61	51
Two year	41	39	34	34	32	35
Three year	12	14	17	16	7	14

Source: 'Narodnye universitety v SSSR', *Vestnik statistiki,* 1988, no. 3, p. 79.

The form, content and processes of higher education since 1987

Some serious steps have been taken to improve the experience of students in higher education, principally by identifying those least likely to profit from it. While improved evaluation was a key feature of the 1986–7 reform proposals, officials in the system of higher education must have been shocked by the information that began to be collected and disseminated about the sorry state of preparation among many *vuz* students. Statistics suggest that standards have been tightened up, allowing fewer students to gain entry into higher education (Table 9.2).

Unfortunately, the tightened standards have meant that the proportion of workers' and collective farmers' children among students continued to decline. During this period, fewer places were made available in engineering

Table 9.2 Vuz student admissions and social origins, USSR, 1988–9

	1988	1989
Entrance examination pass-rate (%)	57.3	52.1
Applicants per 100 openings	202.4[a]	235.9
Students from worker families (%)	44.3	42.5
Students from collective farmer families (%)	6.9	6.6

Source: 'Nekotorye itogi priema v vuzy', *Vestnik vysshei shkoly,* 1989, no. 12, p. 89.
[a] Another source, *Narodnoe obrazovanie i kul'tura v SSSR,* Moscow, Finansy i statistika, 1989, p. 229, puts the overall figure at 192 (Ed.).

generally, probably in an attempt to 'dry up' a field that had become over-crowded with poorly prepared graduates, but more openings were made available in engineering-related 'deficit specialisms' such as instrument design and production.

Even more shocking are the figures that have emerged indicating the abysmally low levels of preparation of secondary school graduates in certain parts of the country. When externally administered achievement tests were given to students at the Karaganda Cooperative Institute, for example, not one student passed the exam in 'Trade in the Non-Food Sector', while 97 per cent failed a companion course in 'Trade in Food Goods', and 73 per cent failed economics. Of students on the book-keeping course, 92 per cent proved unable to answer correctly basic 'sixth-form-type' questions regarding percentages. And 62 per cent of first- and second-year students failed 'fifth-form-type' dictation work.[16] A similar evaluation report, based on a sample of 16,000 students from 63 *vuzy* around the country in October 1987, found that 25 per cent failed basic secondary-level exams in mathematics, physics, chemistry, biology and history of the CPSU. High school students, noted the author with disapproval, are now apparently accustomed to 'lightning-like learning' but they also forget the material just as fast.[17]

Pedagogical approaches in higher education have been discussed extensively in the press. Some observers note that the entire existing system is geared toward a traditional, 'group-focused' instruction in which subject matter is completely pre-defined for both teacher and student. Those who try to go beyond the usual face difficulties not only with administrators but also with party, Komsomol, trade union, and legal (*yuriskonsul'ty*) officials, who are disinclined to admit the possibility of new approaches.[18] That students and lower-level academic staff find daunting the prospects of trying to bring about real change in their own classes is not surprising; traditionalism abounds in higher education, even at a time when it is being shed or at least disguised in other parts of society. Consider, for example, the subject priorities established for continuing education of teachers in 1988: in the number one position was 'party-mindedness' (*partiinost*'),[19] a ranking for that topic that many teachers would have found laughable at best.

One clear barrier to teachers in higher education wishing to improve their instructional approaches is lack of time and facilities. Indeed, the crushing teaching loads that many academic staff must cope with would seem to prevent much out-of-class experimentation at all: Kigel' notes that the proposed reduction in numbers of students at *vuzy* has not occurred; instead, their numbers at many institutions have risen, but numbers of instructors have remained constant, resulting in *increased* loads.[20] For a beginning-level lecturer (*assistent*), the typical load is 800–1000 class contact hours per year (rough US equivalent: 9–11 courses per semester), all for the munificent wage of 233 roubles per month. Nor have graduate students been provided with the basic course on instructional techniques that they were promised as part of the 1987 reform package. While some *vuzy* offer an open 'pedagogical seminar', some see a more organized approach stressing the works of such theorists as Vygotsky and Davydov as more valuable.[21]

With the growth of glasnost, it should not be surprising that surveys of students' opinions and values have increasingly appeared in the press. One of these makes it clear that those goals of the 1987 reform that dealt with improvement of students' living conditions have still not been satisfied: better access to goods and housing topped the list of concerns, as Table 9.3 demonstrates.

Another survey asked both students and staff to indicate their feelings about reform of the educational system itself. Some 95 per cent of both staff and students approved of the idea, but only 16 per cent of staff (24 per cent of students) approved of the ways in which change was actually being carried out.[22]

Table 9.3 Soviet student concerns, April–May 1988 (per cent)

Improved living standards (goods, housing)	80
Lawfulness in society	72
Social democracy	68
Better services	62

Source: 'Sotsial'nyi oblik studenta', *Vestnik vysshei shkoly*, 1989, no. 10, p. 75 (at 57 *vuzy* in 52 towns).

Organization and administration of higher education since 1987

One clear goal of the 1987 reforms was to provide rectors with the power to review academic staff on a regular basis, and to have the power also to remove those who were not productive. The prospect, needless to say, was not attractive to academics, but administrators (and some staff) clearly felt that it was needed. Application of the corresponding power, however, has not been uniform: of the 400,000 academic staff in *vuzy* around the country, some 1,500 (full) professors (*professora*) and 5,000 senior lecturers or associate professors (*dotsenty*) were evaluated between September 1987 and June 1988.[23] This represents less than 2 per cent of all academic staff members nationally, and perhaps reflects more accurately the real intent of the new laws: to give rectors the opportunity to remove the most egregious cases of 'dead wood'. As a professor at the Lenin Pedagogical Institute in Moscow noted, 'It's no secret that competition for reselection [of staff] doesn't occur if there's no conflict with the administration', and if there is a conflict, why should the administration wait five years to resolve it? The new system, he noted, only increases the kind of cringing attitude toward 'bosses' that was common thirty years ago.[24]

The material conditions faced by teachers and students in *vuzy* have not improved as had been hoped in 1987. Computers and other 'new technologies' of instruction have become somewhat more widespread, and there have been some visionary statements about their possible role in the long-term improvement of education, including not only instruction but also access to information more generally. There is clearly a hope by some that creating an 'information environment' in educational institutions will reduce the bureaucratic power traditionally wielded by educational bureaucrats.[25] These documents go far beyond the earlier cautious statements about the need for all specialists to be computer-literate, or the still-popular attempts to use computers as glorified testing machines.[26] Practice, once again, lags well behind what the vision suggests. In one institute that was evaluated, students received only 30 *minutes* on a computer per year, a far cry from the minimum of 40 *hours* for non-engineering students suggested in 1987.[27] Anecdotal accounts indicate that computers (especially working ones) are still the exception for academics, to say nothing of students. The second issue of *Poisk (Quest)*, the new newspaper (to be considered below) for workers in higher education, carried an article on 'computer crime' that dealt not with electronic breaking-and-entering or illegal funds transfer but rather with the growing number of thefts of computers and their high value on the black market.[28]

The hoped-for greater integration and control over the activities of the various higher education institutions that was to result from the 1987 reforms has not really materialized at this point. Most of the earlier institutional isolation, the jealous control over individual *vuzy* by ministries, that was to have been done away with by the 1987 reform appears to have remained. Rectors still complain about the flow of instructions and directives from on high, and the fact that they are more and more frequently subject to conflicting requirements from ministries and the State Committee, agencies that may not see eye to eye on what needs to be done in any particular case. There are still far too many instances in which administrators reply, 'The changes have been made!' or 'We've taken measures!', even when nothing has really changed.[29]

One arena in which there has been some notable activity is in the selection of rectors for *vuzy*. Whereas formerly these top administrators were simply appointed to their positions, they are now increasingly elected. Feliks Peregudov, the First Vice-Chairman of the State Committee on Public Education, reported in 1988 that 139 of 898 *vuz* rectors had, at that time, been elected to their positions.[30] Whether election of a key administrator is necessarily the best way to identify top academic leaders is, of course, open to some question. One has to conjecture that in many cases academics will elect administrators who seem not to threaten their own self-interests and who will maintain whatever arrangements and standards have furthered their own careers. And there are many anecdotal reports from Soviet scholars which suggest that this is true in at least some of the cases. It remains to be seen whether tough academic leaders will emerge and be elected if Soviet higher education institutions come to the point of having to make hard choices on their own about, say, the types of research to be conducted, or the numbers of students to be served, or the ways in which internal resources are allocated.

Summary: stasis in a changing context

While the reform of 1987 promised many changes for higher education, it has delivered relatively few. There have been some serious efforts at least to evaluate the sorry state of students' basic preparation and to provide rudimentary opportunities for continuing education. Administrators have gained some new power to distribute resources internally and to call poorly performing academic staff to account. And academics have achieved at least some form of control through rectorial elections. But the large shifts in the relationships among universities, institutes, and the economy that were intended in 1987 have not come to pass, nor have the barriers that would allow new arrangements to flower been removed. Meeting the demand that more and better research be done has been hindered by staff attitudes and the primary constraints of a crushing workload and lack of basic facilities. Public conferences and meetings called to address these issues seem to have had no great effect; the long-awaited National Congress of Education Workers in December 1988 produced few concrete results and left almost as many *vuz* workers dissatisfied as happy.[31] As one critic noted, 'The restructuring of higher education to date has been much like an attempt to turn a cart into a motor car without making radical changes in construction.'[32]

But if bureaucratic fiat and the heritage of the Stalinist 'command-and-administer' system still powerfully determine the dimensions of the possible for those who work in Soviet *vuzy*, there are also some new developments which were not anticipated in the 1987 reforms. This should not be too surprising, since those involved in the reform three years ago could not have foreseen the rapid change that was to take place in other parts of Soviet society between 1987 and 1990.

HIGHER EDUCATION SINCE 1987: THE RISE OF RADICAL RECONSTRUCTIONISM

If the changes intended by the 1987 reform have been slow to materialize, there have been other changes in the intervening three years that have rolled over Soviet institutes and universities, changes connected with the larger shifts taking place in Soviet society, and changes that over the longer run may be more significant for the educational system of the USSR. We will consider briefly here several of these trends.

The appearance of 'informal' groups

One surprising development recently has been the appearance of a number of 'informal' groups, organizations and unions in Soviet academe. These include an Association of *vuz* Teachers and a Union of Scientists paralleling a similar spirited group among school teachers, the Creative Union of Teachers.[33] Institutions and professional societies have also formed new connections and interest groups: an Association of Universities and a Union of Scientific and Engineering Societies have appeared. To date these groups have been concerned mostly with organizing themselves and trying to decide their role. There are indications, however, that they will emerge as a significant set of forces for the government to deal with as they find their own voices.

Even traditional and formal organizations have changed and become more vocal. The appearance in early 1989 of *Poisk*, the aforementioned weekly newspaper for scientists and *vuz* academic staff, has provided a new outlet for these groups. Published under the joint auspices of the Academy of Sciences, the State Committee on Public Education and the Science and Education Workers' Trade Union, the paper is small – typically only eight pages – but the content has been varied and reflects the changing constellation of interests among Soviet academics. The topics covered during the first year of publication might be described as a mixture of the economy, history, and the activities of the new parliament and its various sub-committees, together with reports of 'What's happening in the United States', computer news, portents of ecological disaster and sympathetic stories about new cooperatives.

The emergence of higher education as a political interest group

The establishment of the new Congress of Peoples' Deputies in the spring of 1989, and later of its new Supreme Soviet, was of great interest to those working in higher education, since it suggested the possibility that their voices might at last be heard more clearly by those making critical decisions about allocation of budgetary resources. Almost immediately after the first meetings of the Supreme Soviet, Yu.A. Ryzhov, the Chairman of its Committee on Science, Public Education, Culture and Upbringing, noted that rectors should have more power (especially the chance to redirect financial resources) and that the roles of the State Committee on Education and the Ministry of Finance should be minimized.[34] By early 1990, a formal Academic Deputies' Group had been formed.[35]

Deputies from Soviet universities have not limited their interest to matters of purely academic concern. A notable example is A.A. Sobchak, a professor of jurisprudence at Leningrad State University, and now (1991) Mayor of Leningrad, who entered the limelight in late 1989 as chairman of a special commission to investigate the 'Tragic Circumstances in Tbilisi' in April 1989. Sobchak refused to treat the events lightly; noting that a muddled governmental chain of command and politically 'riskless' decision structure led to the crisis, he demanded that a system be created that would allow responsibility for problems to be assigned clearly.[36] The Deputies' Group has also spoken out on the possibility that national tensions in the USSR could lead to nuclear catastrophe.[37]

A dramatic example of the potential power of higher education as an interest group is seen in a meeting held in Moscow in May 1990. The gathering of several hundred rectors and other top education officials was held under the auspices of the Council of Moscow Rectors and the national Association of Engineering Institutes. Gorbachev attended part of the meeting and admitted that the 1987 reform was a failure. Those present petitioned the government for a promise that their needs would be more carefully addressed and that the position of education on the national agenda would be improved. Avoiding the possibility that higher education institutions might be taxed was one top agenda item; costs of providing education for students was another. While a national rectors' group does not yet formally exist, this meeting may well have set the stage for the creation of such a coalition in the near future.[38]

The creation of a 'civic culture': academics and society

Members of Soviet academe are participating in social organizations other than the political. The sorry state of the environment has been a strong motivator for many scientists and teachers to become more actively concerned about social problems than has been the case in recent memory. Part of the reason may be the sense that if science created the mess, then science has at least some responsibility to clean it up. Management of scientific and technological progress in an economic context has therefore become a key topic for reformers.[39] The desire to foster glasnost has also led to a kind of national conscience-purging on the part of those who have had some hand in concealing the history or current status of the country.[40]

Education in the lower grades has been seen by many as another disaster area, and many professors and other representatives of the intelligentsia have been instrumental on commissions and groups to improve the schools. N.P. Nikolaev, for example, commented on the deep educational problems created over the years of Soviet power, leading ultimately to 'teachers who don't know how to teach and students who don't want to learn'.[41] Metaphorically linking the concern with ecological matters to the situation in the schools, he observed that 'the extinguishing of morality is also a catastrophe and a total crisis for the ecology – the ecology of culture and morals'. The plight of children under conditions of changing family structure, divorce, and drug and alcohol abuse has also surfaced as an issue, and a number of intellectuals have become engaged in seeking solutions.

Schools are one social arena in which Soviet academics have become increasingly active, perhaps because they see the educational bureaucracy as being unusually unresponsive to demands for change. Some see the problems here as simply insoluble.[42] But the radically new VNIK proposal for new curricula and the plan for local school councils have drawn positive responses from academe.[43]

The move towards a market economy

Soviet scholars have joined the budding class of entrepreneurs created by the relaxation of economic controls. The pages of *Vestnik vysshei shkoly* (*Higher Education Courier*) and *Poisk* are routinely occupied with advertisements for the products and services of one or another cooperative. Many of these concern the preparation and installation of computer-based systems, either for instructional purposes[44] or for research. What contribution such cooperatives might make to the economy's need for more serious revitalization remains to be seen.

The reintegration of Soviet science with the international scientific community

It should come as no surprise that Soviet scholars are extremely eager to reintegrate their own work with that of their colleagues elsewhere. There is a palpable longing for contact, for close associations to allow rapid shedding of the paranoid isolation that gripped so many branches of Soviet science during the past fifty years. Computer networks are one tool for doing this, and it is interesting how rapidly initial attempts have sprung up to use such tools to establish new international relationships.[45]

Other new groups have been established in the social sciences, long a dumping ground for the least talented among the Soviet professorate. The

Academy of Sciences has put new emphasis on training in sociology and management. New institutes have been created, for example for the 'Study of the Person'. And discussion of a new Academy of World Civilizations in Moscow noted prominently the role to be played by various religious groups in its creation.[46]

CONCLUSION: HIGHER EDUCATION REFORM AND THE DILEMMAS OF SOCIAL CHANGE

The changes that Soviet higher education planners undertook in 1986–7 have not all come to pass, but there have been other new initiatives affecting Soviet institutions of higher education which were not foreseen at that time. While education has not become the carburettor for the engine of the economy that many hoped, its problems are at least now more clearly recognized and more openly discussed. Academic staff members have become more outspoken and have begun to participate in the country's intellectual and social life in ways not seen since the 1920s. Students too have gained a voice, and their concerns are now listened to more closely than in the recent past. New ventures of various kinds, both internal and international, suggest the ways in which higher education might flower in the future, if given more leeway to do so.

Yet there remain serious contradictions in the attempts to change higher education in the USSR. Two of these – interrelated, but distinct – stand out especially: where ideas about change originate, and where the responsibility for putting changes into practice lies.

'Reform documents' and the future of Soviet education reform

The 1986–7 reform of higher education could come to be seen as the last major reform effort promulgated from above. Events since 1986 have significantly altered the role of formerly omnipotent bodies such as the Communist Party and the ministries and state committees. This is not to say that these groups are now powerless – far from it – because they do in fact still largely control the specifics of any new practices to be introduced. But the sense of 'where new ideas come from' has changed, and it is doubtful now that a reform of the early 1980s variety, promulgated from the centre and instituted after minimal public discussion, could be carried out in quite the same way again. Future reform efforts may represent at least the beginnings of a collaborative effort, still with important input from central planners and government offices, but with new and powerful roles played by the Supreme Soviet and its constituent committees, by the independent associations and unions that now attract an increasing percentage of academic staff and rectors, and by local *vuz* councils and staff groups. The setting of the agenda for higher education will now be a job for many groups, not just one or two.

160

The responsibility for implementing reform

If the source of ideas about reform changes, then too may the sense of where responsibility lies for carrying out reforms in practice. In many of the documents and articles published since the 1987 reform, there is a kind of wistful desire that centralization should be strengthened, just for long enough to allow old practices to be swept aside and new, enlightened models to be put in their place. But as the economy begins to move toward some form of regulated open market, so too may the intellectual market for educational change need to recognize the importance of individual incentives, academic market mechanisms and the legitimacy of individual choices.

Until these contradictions are resolved, it seems unlikely that deep change can occur in Soviet higher education. The mechanisms are now beginning to be put in place that will allow the dilemmas to be addressed, but it will probably take some time for them to become more finely tuned. What has happened in the past few years in the USSR has been the rapid destruction of a system of higher education that people knew and understood, albeit rarely liked. What has yet to emerge is a fully articulated alternative system. Constructing that system will be difficult and frustrating. Soviet teachers and scientists need both good wishes and real collaborative support if the potential of Soviet academic life is to be better realized.

NOTES AND REFERENCES

1 See, for example, J. Dunstan (ed.), *Soviet Education under Scrutiny*, Glasgow, Jordanhill College Publications, 1987; S.T. Kerr, 'Reform in Soviet and American education: parallels and contrasts', *Phi Delta Kappan*, 1989, vol. 71, no. 1, pp. 19–28; B. Szekely (ed.), 'The adoption of new Soviet school reforms', *Soviet Education*, 1985, vol. 27, no. 5, pp. 1–102.
2 For further details on the plan and the public debate around it, see R.B. Dobson, 'Objectives of the current restructuring of Soviet higher and specialized secondary education', *Soviet Education*, 1987, vol. 29, nos. 9–10, pp. 5–25, and S.T. Kerr, 'The Soviet reform of higher education', *Review of Higher Education*, 1988, vol. 11, no. 3, pp. 215–46.
3 F.I. Peregudov, 'Uspekh zavisit' ot kazhdogo', *Vestnik vysshei shkoly* (hereafter *VVSh*), 1988, no. 8, pp. 3–10.
4 S.K. Yakubovich, '"Vse, chemu tebya uchili v institute, zabud'" . . . ', *VVSh*, 1988, no. 11, p. 13.
5 A.A. Logunov, 'Chto nuzhno universitetu?', *VVSh*, 1989, no. 10, pp. 9–13.
6 A. Saltychev, Yu. Akimov and E. Burykin, 'Itogi attestatsii', *VVSh*, 1990, no. 1, pp. 52–3.
7 V.E. Shukshunov, 'K novomu kachestvu vuzovskoi nauki', *VVSh*, 1989, no. 8, pp. 3–15.
8 N.N. Kutergin, 'Shag za shagom (iz opyta perestroiki odnogo vuza)', *VVSh*, 1989, no. 11, p. 10.
9 I. Grekova and A.D. Myshkis, 'Ot imitatsii deyatel'nosti – k zhivomu delu', *VVSh*, 1988, no. 10, p. 11.
10 N. Aleshin, L. Breslav and A. Ginzburg, 'Kak opredelit' stoimost' spetsialista',

VVSh, 1990, no. 2, pp. 6–11; V. Galanov and V. Kuzmin, '"U poetov est' takoi obychai"', *VVSh*, 1990, no. 2, pp. 6–8.

11 Peregudov, op. cit.

12 Yu.G. Tatur, T.G. Mikhaleva and N.G. Pechenyuk, 'Novye aspekty starykh terminov (kvalifikatsionnaya kharakteristika segodnya)', *VVSh*, 1989, no. 12, pp. 3–9.

13 D.C. Lee, *The People's Universities of the USSR*, New York, Greenwood Press, 1988.

14 L.S. Gur'eva, V.A. Zagarov and K.M. Skobov, 'O soglasovanii zven'ev sistemy obrazovaniya', *VVSh*, 1989, no. 7, pp. 55–9.

15 'Nepreryvnoe obrazovanie – velenie vremeni', *VVSh*, 1989, no. 5, pp. 20–6.

16 Saltychev *et al.*, op. cit.

17 Peregudov, op. cit.

18 N.F. Metlenkov, 'Kak zashchitit' pedagoga-novatora', *VVSh*, 1989, no. 9, pp. 9–11.

19 V.G. Onushkin, Yu.N. Kulyutkin and V.Yu. Krichevsky, 'Povyshenie kvalifikatsii pedagogov v sisteme nepreryvnogo obrazovaniya', *VVSh*, 1988, no. 12, pp. 27–32.

20 R. Kigel', 'Vopros i teoreticheskii, i prakticheskii', *VVSh*, 1990, no. 1, pp. 49–51.

21 L.G. Sagatovskaya, 'O novom kurse dlya aspirantov', *VVSh*, 1989, no. 1, pp. 29–32.

22 A.A. Ovsyannikov, M.V. Lisauskene, D.G. Rotman, T.N. Kuchtevich, V.I. Dobrynina, R.F. Shakhova, A.I. Veretskaya, P.I. Babochkin, V.P. Chebunin, L.L. Antonova, I.A. Konopak and V.P. Trufanova, 'Politicheskaya kul'tura, obshchestvennye nauki, sotsial'naya praktika', *VVSh*, 1989, no. 10, pp. 13–18.

23 Peregudov, op. cit.

24 V. Gurevich, 'Interes lichnosti – prezhde vsego', *VVSh*, 1990, no. 1, pp. 20–2.

25 'Kontseptsiya informatizatsii obrazovaniya', *Informatika i obrazovanie*, 1988, no. 6, pp. 3–31; F. Peregudov, 'Sistemnaya deyatel'nost' i obrazovanie', *VVSh*, 1990, no. 1, pp. 9–15.

26 See, for example, the sharp criticism by a reviewer of one such project: G.I. Kornilov, 'Zaklyuchenie retsenzenta', *Problemy vysshei shkoly*, 1988, no. 66, p. 84. (Response to L.G. Soluyanov and I.A. Kutsenko, 'O sisteme avtomatizirovannogo oprosa na baze mikro-EVM "Iskra-555"', ibid., pp. 78–83.)

27 Saltychev *et al.*, op. cit.

28 D. Mysyakov, 'Pochemu rastet "komp'yuternaya prestupnost"?', *Poisk*, 1989, May, no. 2, p. 5.

29 Grekova and Myshkis, op. cit.

30 Peregudov (1988), op. cit.

31 'Vremya voprosov (ob itogakh Vsesoyuznogo s"ezda rabotnikov narodnogo obrazovaniya)', *VVSh*, 1989, no. 4, pp. 3–9.

32 A.I. Polovinkin, 'S pozitsii mirovogo urovnya', *VVSh*, 1988, no. 9, pp. 7–9.

33 V. Gurevich, 'Esli rektorat ne sdaetsya', *Poisk*, 1990, 25–31 January, no. 4(39), p. 5; A. Sosnov, 'Soyuz, a ne klub', *Poisk*, 1989, 9–15 November, no. 28, p. 1.

34 Yu.A. Ryzhov, 'Na perelome', *VVSh*, 1989, no. 8, pp. 16–21.

35 '. . . A istina dorozhe', *Poisk*, 1990, 4–10 January, no. 1(36), p. 1.

36 A.A. Sobchak, 'Uroki S"ezda', *Poisk*, 1990, 18–24 January, no. 3(38), p. 6.

37 'V nomer', *Poisk*, 1990, 1–7 February, no. 5(40), p. 2.

38 A. Konovalov and B. Pasternak, 'Za gran'yu riska', *Poisk*, 1990, 11–17 May, no. 19(54), pp. 4–5; S. Massey, 'Gorbachev hears academic officials plead for more aid to education', *Chronicle of Higher Education*, 1990, 23 May, p. A36; 'Obrashchenie rektorov vuzov strany k narodnym deputatam', *Poisk*, 1990, 11–17 May, no. 19(54), p. 4.

39 'Fevral'skie nadezhdy', *Poisk*, 1990, 1–7 February, no. 5(40), p. 1.

40 See, for example, the discussion by a leading statistician of the need for such openness: 'Za glasnost' v statistike', *Vestnik statistiki*, 1990, no. 3, pp. 61–2.
41 N.P. Nikolaev, 'Vystrel v budushchee (zametki o sud'bakh intelligentsii i gumanitarnogo obrazovaniya)', *VVSh*, 1989, no. 9, pp. 15–25.
42 See, for example, Z. Gel'man, 'Ostavat'sya li nam "akademicheskim oazisom"?', *VVSh*, 1990, no. 2, pp. 32–42, on the seeming impossibility of reforming the Academy of Pedagogical Sciences.
43 'Shkola i obshchestvo', *VVSh*, 1988, no. 11, pp. 3–7.
44 For example, an announcement for a mathematics program notes that it 'generates 2.1 million problems'; see *VVSh*, 1989, no. 10, inside cover.
45 V.V. Ivanov, 'Osnovnaya zadacha obshchestva', *VVSh*, 1989, no. 7, pp. 3–6.
46 P. Formen, '"Vash primer vpechatlaet . . . "', *VVSh*, 1989, no. 7, pp. 27–30.

10

EDUCATING SCIENTIFIC-TECHNICAL REVOLUTIONARIES?: CONTINUING EFFORTS TO RESTRUCTURE SOVIET HIGHER EDUCATION

Harley D. Balzer

INTRODUCTION

Education continues to be an excellent barometer for measuring the pressures of perestroika. Education touches virtually everyone, and, even more than other social and economic institutions, the education system resists short-term fluctuations. To 'produce' a specialist with a degree requires fifteen or sixteen years of education. Few education systems in the modern world can resist reform for that long a period. The acceptance of reformers' changes by those in the classrooms, however, is a very different story. Frequently what academics do reflects what they are used to doing rather than what the current administrators tell them to do.

There is also an inherent contradiction to education reform in a social system that seeks to manage creativity. Most Soviet educators are now convinced that in the modern world it is not enough to train students to memorize and repeat assigned materials. But teaching students to think inevitably requires permitting them to express their thoughts, and no one has yet discovered a system that allows real thought control.

Despite its value as a lens to view society, Soviet education has become far less easy to study or categorize than in the past. The centralized system we had come to love/hate is rapidly losing even the veneer of homogeneity that seventy years of Soviet power had imposed. The system, of course, was never homogeneous. But central authority at least made the formal rules and structures, the official curriculum, and other elements of the system fairly similar throughout the country. This is now (1991) changing in a way that will render it impossible for anyone to write about 'Soviet education' in the future. No one would have the hubris to attempt a single monograph purporting to summarize all of 'American education'. The same will soon be true in the USSR. In this respect the education system reflects fundamental changes in Soviet political and social life, most notably increasing diversity, along with greater local involvement and control.[1]

This chapter concentrates on two broad topics that permit some insights into the implications of higher education reforms for science and technology. First, it looks at the overall statistical portrait of the education system, using some data that have only recently become available in the West. Then it focuses on why higher education has been regarded as making an inadequate contribution to Soviet science, and on some specific measures that are being taken in an attempt to remedy the problems.

STATISTICS

Examination of the raw numbers of students admitted to, registered at and graduating from Soviet institutions of higher education (*vysshie uchebnye zavedeniya* or *vuzy*) reveals a number of shifts during the decade of the 1980s. First of all, we can see that the total number of students attending Soviet *vuzy* has been declining by about 1 per cent per year since the 1982/3 academic year (Table 10.1). The drop in registrations, however, was not initially accompanied by a decrease in admissions. Rather, the number admitted to *vuzy* continued to increase until 1985 (Table 10.2). Most of the reduction in overall registrations, at least initially, was the result of attrition: the weeding-out of weak students who were not able to handle the heavy courseload. Even after 1985, when admissions began to decrease, the reduced number admitted did not account for the total drop in *vuz* registrations (Table 10.3).

Further evidence that reductions in the number of student registrations have come mainly through attrition can be seen in statistics on graduations, which show a decline in 1986 and a steep drop in 1987. There has been a rise in the number graduating since that time, but the total is not back to the 1985 level (Table 10.4). Soviet sources rarely provide data on the proportion of students who graduate, and variations in the length of time required to complete programmes of study and in the type of education (full-time or part-time) make it difficult to calculate such data with any degree of accuracy. It appears, however, that in the period 1985–90 the absolute number and proportion of students graduating declined.

Unlike secondary school registrations, which fluctuate in direct proportion to population changes, the decline in numbers of *vuz* students cannot be attributed solely to demographics; conscious policy choices are involved here. Central planners, education officials and branch ministry representatives opted to reduce the number of students in an effort to improve quality. The changes are not because of any reduction in the number of *vuzy*, despite such cuts having been promised in the reform documents of 1987. In fact, the number of institutions of higher education has remained the same or increased every year since 1985.[2] The best known case of a *vuz* being closed was the Baku Economics Institute. Typically, a branch of the Leningrad Engineering-Economics Institute was quickly established in Baku, occupying the Economics Institute premises and employing many of the same academic staff.

It is likely that opportunities for higher education will increase in the 1990s, reflecting the demand for more higher education on the part of students and local government officials. As regional and local governments have become more involved in the education system, they have manifested a tendency to favour expanding the system of higher education, both out of local pride and to satisfy the wishes of their constituents – a phenomenon also seen during earlier periods of Soviet history.[3]

There does not seem to be any significant decline in the aspiration for higher education in most areas of the USSR. This is a somewhat contentious issue. Demographics may account for some of the decrease in admission pressure in some regions, but parental education level remains the single strongest indicator of aspirations for higher education, and the proportion of the Soviet population with higher education continues to increase.[4] Overall competition to enter *vuzy* declined somewhat in the mid-1980s, but became slightly more intense at the end of the decade (Table 10.5). When we examine the situation in particular regions and specialisms we find that competition in the most desirable fields remains quite stiff. Technical institutes frequently have about as many applicants as there are places, but the competition in cultural, economics, medical and legal specialisms remains intense (Table 10.6).

Regional breakdowns indicate that the patterns of student aspirations differ among republics. The numerically least competitive admissions are in the Baltic republics and Belorussia; the largest numbers seek admission in Central Asia and the Caucasus (Tables 10.5 and 10.7). However, statistics on the 'effective' demand, that is, those passing the entrance exams, present a different picture (Table 10.7). At least for 1989, the Lithuanian and Moldavian *vuzy* had the highest proportion of successful examinees per opening in the entire USSR.

The republic-level figures often veil specific conditions in individual regions and specialisms. For example, medical *vuzy* in Azerbaidzhan and Tadzhikistan, education institutes in Turkmenia, art and cinematography *vuzy* in the RSFSR and economics institutes in Tadzhikistan all had high levels of competition for admission – between four and seven applicants per opening. Latvian and Belorussian transport institutes had virtually no competition, with an almost equal number of applicants to openings, and the number passing the entrance exams was less than the number of places available.[5] To evaluate the situation properly, we shall need statistics on individual institutes. We shall probably see serious competition at top institutes and in popular specialisms, and a continued lack of competition at weak *vuzy* and in unfashionable disciplines. In addition, a growing number of students are manifesting aspirations for education outside the USSR, now that this has become a possibility. Applications by Soviet students to universities in the USA and UK have increased geometrically, and will rise even more if the new law on foreign travel is implemented.

A trend in the figures that should be disturbing to Soviet educational administrators is the relative increase in the proportion of admissions, registrations and graduations in the correspondence (*zaochnyi*) divisions of *vuzy*. This form of education has been regularly criticized as the weakest and most problematical type of training offered in the Soviet system.[6] Both daytime and especially evening (*vechernii*) registrations have declined at the same time that correspondence divisions have increased their role. The decline of evening education relative to correspondence courses should be a source of particular concern, since this form of training has been rated favourably by Soviets in technical specialisms who praised the opportunity to integrate the material that they were studying with their direct work experience. Evening education has receded, however, as the correspondence share has increased, presumably because the correspondence variant is less expensive and takes workers away from their workplace for less time.

Recently declassified statistical materials permit us to examine the role of these three types of education in different specialisms and regions (Tables 10.8 and 10.9). Unfortunately, the available data pertain only to the 1989/90 academic year. Longitudinal data would permit us to examine the trends more completely. But even the data currently available enable us to note that, after Uzbekistan, the proportion of *vuz* students on full-time courses is lowest in the RSFSR, the republic with the greatest number of students and, after Armenia, the highest proportion of students per 10,000 inhabitants. Comparing the proportion of students admitted to daytime divisions with the proportion among total registrations suggests that the attrition rate may be higher on the full-time courses. Confirmation of this hypothesis, however, must await longitudinal data.

In examining all of the statistics pertaining to higher education, it is important to note that the 1989/90 academic year represents a 'blip', owing to the release from military service of some 300,000 men who had been conscripted after beginning their higher education. In the summer of 1989 the Supreme Soviet, in a highly emotional session, voted to allow these students to return to their studies despite the objections of Minister of Defence Dmitri Yazov. The great majority, 272,000, returned to regular daytime divisions of *vuzy*. The result has been a nightmare for *vuz* administrators and for those of us who try to deal with Soviet education data. One faculty member notes that the Supreme Soviet decision to have students return to the classroom was taken in the summer, during the vacation, and at a time when plans for the next academic year were already set. Allocations for classrooms, equipment, teaching staff, textbooks, residential accommodation, stipends and so on, had been determined by then. It was impossible to change the arrangements to provide for the additional students. The resulting mass of problems caused a further decline in the level of education of graduates, 'although many were certain that it could not possibly get any worse'.[7]

The Orenburg Medical Institute, for example, as of 1 September 1989 had 207 students above its limit and also had to open an evening division for fifty students from Uzbekistan. But classroom space, equipment and resources remained as they were before. And despite promises by the State Committee for Education that the staff–student ratio would decrease to 1:8, and in the 1990s to 1:5, it is now in fact worse than in the period of stagnation. The number of students who staff believe cannot cope with their work in second-year courses has increased to 25–30 per cent, and there has been a significant rise in the number of students who should be dropped from the institute.

The situation varied at different *vuzy* (and we would expect *Sovetskaya Rossiya* to seek out articles comparing current conditions unfavourably with the 'good old days' of stagnation). Some of them managed to prepare themselves, forming special groups of returning servicemen who were given extra attention. Some *vuzy*, or at least some faculties, barely noticed the influx. But at many of them, it seems, there will be a 'bubble' of these students – most of whom returned to the second or third year of the course – that will take several years to move through the system. No one provided teachers, classrooms, living accommodation, grants, books, food allocations, for example, and it seems that serious difficulties were created at many *vuzy*.[8]

Serious difficulties will certainly persist in interpreting statistics on Soviet higher education for three to five years. All of our statistical tables will now require asterisks. Data on registrations, graduations, dropout rates and specialism distributions will all be affected. So will indicators of quality, given that returning servicemen have generally (as a group) performed less well than other students, particularly in maths and science – a condition usually attributed to their having forgotten much of what they learned in secondary school during two years of military service.

One place where the influx of military returnees has already had a marked impact is on the gender distribution of *vuz* students (Table 10.10). The female proportion of the *vuz* student body had been increasing slowly for more than a decade. It increased more rapidly when draft deferments for students were curtailed in the mid-1980s, reaching a high of 56 per cent in 1986/7. The influx of returning servicemen has brought the *vuz* student body closer to gender parity than it has been at any time since 1975. Yet here too we must consider regional, local and disciplinary variations (Table 10.11). The proportion of women in the *vuz* student body is greatest in Latvia, Moldavia and Kirgizia, and remains above average in the RSFSR, Belorussia, Kazakhstan and Lithuania. It is near the all-Union average in the Ukraine and Estonia. The greatest proportion of males are in the *vuzy* of Tadzhikistan, Uzbekistan, Turkmenia and Azerbaidzhan, and there are high numbers in Georgia and Armenia as well.

Specialism distributions show few major shifts over the past five years, or even the past twenty years. The shares of the total number being admitted, trained and graduated still reflect the admissions plans of the various *vuzy* and their administrative patrons. The influence of students and their families is felt more in the intangible area of quality. Competition for admission in some specialisms in fact no longer exists, for example in Latvian and Belorussian transport institutes, as mentioned above, Lithuanian economics *vuzy*, and Estonian, Belorussian and Moldavian agricultural institutes. In other disciplines competition remains quite stiff, particularly at Azerbaidzhani and Tadzhik medical institutes, Turkmenian education institutes, and art and cinema *vuzy* in the RSFSR. For the USSR as a whole, the most popular specialism has shifted from culture to law. The variations in admissions competition inevitably have an impact on the level of education and the quality of graduates in different specialisms and at individual institutes. Here we enter a realm that is not illuminated very much by overall statistics.

If we have only anecdotal data about the quality of specialists in different disciplines and from different regions, we do now have more data on the overall distributions by branches and specialisms (Tables 10.12–16). These data show remarkable stability through the post-Khrushchev period, reflecting the economic syndrome of 'planning from the achieved level'. It will be important to monitor these series over the next Five-Year Plan, to see if increased individualization of instruction and greater local autonomy result in significant quantitative changes.

In one key area affecting science and technology – computer education – progress remains halting, for both quantitative[9] and qualitative reasons (see Chapter 3). Quality is also the most serious problem in training specialists with advanced degrees. VAK (*Vysshaya attestatsionnaya komissiya*, the Higher Attestation Commission) has never satisfied critics that its quality control function was being carried out in a satisfactory way. The 1987 reform shifted the burden of ensuring the quality of *kandidat* dissertations (roughly equivalent to PhD) from VAK to the individual Scientific Councils, with the threat that Councils that approved weak dissertations could lose their right to confer degrees. Thus far, however, there does not appear to have been much impact on the 3,000 or so Scientific Councils. Criticisms are again being voiced regarding their failure to impose tough standards, and also about the lax supervision of new arrangements permitting them to award degrees without a formal defence and even without examinations.[10]

In conditions of increased decentralization, it will be more and more difficult to impose central standards. Local interests are likely to engage in more credential inflation, and it is likely to be even more important to know where and when people did their graduate work, and with whom, in attempting to evaluate their qualifications. One Goskomstat official confided to me that under current conditions they expect *kandidat* degrees to sprout 'like mushrooms after rain'. Statistics already suggest an increase in the number of *kandidat* degrees being awarded, at least to full-time students (Table 10.17). Inevitably, increased numbers and new mechanisms for awarding higher degrees raise concerns about quality.[11]

IMPROVING *VUZ* SCIENCE

If perestroika in general, and the reforms of secondary and higher education in particular, were intended to produce a rapid improvement in educational quality, their overall impact has been a sad disappointment. This is hardly a surprise. It now takes ten or eleven years of general education and five years at a *vuz* to produce a specialist, and another three years of 'practical work' to hone his or her skills for certification. Even if a thorough overhaul of the entire education system had been accomplished in the 1980s, no one should expect dramatic qualitative changes in less than a decade, and perhaps not for twenty years.

Yet the overwhelming perception of conditions in Soviet higher education is that very little has changed. The increased resources made available for *vuzy* amounted to a drop in the proverbial bucket. Hopes that enterprises and research institutes would behave in an enlightened manner, recognizing that their future depended on having a pipeline of new talent and providing financial assistance accordingly, have generally been misplaced. The approach was a conceptual disaster. Support for education in corporate America is a sometime thing, recognized as valuable both for public relations and self-interest, but subject to profitability. Among Soviet enterprises that are thrashing about in an attempt to cope with a new world of economic self-financing/cost accounting, diverting funds to educational purposes often seems a luxury.

There have been some positive improvements in eliminating required courses in Marxism, adopting more individualized programmes of study that permit at least some students to design customized curricula, and encouraging more interaction both among Soviet institutions and with the international scientific community. But the overwhelming impression is one of crisis.

If Soviet education for science and technology is in serious difficulty, how did it happen, and what might be done to rescue it? One reason for the problems is that research has never been a top priority at higher education institutions in the Soviet period.[12] Even during NEP, the state paid *vuz* staff for their teaching, not for doing research. The system introduced during the I Five-Year Plan (1928–32) was geared to training vast numbers of narrow specialists for the specific needs of individual commissariats. This approach virtually destroyed whatever remained of the pre-revolutionary tradition of *vuz* scientific research.

During and after World War II, the importance of research was once again acknowledged. But the 1944 decree on this topic increased the quantity of work done at *vuzy* without addressing any of the fundamental problems inhibiting its effectiveness. The structure of *vuz* departments (*kafedry*) continued to reflect the 'consumer' interests of the ministries, unrelated to emerging lines of scientific research. Contract work consisted mainly of 'small themes' that could be completed within a single annual planning cycle. And, most important, the research done at *vuzy* was contracted and remunerated independently from any ties to its introduction into production or its benefits for society. Additional decrees in 1956 and 1967 also brought quantitative growth without changes in the basic patterns.

The 1967 decree also resulted in major expansion of research departments at *vuzy*: by 1977 there were 540 problem laboratories and 770 branch laboratories. The number of these scientific institutions doubled in 1964–7, and the increase from 1957 to 1967 was eightfold. The number of *vuz* scientific workers doubled in the 1970s, overwhelmingly on the basis of contract work. In 1974 the amount of state budget research was 260 per cent of the 1964 level, while contract research was 428 per cent of the 1964 level.

Thus the rapid growth in the *vuz* science sector came in the period 1965–70, when the overall growth in scientific personnel had begun to stabilize. *Vuz* science came to have a dual meaning, encompassing both the specialized research laboratories and the research activity of academic staff and students. It should also be noted that this explosion came at a time of overall decline in the proportion of resources devoted to higher education, from 1.6 per cent of national income to 0.8 per cent.

Yet another decree in 1978 was aimed at deriving a greater 'scientific return' from *vuzy*, and included a provision for increasing the material resources devoted to higher education. This initiative sought to involve ministries and departments. Most promisingly, it also included resources for development of inter-*vuz* centres to pool complex equipment, especially computers, and experimental and testing facilities. The first of these complexes was established in Dnepropetrovsk in 1980, followed by the creation of similar organizations in Chelyabinsk, Rostov, Tomsk, Tashkent, Odessa and other cities.

The Russian Republic Ministry of Higher Education (MinVuz RSFSR) responded to the 1978 decree by creating a 'Contractual Scientific Association' (*Khozraschetnoe nauchnoe ob"edinenie*) combining eighty-seven *vuzy*, thirty-eight scientific research institutes (NIIs), twenty-four design bureaus (KBs) and thirty-five experimental plants. But *vuzy* still were obliged to solicit orders from enterprises and ministries, and they were still concluding agreements for the research itself, not for the actual results of introducing that research into production. As in branch science, emphasis was on the contract, not the product.[13]

In these conditions, *vuz* science tended to repeat, with some lag, the development of science in the country generally. Soviet educators have been unable to resolve the contradiction between the educational and scientific roles of the *vuz*, and in particular have not found ways to make them reinforce each other.

Until 1988, *vuzy* were not considered administratively part of the system of 'science and science services' but rather were in the sphere of 'public education', which received a lower priority in the allocation of equipment. This resulted in a terrible technical supply situation. Requests for equipment were satisfied at a rate of 10–15 per cent, and renewal of facilities took place at a rate of 1.5–2 per cent per year. *Vuz* science is equipped at one-fifth the level of the Academy. As one observer notes, 'here is the source of the contradiction between rich intellectual and weak technical possibilities'.[14] The weak experimental and testing base at *vuzy* is a particular problem. In 1986 only 20 per cent of *vuzy* had their own testing facilities, while 63 per cent had none and were not able to utilize those of enterprises.

The number of scientific research institutes affiliated with *vuzy* has not grown much: there were forty such institutes in 1922 and fifty-eight at the beginning of the 1980s. Institutes of this type have a special advantage in their capacity to provide industry with young graduates who participate in developing new processes, along with the new technologies themselves. A leader in this area has been the Tomsk Institute of Automated Control Systems and Radioelectronics.[15]

There is also tremendous potential for cooperation between *vuzy* and scientific research institutes. These possibilities are increased when *vuzy* are included in complex scientific-technical projects. In 1986 MinVuz RSFSR approved thirty-three such initiatives, many on regional principles, such as the branch-territorial project at Tomsk Polytechnical Institute. The North Caucasus has been a leader in inter-*vuz* cooperation.

There are still many instances, however, where introduction of *vuz* innovations is blocked by ministerial research institutes that insist on a monopoly for their own efforts in a particular field. A similar problem exists in fundamental science, where Academy institutes seek to monopolize basic directions in science. As Lakhtin notes, 'one of the unresolved problems remains finding for *vuz* science its sphere of activity, corresponding to its special characteristics'.[16] A 1987 decree includes provisions for an increase of three or four times in the amount of contract work at *vuzy*, but this will produce genuine results only if students are involved in the research and if the research is actually used in the economy.

Overall, there are few signs that genuine improvements have taken place, either in training or in the contribution of the *vuz* sector. Some Soviet observers put great hopes in education-science-production complexes, which they say mark a shift from instances of one-time joint activity to genuine cooperation (*sotrudnichestvo*). The first such complex was established in 1959, combining the Leningrad Institute of Water Transport Engineering, the Central Scientific Research Institute of the Navy, and the Ministry of Inland Navigation's experimental research plant. Many heads of departments at the Engineering Institute became directors of scientific-technical projects for the Ministry. Another example of close cooperation was between the Leningrad Polytechnical Institute and the Elektrosila enterprise. But these are 'experiments' and have not been replicated on a broad scale.

What we have seen thus far in Soviet higher education reform is a continuation of two trends. One is the 'experiment syndrome'. The other is an increasing disparity between a few élite institutions and the bulk of scientific and educational activity.

In the Soviet economy, and in other areas of Soviet society, limited experiments have frequently been successful. They receive resources, attention and priority. Not only do those involved know that they can get extra help to deal with difficulties, fundamentally changing their decision-making priorities, but simply being part of an experiment influences attitudes and expectations. When these experiments have been extended to a greater number of institutions, it has been impossible to maintain the 'hothouse' environment, and systemic dysfunctions have eroded the successes. Priority by its very nature cannot be broadly disseminated.

Not all of the experiments have been failures. A growing number of *vuz*, institute and cooperative personnel have been seeking new forms of activity that both improve scientific research and aid the education system. These are the greatest sources of optimism in any overview of Soviet higher education. But successful experiments and integration of students into genuine research remain the exception. Student participation in scientific research has not spread very far. A survey of thirty-five *vuzy* in 1989 found that two-thirds of the students do not participate in scientific research.[17] Only in Latvia and Estonia does the figure approach half the *vuz* students. For the USSR as a whole it is barely more than one-quarter, and for the RSFSR it is only one-third (Table 10.18).[18]

Statistical evidence also reveals that only a small proportion of *vuz* students are studying under contracts with enterprises. In 1989/90, just 15 per cent of the students in daytime divisions of *vuzy* were studying on the basis of contracts (*obuchaetsya na osnove zaklyuchennykh dogovorov*). Once again, there is significant regional variation. The greatest number are in the Ukraine (33.6 per cent of daytime students) and Latvia (15.2 per cent). In Tadzhikistan and Armenia the number is insignificant (0.1 per cent).[19] Those institutes that have concluded contracts are learning some rough lessons about the market for specialists. One Moscow energy *vuz* held an 'auction' of its graduates for enterprises, only to find that male specialists were highly sought after, while women were boycotted by all the enterprises and ministries.[20]

There continue to be signs of hope amidst the chaos. The head of the English department at one Tomsk technical institute states that *all* students at the institute are now studying English. International contact and cooperation are increasing. Many of us have Soviet graduate students and undergraduates registered at our universities. Yet these remain, thus far, isolated cases.

173

CONCLUSION

In developing the secondary and higher education reforms of 'early pere-stroika', Soviet officials were caught on the horns of a dilemma stemming from a simultaneous labour shortage and need for more education to cope with an increasingly complex scientific and technical environment. At least now they may see a situation in which fixing the economic problems could help, since so many people are underemployed and so many enterprises are overstaffed. Unless the economic difficulties can be resolved, and in the near term even if they are, the Soviet education system will continue to manifest extremes of uneven development.

Table 10.1 *Vuz* students by division, USSR, 1980–9
(thousands, start of academic year)

Division	1980	1981	1982	1983	1984	1985	1986	1987	1988	1989
Total	5235	5284	5315	5301	5280	5147	5088	5026	4999	5178
per cent[a]	100	100	100	100	100	100	100	100	100	100
Day	2978	3011	3023	2986	2932	2763	2688	2675	2721	2991
per cent	56.9	57.0	56.9	56.3	55.5	53.7	52.8	53.2	54.4	57.7
Evening	649	648	645	641	636	634	620	584	548	509
per cent	12.4	12.3	12.1	12.1	12.0	12.3	12.2	11.6	11.0	9.8
Correspondence	1608	1625	1647	1674	1712	1750	1780	1767	1730	1678
per cent	30.7	30.8	31.0	31.6	32.4	34.0	35.0	35.2	34.6	32.4

[a] Owing to rounding, percentages may not total precisely to 100

Source: Narodnoe khozyaistvo SSSR – various years, Moscow, Finansy i statistika.

Table 10.2 *Vuz* admissions by division, USSR, 1980–9
(thousands, start of academic year)

Division	1980	1981	1982	1983	1984	1985	1986	1987	1988	1989
Total	1051.9	1062.4	1070.3	1075.7	1087.2	1104.0	1102.5	1092.5	1075.8	1050.0
per cent[a]	100	100	100	100	100	100	100	100	100	100
Day	639.9	644.0	644.4	645.7	643.5	649.9	653.8	655.2	661.9	654.8
per cent	60.83	60.62	60.21	60.03	59.19	58.87	59.30	60.00	61.52	62.36
Evening	134.3	135.4	135.2	134.2	136.3	137.5	131.7	121.5	108.7	102.0
per cent	12.77	12.74	12.63	12.48	12.54	12.45	11.95	11.12	10.10	9.71
Correspondence	277.7	283.0	290.7	295.8	307.4	316.6	317.0	315.8	305.2	293.2
per cent	26.40	26.64	27.16	27.50	28.27	28.68	28.75	28.90	28.36	27.92

[a] Owing to rounding, percentages may not total precisely to 100

Source: *Narodnoe khozyaistvo SSSR* – various years, Moscow, Finansy i statistika.

Table 10.3 Net change in *vuz* enrolments from previous year, USSR, 1981–9

Year	Change in admissions	Change in enrolments
1981	+10,500	+ 50,000
1982	+ 7,900	+ 30,000
1983	+ 5,400	− 14,000
1984	+11,500	− 21,000
1985	+16,800	−133,000
1986	− 1,500	− 59,000
1987	−10,000	− 62,000
1988	−16,700	− 27,000
1989	−25,800	+179,000 [a]

[a] This includes students freed early from military service.

Source: Computed by the author from the data in Tables 10.1 and 10.2.

Table 10.4 *Vuz* degrees awarded by division, USSR, 1980–9
(thousands)

Division	1980	1981	1982	1983	1984	1985	1986	1987	1988	1989
Total	817.3	831.2	840.8	849.5	855.0	858.9	839.5	768.1	775.2	792.5
per cent[a]	100	100	100	100	100	100	100	100	100	100
Day	518.0	527.5	537.3	545.6	550.6	549.1	527.0	451.5	447.1	444.0
per cent	63.4	63.5	63.9	64.2	64.4	63.9	62.8	58.8	57.6	56.0
Evening	85.3	85.8	84.4	83.4	84.0	83.1	80.4	79.2	77.7	78.6
per cent	10.4	10.3	10.0	9.8	9.8	9.7	9.6	10.3	10.0	9.9
Correspondence	214.0	217.9	219.1	220.5	220.4	226.7	232.1	237.4	250.4	269.9
per cent	26.2	26.2	26.1	26.0	25.8	26.4	27.6	30.9	32.3	34.0

[a] Owing to rounding, percentages may not total precisely to 100

Source: Narodnoe khozyaistvo SSSR – various years, Moscow, Finansy i statistika.

Table 10.5 *Vuz* entrance exam competition by Union Republic, 1980–9
(applicants per 100 places)

	1980	1985	1987	1988	1989
USSR	204	182	196	192	228
RSFSR	188	166	180	169	204
Ukraine	203	181	188	187	217
Belorussia	188	173	183	177	201
Uzbekistan	263	235	280	291	342
Kazakhstan	230	212	211	226	277
Georgia	346	266	341	394	357
Azerbaidzhan	312	248	264	307	320
Lithuania	173	157	168	164	192
Moldavia	199	194	189	195	223
Latvia	181	164	158	159	171
Kirgizia	286	249	280	304	337
Tadzhikistan	261	277	324	328	369
Armenia	264	221	245	245	248
Turkmenia	256	242	273	301	381
Estonia	146	133	154	154	200

Sources: Narodnoe obrazovanie i kul'tura v SSSR, Moscow, Finansy i statistika, 1989, p. 230; *Narodnoe obrazovanie v SSSR – 1989/90 uchebnyi god*, Moscow, Gosobrazovanie, 1990, p. 13.

Table 10.6 *Vuz* entrance exam competition by branch of educational institution and division, USSR, 1980–8 (applicants per 100 places)

	1980	1985	1987	1988
For all educational institutions — for the following divisions:	204	182	196	192
day	212	180	199	201
evening	181	161	162	157
correspondence	198	191	203	186
In the educational institutions of: — industry and construction	176	149	153	148
day	176	142	151	147
evening	168	147	143	143
correspondence	184	174	167	154
— transport and communications	193	159	165	156
day	191	152	164	155
evening	181	165	163	152
correspondence	198	166	167	158
— agriculture	210	167	171	160
day	224	164	162	157
evening	–	–	–	–
correspondence	188	171	184	165
— economics and law	265	229	244	242
day	295	228	262	287
evening	260	238	235	211
correspondence	247	229	233	214
— health, phys. ed. and sport	246	225	254	236
day	249	226	257	241
evening	238	268	200	175
correspondence	177	200	244	214
— education	212	207	237	236
day	223	209	242	252
evening	202	185	207	198
correspondence	191	209	232	210
— art and cinematography	430	373	346	357
day	479	416	383	403
evening	259	223	253	213
correspondence	274	267	254	237

Source: *Narodnoe obrazovanie i kul'tura v SSSR*, Moscow, Finansy i statistika, 1989, p. 229.

Table 10.7 Vuz entrance exam competition and admissions to day divisions by Union Republic, 1989

	Those who took the exams (thousands)	Applicants per 100 places	Those who passed the exams (thousands)	Number per 100 places	Those accepted (thousands)
USSR	1495.5	228	788.7	120	654.8
RSFSR	744.9	204	436.8	120	365.4
Ukraine	235.9	217	135.5	125	108.8
Belorussia	50.3	201	29.2	117	25.0
Uzbekistan	124.5	342	42.5	117	36.4
Kazakhstan	104.8	277	43.3	115	37.8
Georgia	40.0	357	14.2	127	11.2
Azerbaidzhan	35.2	320	12.6	115	11.0
Lithuania	17.7	192	14.0	152	9.2
Moldavia	16.5	233	9.7	131	7.4
Latvia	10.6	171	7.8	126	6.2
Kirgizia	29.3	337	9.8	113	8.7
Tadzhikistan	35.8	369	12.0	124	9.7
Armenia	22.6	248	10.7	118	9.1
Turkmenia	20.2	381	6.0	113	5.3
Estonia	7.2	200	4.6	128	3.6

Source: Narodnoe obrazovanie v SSSR – 1989/90 uchebnyi god, Moscow, Gosobrazovanie, 1990, p. 13.

Table 10.8 *Vuz* students by division and Union Republic, 1989
(thousands, start of academic year)

	Total	Day	%	Evening	%	Correspondence	%	Number of students per 10,000 people
				Division				
USSR	5178.2	2990.8	57.8	509.1	9.8	1678.3	32.4	181
RSFSR	2861.0	1624.1	56.8	310.5	10.8	926.4	32.3	194
Ukraine	888.8	510.7	57.5	75.5	8.4	302.6	34.0	172
Belorussia	189.4	113.8	60.1	7.1	3.7	68.6	36.2	186
Uzbekistan	331.6	174.3	52.6	45.1	13.6	112.2	33.8	167
Kazakhstan	285.6	170.8	59.8	13.1	4.5	101.7	35.6	173
Georgia	93.0	57.8	62.2	13.1	14.0	22.1	23.7	171
Azerbaidzhan	99.7	57.5	57.7	17.2	17.2	25.0	25.0	142
Lithuania	69.4	43.2	62.2	6.4	9.2	19.8	28.5	188
Moldavia	55.5	34.4	62.0	0.6	1.0	20.5	36.9	128
Latvia	45.6	28.1	61.6	3.5	7.6	14.0	30.7	170
Kirgizia	59.3	40.4	68.1	3.9	6.5	15.0	25.2	138
Tadzhikistan	65.6	44.5	67.8	3.4	5.1	17.7	26.9	128
Armenia	65.4	46.0	70.3	7.0	10.7	12.4	18.9	199
Turkmenia	42.0	28.0	66.7	1.1	2.6	12.9	30.7	119
Estonia	26.3	17.2	65.4	1.6	6.0	7.5	28.5	167

Source: Narodnoe obrazovanie v SSSR – 1989/90 uchebnyi god, Moscow, Gosobrazovanie, 1990, p. 16.

Table 10.9 Vuz admissions by division and Union Republic, 1989
(thousands)

				Division			
	Total	Day	%	Evening	%	Correspondence	%
USSR	1050.0	654.8	62.4	102.0	9.7	293.2	27.9
RSFSR	602.7	365.4	60.6	69.3	11.4	168.0	27.8
Ukraine	174.9	108.8	62.2	14.5	8.2	51.6	29.5
Belorussia	38.3	25.0	65.3	1.1	2.8	12.2	31.8
Uzbekistan	59.4	36.4	61.3	6.6	11.1	16.4	27.6
Kazakhstan	58.1	37.8	65.1	2.5	4.3	17.8	30.6
Georgia	17.4	11.2	64.4	1.5	8.6	4.7	27.0
Azerbaidzhan	16.4	11.0	67.1	2.1	12.8	3.8	23.1
Lithuania	13.6	9.2	67.6	1.1	8.0	3.3	24.2
Moldavia	11.4	7.4	64.9	0.2	1.7	3.8	33.3
Latvia	9.3	6.2	66.7	0.7	7.5	2.4	25.8
Kirgizia	11.5	8.7	75.7	0.6	5.2	2.2	19.1
Tadzhikistan	13.4	9.7	72.4	0.5	3.7	3.2	23.8
Armenia	11.5	9.1	79.1	0.8	6.9	1.6	13.9
Turkmenia	6.9	5.3	76.8	0.1	1.4	1.5	21.7
Estonia	5.2	3.6	69.2	0.4	7.6	1.2	23.0

Source: Narodnoe obrazovanie v SSSR – 1989/90 uchebnyi god, Moscow, Gosobrazovanie, 1990, p. 9.

Table 10.10 Women as percentage of *vuz* students, USSR, 1970–89
(start of academic year)

	1970	1971	1972	1973	1974	1975	1976	1977	1978	1979
Percentage of total	49	49	NA	50	50	50	51	51	51	52
	1980	1981	1982	1983	1984	1985	1986	1987	1988	1989
Percentage of total	52	52	52	53	54	55	56	55	54	50.7

Source: Narodnoe khozyaistvo SSSR – various years, Moscow, Finansy i statistika.

Table 10.11 Vuz students by gender and Union Republic, 1989 (thousands, start of academic year)

| | All students | Of whom: | | Percentage | |
		Men	Women	Men	Women
USSR	5178.2	2552.1	2626.1	49.3	50.7
RSFSR	2861.0	1376.3	1484.7	48.1	51.9
Ukraine	888.8	433.5	455.3	48.8	51.2
Belorussia	189.3	88.8	100.5	46.9	53.1
Uzbekistan	331.6	194.0	137.6	58.5	41.5
Kazakhstan	285.6	136.0	149.6	47.6	52.4
Georgia	93.0	48.3	44.7	51.9	48.1
Azerbaidzhan	99.7	58.1	41.6	58.3	41.7
Lithuania	69.4	32.4	37.0	46.7	53.3
Moldavia	55.5	24.8	30.7	44.7	55.3
Latvia	45.6	19.6	26.0	43.0	57.0
Kirgizia	59.3	27.5	31.8	46.4	53.6
Tadzhikistan	65.6	40.3	25.3	61.4	38.6
Armenia	65.4	35.1	30.3	53.7	46.3
Turkmenia	42.0	24.2	17.8	57.6	42.4
Estonia	26.3	13.2	13.1	50.2	49.8

Source: Narodnoe obrazovanie v SSSR – 1989/90 uchebnyi god, Moscow, Gosobrazovanie, 1990, p. 25.

Table 10.12 *Vuz* students by branch of educational institution and division, USSR, 1980–8
(thousands, start of academic year)

	1980	1985	1987	1988
Total	5235.2	5147.2	5025.7	4999.2
— including educational institutions of:				
— industry and construction	2088.2	1996.8	1875.4	1835.6
day (%)	57	53	52	54
evening and correspondence (%)	43	47	48	46
— transport and communications	300.5	290.5	273.2	264.4
day (%)	49	46	43	44
evening and correspondence (%)	51	54	57	56
— agriculture	533.8	532.8	520.3	513.3
day (%)	53	48	47	49
evening and correspondence (%)	47	52	53	51
— economics and law	377.0	383.2	372.0	355.1
day (%)	29	28	29	31
evening and correspondence (%)	71	72	71	69
— health, phys. ed. and sport	378.7	376.0	362.6	368.5
day (%)	94	92	90	90
evening and correspondence (%)	6	8	10	10
— education	1509.0	1519.6	1572.5	1611.8
day (%)	57	54	55	56
evening and correspondence (%)	43	46	45	44
— art and cinematography	48.0	48.3	49.7	50.5
day (%)	73	69	68	68
evening and correspondence (%)	27	31	32	32

Source: *Narodnoe obrazovanie i kul'tura v USSR*, Moscow, Finansy i statistika, 1989, p. 197.

Table 10.13 *Vuz students by branch of educational institution and division, USSR, 1989 (thousands, start of academic year)*

	Total	Division			Day students as percentage of total
		Day	Evening	Correspondence	
Total	5178.2	2990.8	509.1	1678.3	57.8
— including instruction in:					
— industry	1693.9	982.7	325.5	385.7	58.0
— construction	194.6	106.4	25.7	62.5	54.7
— transport	225.7	108.3	18.8	98.6	48.0
— communications	46.6	21.1	5.2	20.3	45.3
— agriculture	534.4	284.3	–	250.1	53.2
— economics	313.8	106.3	27.7	179.8	33.9
— law	34.4	8.9	5.0	20.5	25.9
— health	335.0	318.9	12.2	3.9	95.2
— phys. ed. and sport	60.6	34.3	–	26.3	56.6
— education	1687.2	983.2	87.7	616.3	58.3
of which:					
— universities	627.7	370.1	69.8	187.8	59.0
— pedagogical institutes	984.0	585.4	14.3	384.3	59.5
— art and cinematography	52.0	36.4	1.3	14.3	70.0

Source: *Narodnoe obrazovanie v SSSR – 1989/90 uchebnyi god*, Moscow, Gosobrazovanie, 1990, p. 17.

Table 10.14 *Vuz* admissions by branch of educational institution, USSR, 1980–9
(thousands)

	1980	1981	1982	1983	1984	1985	1986	1987	1988	1989
Total	1051.9	1062.4	1070.3	1075.8	1087.2	1104.0	1102.5	1092.5	1075.8	1050.0
per cent [a]	100	100	100	100	100	100	100	100	100	100
Industry and construction	421.8	425.8	428.9	431.6	433.4	437.0	433.3	424.7	407.4	384.7
per cent	40.10	40.08	40.07	40.12	39.86	39.58	39.30	38.87	37.86	36.63
Transport and communications	56.9	57.2	57.7	58.1	58.6	59.1	59.0	58.2	55.7	49.5
per cent	5.41	5.38	5.39	5.40	5.39	5.35	5.35	5.32	5.17	4.71
Agriculture	103.2	104.0	106.1	107.1	108.5	110.1	107.7	107.7	105.8	99.4
per cent	9.81	9.79	9.91	9.96	9.98	9.97	9.77	9.85	9.83	9.46
Economics and law	80.1	80.7	81.2	80.8	81.4	81.0	81.0	77.1	69.4	69.0
per cent	7.61	7.60	7.59	7.51	7.49	7.34	7.35	7.05	6.45	6.57
Health, phys. ed. and sport	69.3	71.1	71.1	71.3	70.2	69.7	69.6	70.5	72.8	76.1
per cent	6.59	6.69	6.64	6.63	6.46	6.31	6.31	6.45	6.72	7.24
Education	310.7	313.4	315.1	316.5	325.0	337.2	342.0	344.6	354.7	361.1
per cent	29.54	29.50	29.44	29.42	29.89	30.54	31.02	31.54	32.97	34.39
Art and cinematography	9.9	10.2	10.2	10.4	10.1	9.9	9.9	9.7	10.0	10.2
per cent	0.94	0.96	0.95	0.97	0.93	0.90	0.90	0.88	0.92	0.97

[a] Owing to rounding, percentages may not total precisely to 100
Source: *Narodnoe khozyaistvo SSSR* – various years, Moscow, Finansy i statistika.

Table 10.15 *Vuz* admissions by branch of educational institution and division, USSR, 1989
(thousands)

				Division			
	Total	Day	%	Evening	%	Correspondence	%
Total	1050.0	654.8	62.4	102.0	9.7	293.2	27.9
— including educational institutions of:							
— industry	345.9	213.4	61.7	65.7	18.9	66.8	19.3
— construction	38.8	23.9	61.6	4.4	11.3	10.5	27.0
— transport	40.7	20.9	51.4	3.3	8.1	16.5	40.5
— communications	8.8	4.6	52.3	1.0	11.3	3.2	36.3
— agriculture	99.4	61.7	62.1	–	–	37.7	37.9
— economics	61.3	24.8	40.5	5.0	8.1	31.5	51.3
— law	7.7	2.4	31.2	1.1	14.2	4.2	54.5
— health	62.5	56.8	90.9	5.0	8.0	0.7	1.1
— phys. ed. and sport	13.6	8.8	64.7	–	–	4.8	35.2
— education	361.1	229.8	63.3	16.3	4.5	115.0	31.8
of which:							
universities	127.9	81.3	63.6	12.8	10.0	33.8	26.4
pedagogical institutes	217.1	141.2	65.0	2.7	1.2	73.2	33.7
— art and cinematography	10.2	7.7	75.5	0.2	1.9	2.3	22.5

Source: *Narodnoe obrazovanie v SSSR – 1989/90 uchebnyi god*, Moscow, Gosobrazovanie, 1990, p. 10.

Table 10.16 Vuz students by specialism and division, USSR, 1989
(thousands, start of academic year)

	Total	Division			
		2990.8	509.1	1678.3	57.8
Total	5178.2	2990.8	509.1	1678.3	57.8
— including the following groups of specialisms:					
— natural sciences	449.7	338.8	27.0	83.9	75.3
— humanities	643.8	357.5	39.5	246.8	55.5
— labour, physical and aesthetic studies and disciplines	512.9	251.1	7.0	254.8	49.0
— health care	345.8	328.8	12.6	4.4	95.1
— culture and art	129.6	65.4	4.2	60.0	50.5
— general economics	346.3	134.0	35.8	176.5	38.7
— technical economics	238.9	91.2	32.2	115.5	38.2
— geology and mining of minerals	38.0	26.3	1.7	10.0	69.2
— mineral cultivation	61.1	38.3	6.9	15.9	62.7
— power engineering	103.9	59.5	15.4	29.0	57.3
— metallurgy	49.3	33.9	10.2	5.2	68.8
— machine building and metal-works	208.9	106.7	56.3	45.9	51.1
— aviation technology	49.3	36.0	9.6	3.7	73.0

— ship-building	31.2	16.9	2.9	11.4	54.2
— automobiles and tractors	120.2	59.4	25.4	35.4	49.4
— power machine-building	22.2	14.1	4.1	4.0	63.5
— technical machinery and equipment	133.3	73.9	19.9	39.5	55.4
— electrical engineering	37.9	24.3	6.7	6.9	64.1
— instrument making	44.7	28.2	10.5	6.0	63.1
— electronics	46.0	30.0	10.9	5.1	65.2
— automation and control	160.5	90.6	36.2	33.7	56.4
— computer technology and automation systems	101.0	73.2	23.0	4.8	72.5
— radio-technology and communications	155.3	89.4	29.1	36.8	57.6
— transport maintenance	59.6	30.9	3.0	25.7	51.8
— chemical engineering	78.7	51.9	14.1	12.7	65.9
— forestry and timber	28.2	17.6	1.3	9.3	62.4
— food industry	92.8	40.5	5.1	47.2	43.6
— consumer goods industry	92.2	38.3	8.6	45.3	41.5
— construction and architecture	338.4	187.1	49.5	101.8	55.4
— land-surveying and cartography	11.1	8.0	0.1	3.0	72.1
— agriculture and forestry	447.4	249.0	0.3	198.1	55.7

Source: *Narodnoe obrazovanie v SSSR – 1989/90 uchebnyi god*, Moscow, Gosobrazovanie, 1990, pp. 18–19.

Table 10.17 Graduate students (*aspiranty*) by full- and part-time study and place of study, USSR, 1980–9 (end of year)

| | Total number of aspiranty | Of whom: | | Of total: | Of whom: | |
		Full-time	Part-time	Students in vuzy	Full-time	Part-time
1980	96,820	39,666	57,154	58,053	28,290	29,763
1981	97,860	42,011	55,849	58,663	29,968	28,695
1982	98,320	44,228	54,092	59,049	31,703	27,346
1983	98,615	45,898	52,717	59,243	33,040	26,203
1984	97,779	46,306	51,473	58,527	33,222	25,305
1985	97,352	46,239	51,113	57,935	33,119	24,816
1986	96,125	46,168	49,977	57,207	33,030	24,177
1987	95,606	47,238	48,368	57,025	33,679	23,346
1988	97,569	50,426	47,143	58,924	35,806	23,118
1989	95,310	51,260	44,050	51,782	NA	NA

Sources: Goskomstat, *Press-vypusk*, no. 130, 10 April 1988; *Statisticheskii press-byulleten'*, 1990, no. 13, p. 47; *Narodnoe khozyaistvo SSSR* – various years, Moscow, Finansy i statistika.

Table 10.18 Participation of research workers, graduate students and students in work of scientific research divisions of *vuzy*, by Union Republic, 1986 (data from a one-off study)

	Total participants in scientific work (thousands)			Those who conducted work in scientific research divisions of vuzy (% of total participants)		
	Scientific & scientific pedagogical workers [a]	*Graduate students who took leave from work*	*Day students*	*Scientific & scientific pedagogical workers*	*Graduate students who took leave from work*	*Day students*
USSR	481.3	32.4	2673.8	78	71	27
RSFSR	270.8	23.3	1499.9	78	76	34
Ukraine	89.1	4.4	450.1	94	66	21
Belorussia	17.2	0.8	98.8	68	68	23
Uzbekistan	21.6	0.8	138.5	36	49	29
Kazakhstan	21.5	0.9	151.3	73	34	5
Georgia	10.5	0.5	47.6	60	31	12
Azerbaidzhan	10.4	0.3	53.3	81	50	20
Lithuania	6.7	0.3	36.3	63	74	29
Moldavia	4.6	0.1	30.6	79	43	4
Latvia	5.1	0.2	25.0	94	71	47
Kirgizia	5.2	0.2	36.3	48	30	2
Tadzhikistan	5.2	0.2	31.7	66	84	6
Armenia	7.8	0.3	36.9	79	26	5
Turkmenia	2.6	0.1	23.6	51	27	11
Estonia	3.0	0.1	13.9	95	98	46

[a] There is no satisfactory translation of the Russian *nauchnye, nauchno-pedagogicheskie rabotniki*. Most *vuzy* include both full-time researchers and teaching staff also engaged in research

Source: Narodnoe obrazovanie i kul'tura v SSSR, Moscow, Finansy i statistika, 1989, p. 238.

NOTES AND REFERENCES

1 The Baltic republics have been leaders in formulating entire new systems of education. For example, see *Demokraticheskaya perestroika v Litovskoi SSR (1988-1989gg.). Natsional'nye voprosy i prosveshchenie. Sbornik materialov*, Vilnius, Akademiya nauk Litovskoi SSR, 1989.

2 At the beginning of 1989/90, 904 *vuzy* were operating – ten more than in 1985/86. In 1989 new *vuzy* included the All-Russian Academy of Painting, Sculpture and Architecture (*Vserossiiskaya Akademiya zhivopisi, vayaniya i zodchestva*), Moscow; Novosibirsk Architectural Institute; Institute of Cosmic Technology (*Institut kosmicheskoi tekhniki*), Krasnoyarsk Territory; Birobidzhan Pedagogical Institute; Khar'kov Institute of Physical Culture; and the Tashkent Machine-building Institute. The government closed the Przheval'sk Pedagogical Institute.

3 S. Fitzpatrick, *Education and Social Mobility in the Soviet Union, 1921-1934*, Cambridge, Cambridge University Press, 1979, pp. 48-9.

4 H.D. Balzer, *Soviet Science on the Edge of Reform*, Boulder, CO, Westview Press, 1989, chapter 2.

5 Goskomstat, 'Vysshie uchebnye zavedeniya v 1989 godu', *Press-vypusk*, 26 April 1990, no. 172.

6 Balzer, op. cit., pp. 20-9; and most recently T. Krasnenko and A. Shukhov, 'Kogda zhe vspomnyat o zaochnikakh?', *Vestnik vysshei shkoly*, 1990, no. 6, pp. 37-9.

7 V. Vorontsov, 'Vernulis' soldaty v auditoriyu', *Sovetskaya Rossiya*, 17 January 1990, p. 1. (The author is a professor at Orenburg Medical Institute.)

8 Impression based on conversations with a group of Soviet teachers at Georgetown University, 10 July 1990.

9 *Narodnoe obrazovanie i kul'tura v SSSR*, Moscow, Finansy i statistika, 1989, p. 104; *Molodezh' SSSR*, Moscow, Finansy i statistika, 1990, p. 93.

10 V. Kirillov-Ugrumov, at the time chairman of VAK, interviewed in *Izvestiya*, 30 August 1986, p. 3; B. Konovalov, 'VAK v svete glasnosti', *Izvestiya*, 22 February 1990, p. 2. (Konovalov is an *Izvestiya* science reporter.)

11 ibid.

12 This section draws heavily on G.A. Lakhtin, *Organizatsiya sovetskoi nauki: istoriya i sovremennost'*, Moscow, Nauka, 1990, pp. 69-82, and H.D. Balzer, 'Engineers: the rise and decline of a social myth', in L. Graham (ed.), *Science and the Soviet Social Order*, Cambridge, MA, Harvard University Press, 1990, pp. 141-67.

13 The classic sources on information problems in the USSR are J.S. Berliner, *The Innovation Decision in Soviet Industry*, Cambridge, MA, MIT Press, 1976, and R. Amann and J. Cooper (eds), *Industrial Innovation in the Soviet Union*, New Haven, Yale University Press, 1982. For recent evidence that the problems persist, see A.K. Solov'ev, *Nauchno-tekhnicheskaya deyatelnost': faktory intensifikatsii*, Moscow, Znanie, 1989.

14 Lakhtin, op. cit., p. 77. Lakhtin also points out that those who talk about a tremendous unrealized reserve/potential of *vuz* science are ignoring the serious limitations on time of *vuz* personnel. At best, they can devote 22 per cent of their work time to research, and many of the teaching staff have 'neither the training nor the talent' for genuine research (p. 76).

15 These scientific research institutes should not be confused with the approximately 1,300 scientific research laboratories under the system of the State Committee for Education. The laboratories perform mainly contract research, employing scientific workers who are not classroom teachers. Most of the laboratories do not serve a major pedagogical function. See Solov'ev, op. cit., p. 51.

16 Lakhtin, op. cit., p. 79.
17 V. Lisovsky, 'Troika, pyaterka, vuz', *Pravda*, 7 January 1990, p. 4. (Lisovsky is a professor at Leningrad University.)
18 *Narodnoe obrazovanie . . .* , op. cit., p. 238.
19 Goskomstat, op. cit.
20 S. Kirillova, 'Kto bol'she?', *Poisk*, 22–28 July 1990, no. 25, p. 5. The exact words quoted are: *Platit' devchonke, kotoraya cherez god vyskochit v dekretnyi otpusk?* (Why pay a woman, who after one year will drop out due to maternity leave?)

11

THE SOVIET KOREANS: THE POLITICS OF ETHNIC EDUCATION

Youn-Cha Shin Chey

INTRODUCTION

In the world today there are 5m Koreans living outside Korea. The largest number, 1.8m Koreans, live in China, having formed an autonomous state; 700,000 reside in Japan, 1m in the United States, half a million in the Soviet Union and the remainder in Europe and South America. The Soviet Koreans comprise one of a multiplicity of nationalities in the USSR. The majority of them are settled in Kazakhstan and Central Asia. Despite the marked contribution that they have made to the building of Soviet society, the Soviet Koreans have remained until recently a 'silent', 'punished people', and very little has been written about them.

This contribution will describe the recent historical phenomenon of the Korean presence in the Soviet Union and the impact of the politics of ethnic education on the Korean minority under the changing Soviet leadership. Several factors that can be attributed to the facilitation of processes of the sovietization of Koreans will be elaborated, in contrast to the failing efforts to preserve the Korean ethnic identity. The revolutionary policy of perestroika and glasnost put forward by M.S. Gorbachev has precipitated a new surge for ethnic education among Soviet Korean intellectuals and a reevaluation of the importance of ethnically-based educational programmes for the Soviet Koreans. The limitations and barriers that they face, as well as their accomplishments and the prospects for the successful implementation of the programmes, are directly related to the politics of ethnic education in Soviet society.

KOREAN PRESENCE IN THE SOVIET UNION

In the Soviet Union there are over 110 minority nationalities, and 130 languages are spoken within its vast territorial boundary. The 1989 census shows the total population of the USSR as 285,743,000. The Russians form the largest ethnic group, comprising 51 per cent of the total Soviet population.

Aside from the nationalities of the fifteen republics, there are seven ethnic groups whose populations exceed 1m, including Germans, Poles, Jews and Tartars. Koreans are listed as one of nine ethnic groups numbering between 400,000 and 1m.[1] The official census data reveal the growth of the Korean population (see Table 11.1). Thus in 1989 the Soviet Koreans had a population of nearly 439,000[2] with an increase of 12.9 per cent from almost 389,000 in 1979. They ranked twenty-eighth in size of population among the ethnic minorities of the USSR.

Table 11.1 Korean population, Russian Empire and USSR, 1907–89

1907	1923	1959	1970	1979	1989
46,430	106,817	313,735	357,507	388,926	438,650

Sources: S.D. Anosov, *Koreitsy v Ussuriiskom krae,* Khabarovsk, Knizhnoe delo, 1928; *Itogi Vsesoyuznoi perepisi naseleniya 1970 goda,* vol. 4, Moscow, Statistika, 1973, p. 10; *Chislennost' i sostav naseleniya SSSR,* Moscow, Finansy i statistika, 1984, p. 72; 'Raspredelenie naseleniya SSSR po natsional'nosti i yazyku', *Vestnik statistiki,* 1990, no. 10, p. 69.

Kazakhstan and the four Central Asian republics are now the home of the majority of Koreans, as more than two-thirds of them are settled in this area. In 1959 the Koreans in Central Asia and Kazakhstan numbered 220,378 and in 1970 the numbers increased to 250,523. According to census counts from 1959 to 1989 the distribution of Koreans in the five republics was as presented in Table 11.2. Statistics show that the Soviet Koreans in general live in compact groups, mostly in the regions which they were designated to settle since 1937 in Uzbekistan and Kazakhstan. The 1970 and 1979 Censuses give some information on the distribution of Koreans in these two republics (see Table 11.3; a breakdown is available only in the case of regions with major Korean populations). In 1979 some 163,000 (42 per cent) of the Koreans in the Soviet Union were living in Uzbekistan. Of these, an estimated 30,000 were resident in the city of Tashkent – the exact figure is not at our disposal – and almost 74,000 in Tashkent Region. Approximately 92,000 (nearly 24 per cent) were domiciled in Kazakhstan.[3] By 1989 Uzbekistan Koreans numbered roughly 183,000, still about 42 per cent of the USSR total, with over 103,000 in Kazakhstan (again just under 24 per cent).[4] In addition to the large concentration in Central Asia, there are about 40,000 Koreans living on Sakhalin Island who were left behind after World War II by the Japanese, and approximately 30,000 in Vladivostok, Khabarovsk and the Far East. It is reported that around 6,000 Koreans reside in Moscow and Leningrad, and that there are Koreans resident in the Ukraine and the Caucasus as well.

Table 11.2 Korean population, Soviet Central Asian Republics and Kazakhstan, 1959–89

Republic	1959	1970	1979	1989
Uzbekistan	138,453	147,538	163,062	183,140
Kazakhstan	74,019	81,598	91,984	103,315
Kirgizia	3,622	9,404	NA	NA
Tadzhikistan	2,365	8,490	NA	NA
Turkmenia	1,919	3,493	NA	NA

Sources: Itogi Vsesoyuznoi perepisi naseleniya 1959 goda, Moscow, Gosstatizdat, 1963, pp. 116, 128; *Itogi Vsesoyuznoi perepisi naseleniya 1970 goda*, vol. 4, Moscow, Statistika, 1973, pp. 13, 284, 295, 306; *Chislennost' i sostav naseleniya SSSR*, Moscow, Finansy i statistika, 1984, pp. 110, 116; 'Raspredelenie naseleniya Uzbekskoi SSR po natsional'nosti i yazyku', *Vestnik statistiki*, 1990, no. 11, p. 79; 'Raspredelenie naseleniya Kazakhskoi SSR po natsional'nosti i yazyku', *Vestnik statistiki*, 1990, no. 12, p. 70.

Table 11.3 Korean population, Uzbekistan and Kazakhstan, by selected regions, 1970–9

	1970	1979
Uzbekistan		
Tashkent Region	73,349	73,981
Tashkent (city)	18,186	NA
Syrdar'ya	11,661	12,296
Karakalpak ASSR	8,958	NA
Samarkand	7,708	NA
Fergana	6,438	NA
Khorezm	6,368	NA
Kazakhstan		
Kzyl-Orda	13,429	12,503
Karaganda	13,391	10,638
Taldy-Kurgan	12,514	12,215
Chimkent	9,862	11,071
Dzhambul	8,228	NA
Alma-Ata (city)	6,908	NA
Alma-Ata Region	4,391	NA

Sources: Itogi Vsesoyuznoi perepisi naseleniya 1970 goda, vol. 4, Moscow, Statistika, 1973, pp. 215, 217, 218, 220, 233, 241, 247; *Chislennost' i sostav naseleniya SSSR*, Moscow, Finansy i statistika, 1984, pp. 114, 118, 122.

The Korean presence in Soviet Central Asia has a unique history which has not been fully documented to this day. The story begins in another area altogether. The Russian Empire acquired the virtually uninhabited lands of the Far East, 350,000 square miles of territory with only about 15,000 inhabitants, from China in 1860 under the terms of the Treaty of Peking. The territory stretched between the Ussuri and Amur rivers and the Pacific Ocean, and included the Maritime (Primorskii) Territory. This newly secured boundary placed Russia at the back door of Korea, and the new geographical proximity prompted the development of relations between the two countries.

For ten years following the first Korean immigration in 1863, when thirteen families settled in the South Ussuri area, the regional administration was tolerant of the Korean presence in Russia. Koreans provided cheap labour for this sparsely inhabited land, working as *arendatory* (tenant farmers) and *batraki* (farm labourers). Those without any means of support were sent by order of the local Russian administration to various parts of the region along the Ussuri and Amur rivers. Through this government relocation, the first large Korean village, Blagoslovennoe, was formed along the Samarga River in 1872. Thus from the very beginning the formation of Korean settlements was not a purely natural process; the tsarist administration played a part in their placement, using this new source of population to its advantage.[5]

Initially Korean peasants and labourers emigrated mostly for economic reasons. However, after the annexation of Korea by Japan in 1910 and the unsuccessful March the First Uprising in 1919, Koreans fled to Russia for political reasons as well. The last major wave of immigration occurred between 1917 and 1923, with the majority of these new arrivals settling in the Maritime Territory.[6] The tsarist regimes were ambivalent on the Korean question. Government indecision meant that policy depended largely upon the discretion of individual local administrators, who had to consider several conflicting factors. The Koreans represented cheap farm labour. More than 80 per cent of the Koreans in Russia were *batraki*, and they assisted Russia's agricultural development.

The October Revolution was welcomed by many landless Koreans as a way to improve or settle the land question. In October 1917 Korean peasants even formed Red Army detachments and participated in partisan activities, fighting alongside Russian units. The Revolution did not, however, immediately improve their lot. It was only after 1923 that the new Soviet regime began to regulate the dispersal of land among the peasants. By 1926 a majority of the Koreans who had settled in the Soviet Far East had received Soviet citizenship, a prerequisite for obtaining land. Land was essential for the rice cultivation initiated by Korean peasants on the Ussuri plain, by Lake Khanka.

Rice was sown for the first time in the Maritime Territory in 1917 by Koreans who had brought the seeds from Korea, and production rapidly increased. In addition to rice, silkworm breeding was introduced to the region by Koreans. More than 210,000 mulberry tree saplings were brought into the Nikol'sk-Ussuriisk and Vladivostok areas. Koreans also grew beans, barley and maize, and a small number worked in the fishing and lumber industries. During the late 1920s and early 1930s the sizeable settlement by Koreans thus made an important contribution to agricultural development in the Far East, especially on the Ussuri-Khanka plain, by their persistence on land previously thought unsuitable for farming. Their hard work and effort, however, went unrewarded when in 1937 all 182,000 Koreans in the area were ordered by Stalin to be deported to Central Asia and Kazakhstan. It took three months, from September to December 1937, to relocate them by freight trains. Thousands perished on the way and on the barren steppes after the forced transplantation. The Soviet Koreans today are descendants of these 'punished people' who survived. Solzhenitsyn described the event in his *Gulag Archipelago*:

> In 1937 some tens of thousands of those suspicious Koreans – with Khalkin-Gol in mind, face to face with Japanese imperialism, who could trust those slant-eyed heathens? – from palsied old men to puling infants, with some portions of their beggarly belongings, were swiftly and quietly transferred from the Far East to Kazakhstan. So swiftly that they spent their first winter in mud-brick houses without windows (where would all that glass have come from!). And so quietly that nobody except the neighbouring Kazakhs learned of this resettlement, no one who counted let slip a word about it, no foreign correspondent uttered a squeak.[7]

ETHNIC EDUCATION AND THE SOVIETIZATION PROCESSES

Koreans in the Soviet Union call themselves either Koryo Saram (people from Koryo, the name of Koryo Dynasty, 932–1392) or Chosun Saram (people from Chosun, taken from the ancient name for Korea meaning 'Land of Morning Calm'). But the younger generation see themselves as 'Soviet Koreans' with a dual identity: ethnically of Korean nationality but with Soviet citizenship. The transformation in self-identification from Koryo Saram to Soviet Koreans has resulted from the processes of sovietization under Soviet nationality policy.

During the early period of the Koreans' settlement in Russia, their search for ethnic education was evident. Before the 1917 Revolution, despite extreme hardship and pressure of russification, they were able to operate 182 Korean schools in their farming villages, on funds raised among themselves. There were 5,750 pupils and 257 teachers.[8] With the establishment of Soviet government, a free and compulsory public education system was instituted and a policy of educational and cultural pluralism adopted. Following the education reform of 1923, the study of all of the minority languages including Korean was encouraged, in order to eradicate illiteracy. The new Soviet government was intent on reaching all of the nationalities in their native languages, so that the country could be organized and every citizen would be indoctrinated in accordance with party policy.

By 1931 in the Far East there were 380 Korean schools with 33,595 students. The Korean minority operated three secondary schools, two technical colleges and two teacher training colleges. In the same year the first Korean Pedagogical Institute with departments of history, literature, physics, mathematics and biology was established in Vladivostok, and there were 780 students.[9] Textbooks and other books for the general reader were published and available in the Korean language in the 1930s. When the liquidation of the Koreans in the Soviet Far East took place in 1937, the survivors had to rebuild their life on the barren soil of Central Asia with their bare hands.[10] They turned the desert into a cultivated land and, according to a fourth-generation Soviet émigré to the United States, the barren place where Soviet Koreans toiled with sweat and drudgery is now called *tsvetuyushchii gorodok* (little town of blossoms). Many were awarded the title of Hero of Socialist Labour for their work on collective farms such as Politotdel, Polyarnaya Zvezda and Sverdlov. They showed a high degree of efficiency and productivity as Korean pioneers in the formerly uninhabited territory.

It is to be noted that the special settlement restrictions on Koreans and the loss of free mobility nevertheless enabled reinforcement of Korean customs and traditions which in turn strengthened ethnic identity. The Korean language was spoken at home and taught in the schools of the collective farms where Koreans were concentrated. Schooling in the native tongue, however, was given only up to the eighth class (about age 16), all instruction thereafter being either in Russian or in the languages of the republic.[11] Stalin's dictum specified that Soviet culture was to be 'national in form' but 'socialist in content', and the declared goal of the USSR was the creation of a society that 'fuses' all nationalities. In order to achieve this goal the Russian language had to be learned as the official inter-republic language of the Soviet Union. Thus education in Korean has decreased rapidly with less and less demand.

Only since the time of the 'thaw', following Stalin's death in 1953, have the children of Korean collective farmers been permitted to receive higher education in the cities, outside their place of exile.[12] In Uzbekistan in the 1960s there was even the textbook *Chosuno Kyokwaso*, published by Kim Nam-Suk. This was used for classes 3 and 4 (with entry at 9-plus and 10-plus), but it has become unavailable, as it has not been republished for over twenty years. In 1975 there were reportedly fourteen secondary schools and a teachers' institute offering Korean language instruction.

As Koreans gained freedom of mobility, they set a new priority for their children to achieve higher education, which required the mastery of the Russian language. The educational reform of 1958 provided the formal right of parents to choose which type of school their children would attend.[13] In Soviet society a knowledge of Russian is a prerequisite not only for higher education but for employment, career advancement and social mobility. Russian is the language of command in the armed forces. Under these circumstances those transplanted Koreans who had now lost all contact with their motherland chose to educate their children in schools where the language of instruction was Russian rather than their respective republic languages such as Uzbek or Kazakh. The 1989 census data show that only 49.4 per cent listed Korean as their native language, compared to 55.4 per cent in 1979. Nearly half of the total Korean population in the USSR speak Russian as their second language (43.3 per cent). In the case of the Uzbek and Kazakh nationalities, the percentage speaking Uzbek as their native language was 98.3 and Kazakh 97.0, with a decrease of less than 1 per cent within the decade.[14]

The mastery of the Russian language and the high rate of achievement in higher education among the second and third generations of Koreans facilitated the sovietization process in comparison with other ethnic minorities with low educational attainment and lack of fluency in Russian. External factors – the tragic historical event which resulted in abrupt truncation from their motherland and the subsequent territorially restricted living conditions as a secondary minority within the non-Russian republics – provided no support in the quest for ethnic education and left no choice other than accelerated assimilation, predicated by Soviet nationality and language policies.

Another important factor which has weakened the search for ethnic education is the phenomenon of urbanization, which became possible because of the Koreans' achievement in higher education and their socio-economic advancement. In 1959 it was reported that more than 70 per cent of Koreans in Central Asia and Kazakhstan were living in rural areas, whereas in 1970 this figure was down to 41.5 per cent. The city dwellers numbered 62 per cent in the Tashkent Region of Uzbekistan, 64 per cent in Kirgizia, 89 per cent in Tadzhikistan and 71.7 per cent in Turkmenia. Evident since 1960, this shift in residence to urban areas among Koreans has not been witnessed among other nationalities in Central Asia. The growing preference for city dwelling in a multi-ethnic environment for professional occupations instead of labouring on the farms, and for intermarriage among the younger Koreans, hastened the sovietization process and relegated Korean national identity. Thus, in contemporary terms, Koreans in the Soviet Union were becoming active participants in the social processes of formation of the new historical community of 'Soviet people', as stated in the Constitution of 1977.[15]

The socio-economic development of Soviet Korean professionals brought about the emergence of a Soviet Korean intelligentsia. Alexander Solzhenitsyn points out in *The Gulag Archipelago*:

The Koreans prospered even more in Kazakhstan than Germans and Greeks . . . and by the fifties were already in large measure emancipated from serfdom. They were no longer to report . . . and they travelled freely from oblast to oblast, provided they did not cross the borders of the republic . . . They responded very well to education, quickly filled the educational institutions of Kazakhstan and became the main component of the educated stratum in the republic.[16]

During my research in Central Asia in 1985, I was told by Dr Mikhail Wang, a Soviet Korean professor, that of 12,000 Koreans living in Alma-Ata there were thirty who had obtained doctoral degrees and more than 100 with master's degrees. I was also told that of 40,000 Korean residents in Tashkent Region 30 per cent belonged to the Communist Party. Over 100 Soviet Koreans whom I met in Central Asia were academicians, journalists, scientists, administrators, researchers and artists, most of whom were confirmed, committed communist professionals.

It has to be noted that through the efforts of these educated intellectuals the Korean cultural tradition was being maintained, in however limited a fashion, in Central Asia. In the course of urbanization and modernization they have become more ethnically concerned. For them the policy that encourages an appreciation of one's ethnic heritage in one's respective republic has to apply to the Korean minority as well. The historic *Koreiskii teatr* (Korean Theatre) is being maintained, with performances of Korean classical plays. A daily inter-republic newspaper, *Lenin Kichi*, is printed in the Korean language in Alma-Ata, Kazakhstan. In 1985 Korean was being taught again after many years to student teachers at the Nizami Pedagogical Institute in Tashkent, Uzbekistan. Korean-language radio broadcasts go on the air three times a week in Alma-Ata. Some fifty Soviet Korean authors and poets, many of whom are members of the Writers' Union, engage in creative writing in the Korean language and are published in Tashkent, Alma-Ata, Kzyl-Orda and Sakhalin. The Zhazushei publishing house in Alma-Ata has brought out one work in Korean annually: *Haibaragi* (*The Sunflower*, 1982), *Hang boky Norai* (*The Song of Happiness*, 1983) by Yon Song-Yong, *Soom* (*The Breath*, 1985) by Kim Joon, *Ssak* (*The Sprout*, 1986) by Kim Kwang Hyun, and a collection of novels by Kimi Chul. It has been known to take at least ten years for a Korean writer to have a chance to appear in print. A writer has to have two of his or her works published in order to become a member of the Writers' Union.[17] Many Soviet Korean writers manage to publish their work in the literary section of *Lenin Kichi*, which has become popular and is the only such outlet among Korean readers.

The reduction in the circulation of *Lenin Kichi* to fewer than 10,000 copies in 1987 was, however, a matter of grave concern. It indicated the seriousness of the loss of proficiency and interest in the Korean language. During my visit, Korean language instruction was being conducted without any textbook both at Leningrad University and Tashkent Pedagogical Institute. At both institutes there were fewer than ten students on the course. The struggle for the preservation of Korean culture by Korean intellectuals was a task undertaken with little financial and administrative support either from the local government or from the growing number of fourth and fifth generation Soviet Koreans who are further removed from their ethnic roots. As older Koreans (the second generation of Koryo Saram – see above) die out, the processes of sovietization remain, under the circumstances, an inevitable choice for the younger migrant dispersed Koreans. Ethnic education for Koreans in their own culture was quickly reaching the point of no practical significance.

PERESTROIKA AND SOVIET KOREANS' SEARCH FOR ETHNIC EDUCATION

Since Gorbachev's ascendancy to the leadership in March 1985, and with his Vladivostok speech in 1986 as well as his Krasnoyarsk statements, he has 'opened the window' to the Pacific Basin. Under glasnost and perestroika, the Soviet Koreans and Korean studies in the USSR began to experience a very complex period of change. Over the years, Korean studies in the Soviet Union have been extensive, as shown in L.M. Volodina's bibliography on Korea published in 1981. But very little has been written or researched on the lives of Koreans in the USSR.[18] Among work by Soviet Korean specialists, 80 per cent is concentrated on the contemporary problems of, in the main, North Korea.[19] The quantity of publications on South Korea or in the Korean language, apart from selections on Marxism-Leninism and some translations of Russian classical literature, has been minimal.

Bilingualism among non-Russian ethnic groups in the USSR is the stated Soviet language policy. And yet the development of the Korean language and Korean studies in the Soviet Union has been both determined by the socio-political changes that have taken place during the past 125 years and restricted to follow the planned state guidelines. This has resulted in a lack of balance in research, which has suffered from incomplete accuracy and objectivity. The Korean language has not been accorded any significance as a medium for instruction, publication or communication within the Soviet system. The political instability after the death of Brezhnev in 1982 and the ensuing changes in the leadership of the Soviet Union affected academia. Reform-minded Andropov reigned for only nine months, followed by tradition-bound Chernenko. For the period from 1984 to 1985, interest in Korea was extremely low.[20]

Nevertheless, a new direction in the field of Korean studies has taken place under Gorbachev. This is evident from an analysis of new Soviet publications on Korea since 1986 and from G.M. Ageeva's bibliography issued in 1987. Ageeva's bibliography includes a collection of Korean literary works translated into twenty-two different ethnic languages of the Soviet Union, and poems written in the Korean language by Soviet Koreans have been included for the first time.[21]

An analysis of the articles, books and dissertations on Korea that are included in the USSR's monthly bibliographical index of social science publications on South and South-East Asia and the Far East[22] over the period from July 1986 to June 1988 reveals a dramatic increase in the number of volumes issued. This applies in particular to the field of economics, displacing history which predominated in previous years. It is the economic and social development of South Korea that has now become the focus of research. For the first time, writings on South Korea as a new industrial state exceeded those on North Korea.[23]

Even so, Vladimir Li, a professor at Moscow State University and a department head at the Institute of Oriental Studies of the USSR Academy of Sciences, notes that there has been a crisis in the area of Soviet Korean studies in more recent years. It has been especially evident since the death of two renowned Korean specialists, Georgii Kim and Vladimir Tikhomirov, in 1989. Both the subject and the scale of academic studies were affected. In 1988 only two substantial works on Korea were published in the Soviet Union, and not a single book on Korean studies was included in the 1989 plan of the Nauka Academic Publishing House, despite growing interest in contemporary life there. Only one book on Korea, by Kovalev, was scheduled to appear in 1990. Li has also expressed his concern that the number of students of Korea at the colleges and universities is insignificant in the Soviet Union today.[24]

Nevertheless, according to Li, a number of publications are anticipated in future years, and there has been a new research interest in the history of Soviet Koreans. Those engaged in academic research appear to have at least sustained their numbers. In the *Bibliographical Dictionary of Soviet Orientologists* published in 1975, only forty-two specialists in Korean studies were listed. They comprised under 3 per cent of all orientologists, who numbered 1,488 in total.[25] It is estimated that there are now (1991) approximately fifty researchers working on Korea.

A stronger impression of the impact of the policy of glasnost and perestroika on the Soviet Koreans can be obtained if one examines the Korean-language newspaper *Lenin Kichi*. In the absence of any structured programmes of development supported by the government, the newspaper has played a major role in ethnic education, just as it has maintained the use of the language as a tool of communication among Korean-speaking Soviet Koreans ever since 1938. The 28 June 1988 issue of *Lenin Kichi* reported the formation of a new course for training reporters on the Korean-language newspaper at the Kazakh State University. The 6 July 1988 issue reported that a section of the newspaper would be devoted on a regular basis to Korean language instruction for its readers. It has started to print regular and numerous articles on various aspects of Korean culture: clothing, food and customs. As in the past, *Lenin Kichi* features a monthly Korean literary page in order to introduce new creative works and essays by Soviet Koreans. In recent issues there has been a marked openness, including articles critical of the educational system. In the absence of any textbook in the Korean language or literary works in Korean, *Lenin Kichi* has the function of meeting these otherwise unmet needs. It provides a valuable source for understanding the changes taking place in Soviet Korean society.

Furthermore, there is an increased number of schools and *vuzy* (higher educational institutions) where the Korean language is offered. Since 1985, teachers of the Korean language have been trained on a five-year course at Tashkent's Nizami Pedagogical Institute. In September 1989 a Kazakh secondary school began offering Korean. Four secondary schools in Tashkent also started Korean instruction, with approximately eighty students enrolled. It is reported that, since the Seoul Olympics and the establishment of trade offices in Seoul, Korea and Moscow, and the weekly direct flight of Aeroflot and KAL between Seoul and Moscow, there has been an enhanced interest in the contemporary life of South Korea, which has stimulated interest in Korean studies and the Soviet Koreans. Courses at Moscow State University and Leningrad State University include for the first year Korean phonetics, grammar and conversation; for the second year literature and history (ancient history, the Three Kingdoms, Koryo and Yi Dynasty) are offered. At the Institute of Asia and Africa, Moscow University, there are 1,000 students enrolled, but only about ten of them are on the Korean studies course. There are six Soviet Korean academics at Moscow University including Professor Mikhail Pak and Professor Mazur, a second-generation Korean who compiled the Russian–Korean Dictionary and who serves as head of the Korean Department. It is announced that Sakhalin Pedagogical Institute plans to establish a Korean section. The University of Vladivostok also trains Korean-language teachers.

In March 1990, Moscow University and Yonsei University of Seoul established exchange programmes. The Korea University of Foreign Languages in Seoul started exchange programmes with the Pushkin Institute in Moscow. It is reported that the Institute of International Affairs of the USSR Ministry of Foreign Affairs utilizes the *Korea Daily News*, published in Seoul, as its material for Korean language instruction. The largest collection of Korean books is held in the Lenin Library; it has 16,000 books, 10 per cent of which were published in South Korea.

Korean language teaching has been introduced at the newly established Korean Cultural Centres in various cities where Koreans live in large numbers: Tashkent and Samarkand, Uzbekistan; Khar'kov, Ukraine; and Chimkent and Alma-Ata, Kazakhstan. In addition, in May 1990 the National Korean Cultural Association of Soviet Koreans was formed, with an attendance of 300 Soviet Koreans from all parts of the USSR. Its newly elected chairperson, Professor Mikhail Pak, ranks the revival of Korean culture in the Soviet Union as its first priority. According to his report, the possibility of relocation of Soviet Koreans back to the Maritime Territory was to be on the agenda for the next annual meeting.

In the June 1990 issue of *Korea Daily News*, the Ministry of Education of South Korea announced the preparation of Korean conversation and history textbooks to be used for a four-week course, plans for a three-month training programme for Soviet Koreans, and the possible establishment of Korean Educational Institutes in Moscow, Khabarovsk, Tashkent and Leningrad. The implementation of these plans will no doubt assist the efforts to revive Korean cultural identity among young Soviet Koreans, who comprise 70 per cent of the Korean population today and who do not know the Korean language, history or traditions.

PROSPECTS FOR THE SOVIET KOREANS

M.S. Gorbachev stated in his book *Perestroika: New Thinking for Our Country and the World*:

> Every national culture is a treasure which cannot be lost. But a sound interest in everything valuable which each national culture has should not degenerate into attempts to shut off from the objective processes of interaction and rapprochement . . . Even the smallest ethnicity cannot be denied the right to its mother-tongue . . . But at the same time, in our vast multi-ethnic country we cannot do without a common means of communication. The Russian language has naturally come to fulfil this role.[26]

Soviet nationality policy, therefore, reiterated by Gorbachev, is the two-pronged strategy of giving recognition at the local republic level and at the same time of securing central priorities and a Russian preponderance Union-wide. Gorbachev, in supporting Leninist nationality policy, advocates internationalist education with the aim of breeding Soviet patriotism.

The Soviet Koreans, however, constitute an extraterritorial and dispersed secondary group like the Soviet Jews, Soviet Germans and Crimean Tartars, in contrast to the republic nationalities that are territorially-based primary ethnic groups, such as Uzbeks and Kazakhs.[27] Since their forced settlement in Central Asia, the Soviet Koreans as one of the secondary minorities have had practically no administrative or cultural rights or provisions for over half a century.

And yet the Koreans' ethnic communal values and ties persisted in the Soviet Union in spite of enormous injustice and sacrifice inflicted upon them. It was the Korean zeal for educational advancement which enabled them to survive the ethnic policies of the USSR. Their achievement of interethnic linguistic facility and access to higher education altered their socio-economic status and made possible the emergence of their intelligentsia and the process of their urbanization. Young Soviet Korean intellectuals first became role model constituents as *sovetskii narod*, having acquired a new ethnic identity. But the link between education and the development of nationalism began to surface in the consciousness of the Soviet Korean intelligentsia. The noted contemporary writer Anatoly Kim, a third-generation intellectual and member of the Soviet Writers' Union, who thinks, lives and writes only in the Russian language, asserts that happiness is possible only for those whose motherland and fatherland remain identical.[28] A fourth-generation journalist, Kim Brut, in his recently published book *Who are We?*, poignantly describes his agony in the search for his identity, and affirms the importance and urgency of ethnic education.[29]

It is the Soviet Korean intelligentsia, encouraged by the government policy of perestroika, who are calling for perestroika of the Soviet Koreans linguistically, culturally and politically. There is an attempt to redress the historic injustice done to them. They are in pursuit of a revitalization of ethnic education that could prevent the potential extinction of the Korean cultural heritage among the younger generation. At the present time, ethnically based educational programmes are actively promoted on three different levels: (1) through political participation in the local and state processes for the development of curricula at academic and research institutions; (2) by means of the establishment of Soviet Korean Associations and Cultural Centres where Korean language instruction and other cultural activities can be promoted, as well as the community's interests; and (3) in seeking international support, through exchange agreements with foreign institutions, particularly those of South Korea and the United States, and by active participation in international seminars for the exchange of information and discussion of research interests. The prospect of the re-relocation of nearly half a million Soviet Koreans to the Far East, for the establishment of an autonomous republic like the Yon-Byon prefecture in China, is an alternative which is currently contemplated or debated by the Soviet intelligentsia. The Korean question is an ethnic, political and socio-economic issue that remains to be addressed in building the Soviet society of the twenty-first century.

NOTES AND REFERENCES

1 Gosudarstvennyi komitet SSSR po statistike, 'Ob itogakh Vsesoyuznoi perepisi naseleniya 1989g.', *Press-vypusk*, no. 16, 19 January 1990. The nine groups are: Chechens, 957,000; Udmurts, 747,000; Mari, 671,000; Avars, 601,000; Ossetians, 598,000; Lezgians, 466,000; Koreans, 439,000; Karakalpaks, 424,000; Buryats, 421,000. For more details, see 'Raspredelenie naseleniya SSSR po natsional'nosti i yazyku', *Vestnik statistiki*, 1990, no. 10, p. 69.
2 The actual figure is estimated to be higher, as the discrepancy can be explained by the choice of non-Korean ethnicity at the age of 16 in the event of inter-marriage. I am told that in some cases not all household members are registered, to avoid heavy taxes.

3 *Chislennost' i sostav naseleniya SSSR*, Moscow, Finansy i statistika, 1984, pp. 72, 110; M.B. Olcott, *The Kazakhs*, Stanford, CA, Hoover Press, 1987, appendix 1.
4 'Raspredelenie naseleniya SSSR . . . ', op. cit.; 'Raspredelenie naseleniya Uzbekskoi SSR po natsional'nosti i yazyku', *Vestnik statistiki*, 1990, no. 11, p. 77; 'Raspredelenie naseleniya Kazakhskoi SSR po natsional'nosti i yazyku', *Vestnik statistiki*, 1990, no. 12, p. 70.
5 Kim Syn Khva, *Ocherki po istorii sovetskikh koreitsev*, Alma-Ata, Nauka, 1965.
6 S.D. Anosov, *Koreitsy v Ussuriiskom krae*, Khabarovsk, Knizhnoe delo, 1928, p. 8.
7 A. Solzhenitsyn, *The Gulag Archipelago*, New York, Harper & Row, 1976, pp. 386–7.
8 Kim Syn Khva, op. cit., pp. 198, 209, 211.
9 ibid.
10 V. Kim, 'Koreitsy', *Literaturnyi Kirgizstan*, 1988, no. 2, pp. 102–10.
11 N. Grant, *Soviet Education*, New York, Penguin, 4th edn, 1979, p. 19.
12 A. Bohr, 'Breaking the silence: the mass deportation of Koreans under Stalin', *Radio Liberty Research*, RL 397/88, 1 September 1988, p. 4.
13 R. Karklins, *Ethnic Relations in the USSR*, Boston, Allen & Unwin, 1986, p. 104.
14 Gosudarstvennyi komitet SSSR po statistike, op. cit., p. 9.
15 *Konstitutsiya Soyuza Sovetskikh Sotsialisticheskikh Republik*, Moscow, Politizdat, 1977, p. 4.
16 Solzhenitsyn, op. cit., p. 401.
17 V. Klasanov, *Yazyki narodov Kazakhstana i ikh vzaimodeistvie*, Alma-Ata, 1976, p. 198.
18 L.M. Volodina, *Bibliografiya Korei, 1917–1970*, Moscow, Institut vostokovedeniya AN SSSR, 1981. See also *Korean Studies*, Moscow, Academy of Sciences Institute of the Peoples of Asia, 1967; G. Ginsburgs, *Soviet Works on Korea, 1945–1970*, Los Angeles, CA, University of Southern California Press, 1973.
19 I. Kazakevich, 'Vazhnyi uchastok sovetskogo vostokovedeniya', *Aziya i Afrika segodnya*, 1969, no. 10, pp. 54–5.
20 Suh Dae-Sook, *Korean Studies in the Soviet Union: A Review and Update*, Paper no. 12, Honolulu, Center for Korean Studies, University of Hawaii, 1987, pp. 72–3.
21 G.M. Ageeva, *Koreiskaya khudozhestvennaya literatura: ukazatel' perevodov i kriticheskoi literatury, opublikovannykh na russkom i drugikh yazykakh narodov SSSR v 1945–1986 gg.*, issue no. 2, Moscow, Vsesoyuznaya gosudarstvennaya biblioteka inostrannoi literatury, 1987.
22 *Novaya sovetskaya i inostrannaya literatura po obshchestvennym naukam. Yuzhnaya i yugo-vostochnaya Aziya. Dal'nii vostok*, Moscow, Institut nauchnoi informatsii po obshchestvennym naukam AN SSSR, 1986–8.
23 Y.S. Chey, 'Korean studies in the Soviet Union', *Korea Journal* [Seoul, Korean National Commission for Unesco], 1989, vol. 29, no. 2, pp. 4–14.
24 V.F. Li, 'Korean studies in the Soviet Union, a turning point', *Korea Journal*, 1990, vol. 30, no. 1, p. 40.
25 S.D. Miliband, *Bibliograficheskii slovar' sovetskikh vostokovedov*, Moscow, AN SSSR, 1975.
26 M. Gorbachev, *Perestroika: New Thinking for Our Country and the World*, New York, Harper & Row, 1987, pp. 105–7.
27 Karklins, op. cit., pp. 6–7.
28 A. Kim, 'The dream of a seal', *Dong-A Daily News* [Seoul], 1 January 1990.
29 Kim Brut, *Who are We?*, Seoul, Slav Publishing, 1989.

12

PROSPECTS FOR COMPARATIVE EDUCATION EAST AND WEST

Detlef Glowka

INTRODUCTION

This contribution was prompted by the occasion of the sixty-fifth birthday of Professor Dr Oskar Anweiler, director of the Comparative Education Research Unit, Ruhr University, Bochum.[1] Anweiler's scholarly work has won growing appreciation in the West. Soviet scholars, however, have received his work with biting polemic. It was considered to be an expression of a decided anticommunism. He was alleged to have the intention of undermining Marxist ideology and of splitting socialist education; he was accused of ideological 'diversion' and branded a falsifier of the truth.[2] Anweiler's fate was shared by all educational research on the Soviet Union. It was understood either as part and parcel of sovietology or as ideological warfare. In the meantime a profound change in this attitude has been taking place. A tendency is emerging to recognize Western analyses on the condition of the Soviet educational system as serious and useful works, furthering one's own view of oneself. Authors have been contacted and given the opportunity to publish in the USSR. So was truth on our side, and does it now win its deserved appreciation?

In comparative education we in the West may cite the fact that we were not taken in by the palliative Soviet self-image, but always depicted conditions critically. On the whole, it may be said, both the weaknesses and the achievements of the Soviet educational system were adequately described. Nevertheless it is obvious that Western researchers did not discern the full critical extent of developments. There may have been various reasons for this, but one of them probably was that the necessary attention was not paid to the inner erosion of socialism. To a certain degree we researchers on the East have been influenced by the monolithic Soviet self-portraits. Until recently the predominant view was to see changes inside the USSR first and foremost as internal power struggles and as changes of cliques in the leading stratum of society. In the meantime, however, it should have become clear that it was changes in the consciousness and political behaviour of the population which brought about and sustained the process of perestroika. This changing awareness might have been mainly caused by the increased level of education.[3] The full scope of such a function of the Soviet education system has not, however, been recognized by Western researchers. From an educational point of view it is not so much the upheaval of the Soviet political system which is impressive in connection with the processes of perestroika, but rather the changing social awareness expressing itself in them which deserves our attention.

AREAS OF CHANGE

The new situation marked by glasnost profoundly changes the premises of our research. The relevant and accessible sources needed for an analysis of the education system have become more extensive and multifarious. The material made available by Soviet educational research is being augmented quantitatively as well as qualitatively; a wider range of media such as the press, radio and television as well as regional newspapers has to be taken into account; different positions and developmental trends must be identified and their relative significance determined; archives can be utilized to a greater extent; the language of discussion is becoming noticeably more sophisticated (e.g. one has to resort to the dictionary more often in order to understand subtleties of meaning); important material is appearing in the languages of the Soviet republics; basic data prepared or published by the central authorities are losing their explanatory value in relation to the real local and regional conditions – to name but a few issues. Here it must be taken into account that the greater variety of the sources is not only and not even primarily a result of openness, but a consequence of differentiation taking place in the object of research itself. The individual Western researcher will be able to cover the whole area only superficially; one will have to specialize in aspects of the Soviet educational system or in regions of the USSR.

The reconstruction of Soviet society has created several areas of change in the education system. What is new here is manifested with particular forcefulness. Some key problem areas of this kind can already be identified. They reflect a growing international awareness of educational problems and so are worthy of international scrutiny. This in turn has implications for our research priorities. The formerly current Soviet philosophy of education hardly merited any attention; basic conceptions of education as a personal process oriented on the meaning of life had been laid unbearably low by the well-known dogmatization of thought. Today, basic questions concerning education in the Soviet Union are being posed anew.[4]

Let us take an example. In the past the Soviet secondary general school has fascinated the foreign observer because of its uniqueness on an international scale. This model, having failed as had always been foreseen quite

211

clearly in the West, is now being abandoned and is leading to new constellations in the relationship of unity and differentiation in the secondary school system. As there is a satisfactory solution to this relationship nowhere in the world, new and exciting variants of secondary schools are to be expected from developments in the USSR. Experiments have been started in the form of gymnasia (grammar schools), lycées, colleges and single-sex education, along with teaching on the basis of Waldorf pedagogy and other approaches associated with progressive education. (More details of these and further examples of key problem areas are presented in Chapter 2.)

CHANGE IN COMPARATIVE EDUCATION

A further such area with a key function, comparative education, will be dealt with somewhat more extensively. Comparative education in the Soviet Union especially suffered under the dogmatization of thought by being reduced to an instrument of ideological delimitation and self-glorification.[5] The science of confrontation is now to become a science of cooperation. Has perestroika penetrated this area? Apart from the relatively few monographs, it is articles in *Sovetskaya pedagogika* which provide the most important indication of the state of the art of Soviet comparative education. It should be pointed out that the editorial board of this journal (at present comprising seventeen people) had not changed over the three years 1987–9, except for one death and two newcomers. In this period we still find contributions in the old confrontational style.[6]

An attitude of readiness to cooperate with Western comparative education, however, is shown by Z.A. Mal'kova in her report on the World Congress of Comparative Education in Rio de Janeiro.[7] She notes growing international cooperation, but at the same time warns about the falsifiers in the West; according to her, the scientific level of Soviet scholarship is not inferior to the world standard, and a predominant position for Soviet comparativists should be secured. A kind of programmatic change finds expression in an article by B.L. Vul'fson.[8] The position of non-recognition of Western comparative education must be abandoned, as examples of high professional competence can be found there, and certain assessments and conclusions must be corrected, since not all criticism of the Soviet system is ideological subversion. The author, however, still speaks of the crisis of the bourgeois education system and of integration on the part of the 'fraternal socialist countries'.[9]

Writing over a year later, N.D. Nikandrov affirms the principle that with the help of international comparison essential insights can be gained and mistakes avoided, quoting examples by way of illustration.[10] Characteristic of the change taking place in the comparative approach is the number of articles centred on factual reporting, renouncing polemical undertones and visibly treating the subject matter from the angle of what it yields for the solution of one's own problems.[11]

212

The glance cast by Soviet scholars over their own frontiers returns from time to time to scrutinize their own conditions. One may cite V.B. Mironov as an example of how the West is almost unreservedly understood as a positive model, the former habitual criticism being changed into its opposite. It is now held that the development of education in the West takes place in accordance with the productive forces, a high level of qualification of the working population is guaranteed, and competition and carefully directed exploitation (or early selection) of talents is the road to success, as is the prevailing emphasis on individuality in educational processes and the shaping of schools as creative workshops.[12] The reforms which were introduced by the Thatcher administration, so highly controversial in their own country, find a positive response; one simply reads: 'England turns toward world reason. Syllabuses, methodology, textbooks and the character of teaching are changing in line with the spirit of the age.'[13] Mal'kova, because of her former critical stance, is accused of having prevented an appropriate perception of the West.[14]

It is now clear that since 1987 a departure from the attitude of confrontation has taken place. The interest in information on Western countries has led to the first results of careful documentation, of a kind that was almost non-existent before. This development is primarily furthered by the same people who until recently saw themselves as leading figures in the ideological war and owed their prominent position in the scientific hierarchy to this very function. Vul'fson is now committed to opening-up and integration; Mal'kova appears at international conferences in the West, looks for recognition there and indeed finds it. A serious debate on the causes of the former decline of comparative education cannot be detected. It will be intriguing to discover whether, in the forthcoming textbook on the methodology of comparative education, the past is come to terms with or is pushed aside.

Considering the new tasks and possibilities, then, one can hardly call recent results satisfying. As far as one can make out, little is moving in the area of research organization, something that certainly would be a basic requirement of an innovative push. On the one hand a kind of comparative education society has been formed and a programme of work put forward, but on the other hand one can see from the statutes of the society that it is completely lacking in a democratic infrastructure, so that the old Stalinist organizational hierarchy continues, with the formal and informal dependence on it of those tied up in it. To this extent, individual involvement with the West still harbours personal risks for the researcher.

A more interesting picture emerges if one looks at developments at the level of personal contacts in the education sector. Examples of this may be adduced. Following an invitation by the German Institute of International Educational Research, three leading representatives of the Academy of Pedagogical Sciences visited the Federal Republic of Germany: Shadrikov (in 1990 acting president), Razumovsky (vice-president) and Amonashvili (the central figure of the movement for the renewal of education). Their papers contained a message basically of the same tenor: we are open to talks, we are looking for cooperation with the West, we are hoping for an integrating international education. In the meantime this attitude has found expression at a number of meetings: at large and small German–Soviet fora, at meetings at the level of twin towns, in connection with the already proven cooperation between the education authorities of the RSFSR and North Rhine-Westphalia, and at conferences of experts with Soviet participation. The first bilateral research projects have been started. Exchanges of students and apprentice craftsmen and contacts between universities have developed well in a short time. Among others, such contacts are reflected in reports with a personal touch in the Soviet press, e.g. in *Uchitel'skaya gazeta*, where they are often euphorically described. One might speak of a movement and cite many further details. Summing up, it can be said that at the level of individual experience comparative education is rapidly gaining ground.

PROSPECTS FOR WESTERN EUROPEAN RESEARCH ON THE USSR

Let us now turn to Western scientific interest in the Soviet Union. The outlook for future research tasks should be linked to a self-critical review. Such criticism is justified by a discussion in 1989 in the journal *Osteuropa*. Many statements made there seem, even at the time of their publication, and much more so when seen from a short distance in time, to be constantly lagging behind events. They are dominated by the doubt – often packaged in a variety of scholarly arguments – as to whether developments in the USSR can be trusted. A contribution to the effect that one can hardly speak of a 'transformation of the Soviet system', because one has had all of this before and Gorbachev has taken on a 'comparatively modest task' in this respect, is especially blunt.[15] In Buchholz's report on a 'conference on ideology', one can find the opinion that there is no diminution of the party's claim to leadership, that communication and travel are still severely restricted, that the core content of ideology and the Soviet system have so far remained in principle intact, and so on.[16] Similar points of view are upgraded to criteria that have to be fulfilled before one can speak of the Soviet Union as a 'normal state'. It is perhaps sufficient to refer those who have such scruples to the daily press, where in nearly every issue one can find a hint of the disintegration of the traditional Soviet system. What kind of criteria have to be fulfilled before we can speak of a 'change of system'? After all, the USSR not only has not prevented the disintegration of socialism in Eastern Bloc countries but also is constructively helping this development.

Confronted with perestroika in general as well as with recent developments in particular, research on Eastern Europe has proved to be largely incapable of prognostication. Of course the development itself contains unpredictable elements. Obviously some researchers are biased towards the opinion that Soviet society is not to be credited with any capacity for change. They take the attitude that Gorbachev's conception of 'new thinking' – that vision of a world order at peace – is directed exclusively at the dogmatic forces in his own country, for whom it represents an affront. People fail to see that the chances of this vision depend on the spreading of new thinking in the West as well.

There is no need to dwell on evidence of how difficult it is for the West to enter into 'new thinking'. Obviously the present situation encourages widespread ideological prejudice. Advancing European integration and the superiority of the market economy, so dramatically experienced, have repercussions on our perceptual horizon. We lose sight of the fact that the ecological catastrophes threatening us and the explosive socio-economic situation of inequality between countries have been brought about to a large extent by market mechanisms, and that up to now these problems have proved insoluble in the system of the market economy. The EC is built along the lines of an economic model that cannot be commonly applied and that is probably not even durable in the long run. If a larger proportion of humanity were to apply this model, this would imply a demand on natural resources which would quickly lead to a global ecological breakdown. Why is this relevant in our context? It is because if we lack a critical attitude towards our own society we shall hardly understand the processes in Soviet society, one very different from ours.

Change in Soviet society touches upon a further premise of research on Eastern Europe. There used to be a close connection between the distance of researchers from their subject matter and their distance from communism. Now we shall have the experience that even a Soviet society without communism represents something alien to us. Whatever the development in the republics of the USSR is to be, the experiences of the last seventy years will nevertheless continue to make themselves felt; the still more deeply rooted features of national character will become more recognizable without their communist garb, and they will be different from those of Western European countries. Even without the opposition of capitalism and socialism the integration of Western and Eastern Europe will remain a difficult task. Shall we see this distance as an opposition for which we shall lay a 'scientific foundation' in our work, or as a challenge to foster mutual understanding through our work and to help towards the building of bridges?

Up to now the Soviet Union, through its reticence, has forced observer status upon us. Now the country is opening up and there is a chance of entering into a cooperative relationship with the subject of our studies. The prospect of an integrated Europe with a lasting order of peace and an abundant humane culture should not leave the researcher unaffected, least of all in a field such as comparative education, where scholarly competence would then have to stand the test of its capacity for international understanding.

NOTES AND REFERENCES

1 This paper was originally presented at the Meeting for Researchers on Soviet Education organized by the UK Study Group on Soviet Education and the Comparative Education Research Unit (Arbeitsstelle für vergleichende Bildungsforschung), Ruhr University, Bochum, Germany, and held at the IV World Congress for Soviet and East European Studies, Harrogate, 23 July 1990. An extended version of the paper is published as D. Glowka and L. Novikov, 'Perspektiven der Vergleichenden Erziehungswissenschaft zwischen Ost und West', *Osteuropa*, 1990, vol. 40, no. 10, pp. 925–34. We are grateful to the editors of *Osteuropa* for their cooperation.

2 D. Glowka, 'Die westdeutsche Pädagogik in der Sicht sowjetischer Autoren', in B. Dilger, F. Kuebart and H.-P. Schäfer (eds), *Vergleichende Bildungsforschung: DDR, Osteuropa und interkulturelle Perspektiven*, [West] Berlin, Berlin Verlag Arno Spitz, 1986, pp. 410–27.

3 G. Simon, 'Der Umbruch des politischen Systems in der Sowjetunion', *Aus Politik und Zeitgeschichte*, 4 May 1990, pp. 3–15.

4 L. Novikov, 'Anzeichen für Wertelabilität in der sowjetischen Gesellschaft als Herausforderung für die Erziehung', *Zeitschrift für internationale erziehungs- und sozialwissenschaftliche Forschung*, 1988, vol. 5, no. 1, pp. 35–52.

5 D. Glowka, 'Zum Stand der Vergleichenden Pädagogik in der UdSSR', *Vergleichende Erziehungswissenschaft*, 1987, no. 18, pp. 253–63.

6 T.F. Yarkina, 'Moral', politika i burzhuaznaya politika', *Sovetskaya pedagogika* (hereafter *SP*), 1987, no. 1, pp. 116–23; T.F. Yarkina, 'Protivorechiya burzhuaznogo makarenkovedeniya', *SP*, 1988, no. 5, pp. 118–24; A.N. Dzhurinsky, 'Falsifikatsiya istorii sovetskoi shkoly i pedagogiki', *SP*, 1987, no. 6, pp. 128–33.

7 Z.A. Mal'kova, 'Vazhnaya otrasl' pedagogicheskogo znaniya', *SP*, 1988, no. 1, pp. 119–22.

8 B.L. Vul'fson, 'Metodologicheskie problemy sravnitel'noi pedagogiki', *SP*, 1988, no. 8, pp. 130–6.

9 ibid., pp. 131, 133, 134.

10 N.D. Nikandrov, 'Sravnitel'naya pedagogika: uroki i nadezhdy', *SP*, 1989, no. 10, pp. 129–34.

11 M.V. Klarin, 'Individualizatsiya obucheniya v burzhuaznoi pedagogike XX v.', *SP*, 1987, no. 7, pp. 124–9; O.B. Loginova, 'Sravnitel'nyi analiz uchebnykh planov srednei obshcheobrazovatel'noi shkoly', *SP*, 1989, no. 10, pp. 93–8; V.I. Malinin, 'Prodolzhim dialog', *SP*, 1989, no. 11, pp. 133–9; V.G. Razumovsky, 'Soderzhanie obrazovaniya: pedagogicheskii effekt', *SP*, 1989, no. 8, pp. 130–5; I.I. Serebryannikova, 'Kompyuterizatsiya v shkolakh FRG', *SP*, 1987, no. 11, pp. 124–8; N.M. Voskresenskaya and V.S. Mitina, 'Obnovlenie soderzhaniya obrazovaniya v shkolakh kapitalisticheskikh stran', *SP*, 1989, no. 9, pp. 116–22; B.L. Vul'fson, '"Obshcheevropeiskii dom" i obrazovanie', *SP*, 1990, no. 4, pp. 123–31.

12 V.B. Mironov, 'Obrazovanie v stranakh zapada v kontse XX veka', *SP*, 1990, no. 2, pp. 136–42.

13 V.B. Mironov, *Vek obrazovaniya*, Moscow, 1990, p. 97.

14 ibid., p. 119.

15 A. Pradetto, 'Die Zukunft der Sowjetunion und der Ost-West-Beziehungen. Oder: Über die Beliebigkeit zeitgeschichtlichen Denkens', *Osteuropa*, 1989, vol. 39, no. 7, pp. 652–69.

16 A. Buchholz, 'Diskussionen über die Sowjetideologie', *Osteuropa*, 1989, vol. 39, no. 1, pp. 61–7.

INDEX

abilities, 59–60, 77–8, 106–16, 137, 148
Abuladze, T., 86
Academic Deputies' Group, 158
Academy of Pedagogical Sciences, 9–10, 15, 16, 18, 25, 51, 92, 111, 115, 126, 213
Academy of Sciences: 31, 53, 157, 160, 172, 205; Siberian Section, Novosibirsk, 32, 33, 42, 45
Academy of World Civilizations, 160
Adamsky, A., 18, 19
adult education, *see* continuing education
aesthetic education, *see* arts education
Ageeva, G.M., 204–5
agriculture: institutes, 169, 180, 186–9; specialism, 191
Ailamazyan, A.K., 53
aims of education, 5, 8, 72, 81–2
Akhmatova, A.A., attitudes to and study of, 68
Aleksii, Patriarch, 94, 95, 97
algorithms, 32, 34–6, 45, 50, 53–4
Alma-Ata and Region, schools in, 23, 91
alternative schools, *see* cooperative schools
Amonashvili, Sh.A., 8, 15, 16, 17, 18, 22, 90, 97, 119, 213–14
Andropov, Yu., 204
anti-religious education, 83
Antonova, I., 16
Anweiler, O., 210
APN, *see* Academy of Pedagogical Sciences
Armenia: computing facilities in schools of, 37–8, 53; higher
education in, 167, 168, 173, 179, 181–3, 185, 193; religious studies in, 91, 95
art and cinematography: institutes, 166, 169, 180, 186–9; specialism 190
art education, 20, 27, 61, 62–7, 72–5, 77, 87, 89, 94, 190
arts subjects (humanities): 20, 26, 73, 90, 190; and SPTUs, 140
arts education: 20, 58–78, 84; *see also* World Artistic Culture
assessment: of pupils, 5, 67, 68, 70–1, 108; of slow learners, 106, 115, 124; at vocational schools, 132
Association of Engineering Institutes, 158
Association of Social Educators, 25
Association of Universities, 157
Association of *vuz* Teachers, 157
atheism, 82–6, 92–3, 94–101
atheistic education, 82–6, 89, 92, 93, 96, 100, 102(n.4)
atheistic propaganda, 84, 98
atheists and believers: 84, 101, 104(n.77); cooperation between, 86, 98–9
Author Schools, 11, 16, 18, 20, 24, 26, 114, 116
Azerbaidzhan: computing facilities in schools of, 37–8, 53; higher education in, 166, 168, 169, 179, 181–3, 185, 193

backward children, *see* children with learning difficulties
Baku Economics Institute, 165–6

217

SELECTED PAPERS OF THE FOURTH WORLD CONGRESS FOR SOVIET AND EAST EUROPEAN STUDIES, HARROGATE, JULY 1990

Edited for the International Council for Soviet and East European Studies by Stephen White, University of Glasgow

Published by Routledge:

John Dunstan (ed.), *Soviet Education under Perestroika*
  Michael Ellman and Vladimir Kontorovich (eds),
  The Disintegration of the Soviet Economic System

Published by Cambridge University Press:

Anders Aslund (ed.), *Market Socialism or Capitalist Restoration?*
Linda Edmondson (ed.), *Women and Society in Russia and the Soviet Union*
Roger Kanet (ed.), *The Soviet Union in the International Political System*
Marie Lavigne (ed.), *The USSR and Eastern Europe in the Global Economy*
John Massey Stewart (ed.), *The Soviet Environment: Problems, Policies and Politics*
Stephen White (ed.), *New Directions in Soviet History*

Published by Macmillan:

Roy Allison (ed.), *Radical Reform in Soviet Defence Policy*
Ben Eklof (ed.), *School and Society in Tsarist and Soviet Russia*
John Elsworth (ed.), *The Silver Age in Russian Literature*
John and Carol Garrard (eds), *World War II in Soviet Memory*
Zvi Gitelman (ed.), *The Politics of Nationality in the Contemporary USSR*
Sheelagh Graham (ed.), *New Perspectives in Soviet Literature*
Celia Hawkesworth (ed.), *Politics and Literature in Eastern Europe*
Lindsey Hughes (ed.), *New Perspectives on Muscovite Russia*

Walter Joyce (ed.), *Social Change and Social Issues in the Contemporary USSR*

Bohdan Krawchenko (ed.), *Ukrainian Past, Ukrainian Present*

Paul G. Lewis (ed.), *Democracy and Civil Society in Eastern Europe*

Robert D. McKean (ed.), *New Perspectives in Modern Russian History*

John Morison (ed.), *The Czech and Slovak Experience*

John Morison (ed.), *East Europe and the West*

John O. Norman (ed.), *New Directions in Soviet Art and Culture*

Derek Offord (ed.), *The Golden Age of Russian Literature and Thought*

Michael E. Urban (ed.), *Ideology and System Change in the USSR and Eastern Europe*

Published by Nijhoff:

F.J.M. Feldbrugge (ed.), *Papers in Soviet Law*

Other publications:

Laszlo Dienes (ed.), 'The émigré experience': special issue of *Coexistence*

Issues in East European economics: selected issues of *Soviet Studies*

'New directions in Soviet politics': special issue of *Journal of Communist Studies*

Papers in language and linguistics: special issue of *Papers in Slavonic Linguistics*

Papers on publishing: special issue of *Solanus*

Papers on religion: special issue of *Religion in Communist Lands*

Papers on the Revolution and Civil War: special issue of *Revolutionary Russia*

Papers on Slovene studies: special issue of *Slovene Studies*